The Centennial Scandal:
The Election of 1876

© 2021 by Len Sandler

ISBN: 9798719031149

Cover flag canton courtesy of Jeff R. Bridgman, American Antiques & Antique Flags, www.JeffBridgman.com

Table of Contents

Chapter	Title	Page
1.	Slavery in America	7
2.	The Civil War Years	25
3.	The Emancipation Proclamation	47
4.	The War Ends	67
5.	Reconstruction in the South	78
6.	The Republican Convention	103
7.	The Democratic Convention	120
8.	The 1876 Presidential Campaign	130
9.	The Centennial Election	147
10.	Chaos, Confusion, & Corruption	169
11.	The Election Commission	191
12.	The Compromise of 1877	212
13.	The Inauguration	222
14.	The Hayes Presidency	233
15.	Finger-Pointing	249
16.	Lemonade Lucy	256
17.	The Jim Crow Era	269
	Post-Script	281

Foreword

When I was a child, I remember turning on the little black and white television that was set in the oversized, multi-purpose wood cabinet in our living room. There were only three channels back then – ABC, NBC, and CBS. All showed the same horrifying images. Fire hoses were being turned on nonviolent protesters who were exercising their 1st amendment rights to gather. People were being beaten. Yet, they didn't fight back. The police were rushing to the scene to help. But they were coming to help those DOING the beatings. In some cases, it was the police themselves who were carrying out the atrocities. This wasn't happening in violation of the law. It WAS the law in many Southern states.

There were "White Only" signs that prohibited Black people from sitting at lunch counters, drinking from water fountains, or attending schools. Blacks were forced to sit at the back of the bus. This wasn't some far-off country. This was AMERICA. It was happening on MY television! I learned in school that there were federal laws passed during and after the Civil War to give Black Americans their full rights as citizens. Why was this happening, then? Who said it was okay? How can this be legal? Why isn't someone putting a stop to this?

People like to talk about American exceptionalism. The notion is that our country is superior to others and has the obligation to help others become more like us. We've become famous for lecturing other countries about "Human Rights." Yet our own history is replete with examples of individuals and groups of people being grossly mistreated, often by the government itself. You wish you could hold up a giant mirror so Americans can see themselves for what they really are – a flawed nation not unlike others.

We're still paying for the wrong choices made during the Centennial Election. White supremacists were visible, vocal, and often violent at the time. They were backed, or at least tolerated, by many Democrats, the conservative party, which considered them an important part of their base. The Republican party consisted of those who were more progressive and looking for positive change. It's what "Stranger Things," the television show, would call "The Upside-Down."

A full 87 years after the Centennial election, newly-elected Governor George Wallace stepped to the podium in Montgomery, Alabama to deliver his Inaugural Address, written by Ku Klux Klan leader Asa Carter. It was a time when civil rights activists were fighting for equal access to schools, voting booths, and just about any other place you can imagine. Wallace uttered a single sound bite on that January 14, 1963 day that became one of history's most famous rallying cries against racial equality. I remember listening to words that I didn't fully understand but knew they were hateful, nonetheless. They were:

> "Let us rise to the call of freedom-loving blood that is within us, and send our answer to the tyranny that clanks its chains upon the South. In the name of the greatest people that have ever trod this earth, I draw the line in the dust and toss the gauntlet before the feet of tyranny, and I say segregation now, segregation tomorrow, segregation forever." [1]

The "tyranny" he referred to, of course, was the federal government's attempts at implementing de-segregation laws. The central theme of his speech was that the government was trying to oppress the people of Alabama and deprive them of their rights, thus making them the victims. A recurring theme of White supremacists is framing racist policies as an issue of states' rights issue and individual freedom.

The crowd that packed the streets that day roared its approval. Thousands of the attendees were wearing white flowers symbolizing their commitment to White supremacy. If you were there, you might be thinking, "Didn't we fight a Civil War over this? Didn't the South lose?"

James L. Poe Jr., then-president of the Montgomery chapter of the NAACP, recalled that "Indeed, violence quickly followed Wallace's inauguration. We began to feel the sting of the speech. People night-riding and burning crosses. The police beat down people and ran over them with horses, put tear gas on them." (2)

Interestingly, Wallace changed his views on segregation later in life and claimed he regretted the famous line in his speech, calling it his "biggest mistake." He explained it this way in a Washington Post article on September 5, 1991:

> "I didn't write those words about segregation now, tomorrow and forever. I saw them in the speech written for me and planned to skip over them. But the wind-chill factor was 5 below zero when I gave that speech. I started reading just to get it over and read those words without thinking. I have regretted it all my life." (3)

There have been many excuses given for racist rhetoric. Seldom has cold weather been one of them.

Hopefully, the mistakes made during and immediately after the 1876 election can turn into lessons learned, never to be repeated, and help move us closer to earning the distinction of truly being exceptional.

It can be easy to be cynical and disheartened when reviewing events from long ago as well as watching today's news. As the late Congressman John Lewis of Georgia advised, "Do not get lost in a sea of despair. Be hopeful. Be optimistic. Our struggle is not the struggle of a day, week, month, or a year. It is the struggle of a lifetime." (4)

Ch. 1 - Slavery in America

Throughout the 1700s, British colonists were convinced that slavery was an essential element to national prosperity and world power. To justify the practice, they dehumanized Blacks in every way possible. The prejudiced attitudes focused on what they considered their uncivilized and un-Christian nature. Americans won their freedom from British rule in 1776 and a new nation began taking shape. However, freedom was not extended to slaves. Thomas Jefferson, America's 3rd President, came from a wealthy Virginia planter's family and was himself a slave owner, like most of the Founding Fathers. It is believed that he had six children with a slave woman, Sally Hemings. Jefferson freed all six of the children, but never Hemings herself.

Was Jefferson being hypocritical when he proclaimed, "We hold these truths to be self-evident, that all men are created equal" in the Declaration of Independence? Maybe he and the others were only speaking in aspirational terms about what they hoped America would become. Did they have the foresight to realize that what they wanted to achieve would be difficult and require centuries of struggle?

Andrew Johnson, the 17th President, later tried to explain the "all men are created equal" phrase by smugly suggesting, "Mr. Jefferson meant the White race." [5]

At the time of the American Revolution, there was widespread support in the northern colonies for prohibiting the importation of more slaves. However, after the revolution, at the insistence of southern states, Congress would wait more than two decades before finally passing the Act Prohibiting Importation of Slaves of 1807. The law was enacted but smugglers frequently violated it until the Northern blockade of the South in 1861 at the beginning of the Civil War. By the 1780s, slavery was being phased out in the North. But the South stubbornly hung on to it as a cornerstone of its agricultural economy. The plantations relied heavily on the free labor and many could not survive economically without it. Slavery was barely discussed during the Constitutional Convention held in the summer of 1787 in Philadelphia where a new national government and system of justice was shaped.

When the topic of slavery did enter into the discussion at the Convention, it was related to how the first National Census in 1790 should be taken. A key question was whether Blacks should be counted. The census was to be crucial for calculating the number of U.S. House of Representatives from each state, determining how much political influence they would hold. If slaves were to be counted, then the Southern states would have greater political power in relation to the Northern states. The debate raged for days before participants reached a compromise. Black slaves were to be counted as three-fifths of a person. They were still not full humans in the eyes of the law.

That first census showed that 757,000 Blacks lived in the United States, of whom 700,000 were slaves. More than 22% of American families owned at least one slave. The hopes that slavery would fade out of American life were dashed only a few years later. In 1793, Eli Whitney developed a much-improved cotton gin, a machine that separated cotton fibers from seed. The invention made the crop significantly more profitable. Its emergence meant that more slaves were needed to pick the crops because the work once done by hand was now done much faster. New cotton fields spread across the South and slavery boomed. Despite a ban on the importation of new African slaves, the Black population in the United States grew to approximately 4.5 million by 1860. Some 90% of Blacks in America were slaves. However, the number of slave-owning families had dropped to 10% because large cotton plantations had squeezed out smaller farms. Prior to the Civil War, slaves were at the bottom of a de facto caste system. At the top were rich plantation owners. In the middle were merchants, small farmers, and laborers. Slaves lived in housing provided by their owners who would also give them food and clothing. The quality of these basic necessities varied widely. The field laborer would normally work from sunrise to sunset. Ten or more slaves would often live in a single room shack. The beds typically consisted of straw and old rags and the floors were dirt. Slaves were bought and sold on a regular basis. They had no right to marry, vote, carry firearms, own property, learn to read or write, possess books, testify in court against Whites, or speak as equals when talking to Whites.

Hundreds of enslaved people every year successfully escaped to the North. In order to try to stop that, the Fugitive Slave Act was drafted by Senator James M. Mason of Virginia and passed by Congress on September 18th, 1850. It may have been the most hated and openly violated piece of federal legislation in the nation's history. It built upon the earlier Fugitive Slave Act of 1793 which gave southern slave owners the ability to capture escaped slaves from the northern free states and return them to work on the southern plantations. However, the new Fugitive Slave Act set strict guidelines and created additional protections for the southern slave owners. The Act required that all escaped slaves, upon capture, be returned to their masters and that officials and citizens of free states had to cooperate. Abolitionists nicknamed it the "Bloodhound Bill" for the dogs that were used to track down runaway slaves.

The Fugitive Slave Act stipulated that anyone, including government officials, found helping an escaped slave would be punished with a fine of $1,000, which amounts to $33,394 in present-day value, and up to six months imprisonment. It also mandated that law enforcement officers were to arrest anyone suspected of being an escaped slave. This meant that it was easier for slave owners to recapture their lost "property" and afforded fewer protections to the escaped slaves. If captured, escaped slaves were returned based solely on a written statement by the slave owner. All of these conditions combined to create a much more dangerous situation for escaped slaves, and effectively reduced the number of slaves who fled to the Northern free states after 1850. Police everywhere were required to arrest people suspected of being a runaway slave on as little as the claimant's testimony of ownership. No jury was permitted in a trial and the alleged fugitive slave could not testify. The Commissioner before whom the fugitive slave was brought for a hearing was compensated $10 if he found that the individual was proven a fugitive and $5 if he determined the proof to be insufficient. In present-day value, that means a payment of $334 vs. $167. Officers who captured a fugitive slave were often incentivized with a bonus or promotion for their work.

The Fugitive Slave Act helped the economics of the Southern slave owners immensely, as it made escape for the slaves much harder. In fact, the price of slaves after 1850 increased by as much as 30% in the states that bordered the South due to the additional protections given to slave owners.

While southern slave owners supported the Fugitive Slave Act, it angered many who lived in the northern states and were part of the abolitionist movement. Furthermore, northerners, by and large, resented the idea that they were responsible for helping to capture escaped slaves and return them to plantations in the southern states. Harriet Beecher Stowe famously wrote "Uncle Tom's Cabin," which was published in 1852 in response to the conditions of the Fugitive Slave Act. Harriet Tubman, a well-known conductor of the Underground Railroad, helped slaves escape further north to Canada. As part of the British Empire, Canada was not obligated to return escaped slaves. There were a number of well-publicized cases in which "free" Blacks were wrongfully taken and forced into slavery. The Act contributed to the growing polarization of the country over the issue of slavery and is considered to be one of the causes of the Civil War. (6)

The law was tested by a young lawyer named Rutherford B. Hayes, acting as co-counsel along with Salmon P. Chase, representing 16-year-old Rosetta Armstead. Her Kentucky owner, Henry Dennison, had sent her to Virginia accompanied by Dr. Jones Miller in March of 1855. She was going to serve as nursemaid to Dennison's daughter. Due to winter ice still in the Ohio River, however, the two travelers had to disembark from their steamboat and board a train. They ended up staying a night at a hotel in Columbus.

Word of Rosetta's presence spread quickly amongst the Black community. Since Ohio was a free state, Reverend William B. Ferguson rushed to the Franklin County Probate Court where he made a plea for Armstead's freedom. A sheriff arrived at midnight to retrieve Rosetta, and as she was a minor illegally in Miller's custody, place her under the guardianship of Lewis G. Van Slyke, active in the abolitionist movement. The Ohio State Journal reported, "The law had its way and all was quiet." Rosetta was deemed to be free. Unfortunately, her case was not over. While visiting with a friend, she was literally dragged away and put on a carriage by a couple of slave catchers. Rosetta's supporters rushed to the train station where the two "showed, by presentation of revolvers, that they were determined to take her with them." (7)

While awaiting her day in court, Rosetta moved in and out of Cincinnati jails. She was finally tried before U.S. Commissioner John L. Pendry who held that she was not covered by the Fugitive Slave Law because she had not escaped. An agent of her master had brought her into free territory willingly. By the end of April, the court again declared Rosetta Armstead was a free woman. (8) Dennison traveled to Columbus to attempt to convince Rosetta to return as his property to Kentucky, but she refused, staunchly choosing her freedom. Dennison wound up filing a warrant for her arrest with a U.S. Marshal named Hiram Robinson. Her allies filed a habeas corpus writ on her behalf, upon which the judge decided her detainment was unlawful and she would remain free. (9) Habeas corpus requires a person under arrest to be brought before a judge or into court to secure their release unless lawful grounds are shown for their detention.

Robinson was jailed for contempt for re-arresting Rosetta without cause following the previous ruling. The case was brought to Cincinnati's Southern District U.S. Circuit Court to be tried, and following an additional re-arrest of Rosetta, the release of Marshal Robinson, weeks of legal efforts, and a week of deliberation by

Circuit Court Judge John Pendery. Rosetta was ultimately declared to have free status under both U.S. and Ohio law. (10)

Not everyone was happy with the decision to free her. Dennison echoed the sentiments of many of his fellow Kentuckians when he wrote to the Ohio Statesman saying, that "personal rights are dearer to the people of the South than the barren glory derived from a union with strangers." (11)

The Fugitive Slave Act remained in effect until June of 1864 when it was formally repealed. Essentially, the Northern armies stopped forcing escaped slaves back to the South, causing the government to repeal the law. The New York Tribune hailed the action, writing: "The blood-red stain that has blotted the statute-book of the Republic is wiped out forever." According to the Missouri Compromise of 1820, the two new territories of Kansas and Nebraska would have become free states because they were north of the agreed-upon dividing line. But Illinois Senator Stephen A. Douglas sponsored a bill declaring instead that popular sovereignty would determine whether Kansas and Nebraska would be free or slave. In doing so, he hoped to strengthen his bid for the Presidency in 1856 by winning support from Southern Democrats. Douglas would go on to defeat Lincoln in the 1858 United States Senate election in Illinois, famous for the Lincoln–Douglas debates. Kansas would eventually be granted statehood in 1861 and Nebraska in 1867.

The Kansas–Nebraska Act of 1854 was signed into law by the 14th President, Franklin Pierce. The bill was ostensibly passed to open up new lands to development and facilitate construction of a transcontinental railroad but it, significantly, also allowed for the extension of slavery. Opposition to the Kansas-Nebraska Act led to the formation of the Republican Party later that year and revived the failing political career of an Illinois lawyer named Abraham Lincoln. The law is also notable for contributing to a series of armed conflicts known as "Bleeding Kansas."

On May 20, 1856, in the midst of these violent political confrontations, Senator Charles Sumner, an abolitionist Republican from Massachusetts, denounced the Kansas–Nebraska Act, and condemned its authors. He continued his attack in a "Crime against Kansas" speech accusing them of hypocrisy and arguing for the immediate admission of Kansas as a free state. Sumner went on to denounce "Slave Power" as the political arm of the slave owners and alleged that their goal was to spread slavery through the free states:

> "Not in any common lust for power did this uncommon tragedy have its origin. It is the rape of a virgin territory, compelling it to the hateful embrace of slavery; and it may be clearly traced to a depraved desire for a new Slave State, hideous offspring of such a crime, in the hope of adding to the power of slavery in the National Government.
>
> The senator from South Carolina has read many books of chivalry and believes himself a chivalrous knight with sentiments of honor and courage. Of course, he has chosen a mistress to whom he has made his vows, and who, though ugly to others, is always lovely to him; though polluted in the sight of the world, is chaste in his sight - I mean the harlot, slavery. For her his tongue is always profuse in words. Let her be impeached in character, or any

proposition made to shut her out from the extension of her wantonness, and no extravagance of manner or hardihood of assertion is then too great for this senator."(12)

Afterwards, Sumner verbally attacked authors of the Act, Democratic Senators Stephen A. Douglas of Illinois and Andrew Butler of South Carolina. Representative Preston Brooks, a pro-slavery Democrat from South Carolina, was infuriated by the speeches. Andrew Butler was his cousin and he was intent on defending his honor. He claimed that Sumner's speech had been libelous and wanted to challenge him to a duel.

On the afternoon of May 22, two days after Sumner's speech, Brooks entered the Senate chamber, along with two fellow congressmen. He asked people in the chamber to leave. Brooks politely waited for the Senate floor to clear and for the galleries to empty out. He was especially concerned with getting all of the women out of the room so they didn't have to witness what was about to take place. He then approached Sumner at his desk saying calmly, "Mr. Sumner, I have read your speech twice over carefully. It is a libel on South Carolina and Mr. Butler, who is a relative of mine." (13)

As Sumner stood, Brooks brought a thick, heavy walking stick down on his head. The blow was so strong that Sumner was blinded by it, immediately falling to the floor under his desk. As Brooks continued to beat him, Sumner became trapped between the desk, which was bolted to the floor and his chair, which was set into tracks to move back and forth. With blood dripping down his face, Sumner rose to his feet, ripped the desk off the floor, and started to run.

Brooks, however, grabbed him by the lapel, pulled him back to the floor, and continued to beat him.

As the attack was occurring, other congressmen and Senators attempted to help Sumner but were held off by Brooks' accomplices. Congressmen Laurence Keitt of South Carolina and Henry Edmundson of Virginia were each armed with canes of their own and Keitt was waving a pistol, warning everyone against interfering. "Let them be!" shouted Keitt. (14) Eventually, Representatives were able to restrain Brooks, who quietly left the chamber. Charles Sumner was taken to his home to receive emergency medical attention. Brooks was later arrested for assault. The attack demonstrated to the public just how divided the government was. Brooks was seen as a hero in the South for standing up for the rights to own slaves while Sumner was seen as a martyr in the North for defending a slave's right to freedom.

Many southerners mocked Sumner, claiming he was faking his injuries and that the cane used was not heavy enough to inflict severe injuries. They also claimed that Brooks had not hit Sumner more than a few times and had not hit him hard enough to cause serious health concerns. Brooks was praised by Southern newspapers. The Richmond Enquirer editorialized that "Sumner should be caned every morning" and praised the attack as "good in conception, better in execution, and best of all in consequences." It denounced "these vulgar abolitionists in the Senate who have been suffered to run too long without collars" and said, "They must be lashed into submission." Southerners sent Brooks hundreds of new canes in honor of his assault. The Western Democrat, a newspaper based in Charlotte, North Carolina reported that one even had an engraved inscription saying, "Hit him again."

Though Brooks admitted he intended to cause harm to Sumner, who suffered permanent brain damage, he claimed "I hadn't intended to kill him or else I would have used a different weapon." (14) Brooks was arrested, tried in a District of Columbia court, and convicted but received no prison sentence. He was simply fined $300. A motion for his expulsion from the House of Representatives failed. He resigned on July 15, though, saying he wanted his constituents to either ratify or condemn his conduct via a special election. Not surprisingly, they returned him to office.

Keitt was censured by the House for brandishing his pistol and resigned in protest. He was overwhelmingly reelected to his seat within a month. Two years later, he attempted to choke Republican Representative Galusha Grow of Pennsylvania during an argument on the House floor. Fortunately, members of Congress, for the most part, are better behaved these days.

The caning incident became symbolic of the breakdown of reasonable discourse within the government. Sumner was unable to return to Congress for three and a half years as he recuperated from the beating that nearly killed him. Though Sumner recovered, the country did not. Within a few years, the Civil War would begin.

Southern leaders began seriously discussing separating from the United States as early as 1858. One of the precipitating events was the armed conflict at Harper's Ferry which occurred from October 16 to 18 of the following year. John Brown, a White abolitionist, enlisted 22 people on a mission to initiate a slave revolt by taking over the United States Arsenal at Harper's Ferry, Virginia in what has been called "a dress rehearsal for the Civil War." The arsenal was retaken by a company of U.S. Marines commanded by none other than Colonel Robert E. Lee. Among the troops who guarded Brown after his arrest were Stonewall Jackson and Jeb Stewart. One of those who witnessed Brown's execution was a man named John Wilkes Booth.

Abraham Lincoln rose from obscurity to national prominence, claiming the Republican nomination for President in 1860. Prior to the election, the majority of the Southern states were publicly threatening secession from the United States if the Republicans won that election. Following Lincoln's victory as the country's 16th President, South Carolina began secession proceedings. On December 20, their legislature passed the "Ordinance of Secession," which declared that "the Union now subsisting between South Carolina and other states, under the name of the United States of America, is hereby dissolved." (15) After the declaration, South Carolina began seizing forts, arsenals, and other strategic locations within the state.

Over the next six weeks, Mississippi, Florida, Alabama, Georgia, and Louisiana also seceded. In February 1861, delegates from those states convened to establish a unified government. Jefferson Davis of Mississippi was subsequently elected the first President of the Confederate States of America. By the time Lincoln was inaugurated on March 4, 1861, Texas had seceded, bringing the total of rebel states to seven. Virginia, Arkansas, North Carolina, and Tennessee would be added to the list later that year. Four other slave states - Delaware, Maryland, Kentucky, and Missouri – decided to remain in the Union.

Alexander Hamilton Stephens, former Governor of Georgia and Vice-President of the Confederate States explained the outlook of many in the South in what was called his "Cornerstone Speech":

> "The United States rests upon the assumption of the equality of races. Our new government is founded upon exactly the opposite idea; its foundations are laid, its cornerstone rests, upon the great truth that the Negro is not equal to the White man; that slavery subordination to the superior race is his natural and normal condition. This, our new government, is the first, in the history of the world, based upon this great physical, philosophical, and moral truth." (16)

When Lincoln was preparing for his trip to Washington to take the oath of office, threats to his life forced a change in plans. Private detectives uncovered a plot to kill him when he passed through Baltimore, where he would have to travel across town from one train station to another to make the final leg to the nation's capital. Baltimore was a hotbed of Southern sympathy, so Lincoln's team came up with a way to sneak him through town. Lincoln boarded a special train in Harrisburg, Pa., and security agents cut telegraph wires to keep his departure secret. From Philadelphia, accompanied by just two security guards, he took a late-night train to Baltimore, where he arrived undetected at 3:30 a.m., transferred stations and pulled into Washington safely at 6 a.m.

Reporters eventually learned of the subterfuge and mocked him mercilessly, making up details suggesting that he had worn "a scotch plaid cap and very long military cloak" to disguise himself. The New York Herald reported that the new President had "crept into

Washington" like a "thief in the night." But no one was taking his security for granted. During Lincoln's Inauguration, sharpshooters kept watch from roofs, soldiers blocked streets and an artillery unit was deployed to the Capitol.

In the carriage ride to Capitol, outgoing President James Buchanan knew, perhaps more than anyone, what Lincoln was getting himself into. He turned to him and said, "If you are as happy entering the presidency as I am leaving it, then you are a very happy man." (17)

Lincoln steadfastly maintained throughout the war that the secession was illegal and that the newly formed Confederate States of America was not valid as a new nation. He had hoped that the secession would end without conflict. In his first Inaugural Address in March of 1861, he declared that he had "no purpose, directly or indirectly, to interfere with slavery in the States where it exists." (18) By that time, however, the seven Southern states had already left the Union, forming the Confederate States of America and setting the stage for the Civil War. The bloodiest four years in American history began on April 12, 1861 when 50 Confederate shore batteries fired more than 4,000 rounds at Union-held Fort Sumter in South Carolina's Charleston Harbor. The following day, Major Robert Anderson surrendered the devastated fort to Confederate General P.G.T. Beauregard. On April 15, Lincoln called for 75,000 volunteers to serve in the military to help quell the "insurrection."

During the war, approximately two million soldiers fought for the Union and 750,000 for the Confederacy. There were far more deaths in the Civil War than any other American conflict. Estimates of the number of people killed range from 625,000 to 850,000. Even using the lower number, that's more casualties than in World War I, World War II, the Korean War, the Vietnam War, and the Iraq and Afghanistan Wars combined. If the names of the Civil War dead were arranged like the names on the Vietnam Memorial, the wall would stretch over 10 times the memorial's length. At least two percent of the population died, the equivalent of 6 million people today.

Rifles and cannon may have been deadly weapons, but deadlier still was disease which accounted for approximately 2/3 of the Civil War deaths. As armies massed, men once protected from contagion by isolation marched shoulder to shoulder and slept side by side in unventilated tents. Camps became breeding grounds for diseases such as mumps, chicken pox and measles. One million Union soldiers contracted malaria, and uncontrolled epidemics were common. In July 1862, Congress passed the Militia Act, which allowed Black men to serve in the U.S. armed forces as laborers, and the Confiscation Act, which mandated that enslaved people seized from Confederate supporters would be declared forever free. Lincoln also tried to persuade the border states to agree to gradual emancipation, including compensation to enslavers, with little success. When New York Congressman Horace Greeley criticized him for not coming out with a stronger emancipation policy, Lincoln replied that he valued saving the Union over all else:

> "My paramount objective in this struggle is to save the Union and is not either to save or to destroy slavery. If I could save the Union without freeing any slave I would do it, and if I could save it by freeing all the slaves I would do it; and if I could save it by freeing some and leaving others alone, I would also do that. I intend no modification of

my oft-expressed personal wish that all men everywhere could be free" (19)

The North held many advantages over the South during the Civil War. Its population was several times that of the South, a potential source for military enlistees and civilian manpower. The South lacked the substantial number of factories and industries of the North that produced needed war materials. The North had a better transportation network; mainly roads, canals, and railroads, which could be easily used to re-supply military forces in the field. At sea, the Union Navy was more capable and dominant, while the Army was better trained and better supplied. The rest of the world also recognized the United States as a legitimate government, allowing U.S. diplomats to obtain loans and trade concessions. Another disadvantage for the South was it had to worry about its slave population, which posed the threat of rebellion and support of the Northern cause. The South had the benefit of fighting most of the time on their home terrain. They also had a military tradition that encouraged young men to serve in the armed forces or attend a military school. Many had served the U.S. military before the Civil War.

The Union suffered through the first part of the Civil War because a series of senior commanders were not able to exploit the South's weaknesses. Lincoln finally got the Commanding General he needed in Ulysses S. Grant, a man who had a problem with keeping a name. It began when he remained nameless for a full month after his birth. His mother considered calling him Albert but he wound up being Hiram Ulysses Grant, named after his maternal grandfather and the hero of Greek mythology. The prospect of entering West Point with the initials of "H.U.G." written on his foot locker embarrassed him. The new cadet began using the name Ulysses H. Grant so that his the initials would be "U.H.G." Soon after, though, he learned that Representative Thomas L. Hamer, who had arranged for his appointment, erroneously used the name Ulysses Simpson Grant in the application. Grant went along with the change, not having a problem changing the initials to "U.S.G." on the foot locker. Classmates began calling him "U.S." or "Uncle Sam." Thereafter, he was known to his friends as "Sam."

Grant almost didn't make it into West Point. American history likely would have been a lot different if he hadn't. At age 17, he was just 5 feet 1 inch tall, barely over the minimum height requirement. He sprouted six inches by graduation. Grant had bright blue eyes, wavy brown hair, thin lips, a full beard, false teeth, and a piano player's long, slim fingers. He suffered from migraine headaches his entire life. Despite being a relentless, hard-driving General, he was considered soft-spoken, self-effacing, and mild-mannered. He was also very squeamish. Grant couldn't stand the sight of blood, even animal blood. In fact, he would get nauseous if his meat was not well-done. He also had a strange superstition. Grant believed it was bad luck to retrace his footsteps. So, if he inadvertently walked beyond his destination, he would not simply turn around and walk back. Instead, he would keep going further away and return by way of another road.

On March 2, 1864, Lincoln announced he was promoting Grant to Lieutenant General, giving him command of all Union Armies, a total of 533,000 troops. Grant's new rank had only previously been held by George Washington. He was formally commissioned by Lincoln on March 9 at a Cabinet meeting. Grant developed a good working relationship with Lincoln, who gave him the freedom to devise and execute his own military strategy. Grant established his headquarters with General George Meade's Army of the Potomac in Culpeper, Virginia and met weekly with Lincoln and Secretary of War Edward M. Stanton in Washington.

Prior to his taking charge of the Army, Grant had solidified the Union's control of the West in parts of the Mississippi River Basin. He went on to direct the defeat of Southern forces and strongholds and held off determined advances northward by Confederates. From the day of Grant's appointment, the Union Army won all of the remaining Civil War battles.

Grant was known to smoke cigars in excess. He would, in fact, have up to 20 of them in a day and often chew an unlit one, particularly for breakfast. It's said he received more than 10,000 cigars as gifts, more than he could possibly smoke. Tobacco was not his only vice. He started drinking heavily as a cadet at West Point and became legendary for his binges.

When Lincoln was told that Grant had an alcohol problem, he famously replied, "I wish you would tell me the brand of whiskey that Grant drinks. I would like to send a barrel of it to my other Generals." [20] Lincoln was a practical man. He knew that what matters is results.

Ch. 2 - The Civil War Years

Rutherford Birchard Hayes bears a striking resemblance to William Smith, the brother pictured on the right of the old-fashioned Smith Bros. cough drop box. The brand was started in 1872, went out of business in 2016, but was revived later that year by Lanes Brands.

Rutherford B. Hayes (Courtesy National Archives)

Standing 5 feet 8.5 inches tall, he weighed about 180 pounds. Hayes had a high forehead, straight nose, and deeply set blue eyes. As a youngster, he had auburn hair which turned dark brown in adulthood and then gray as he aged. Beginning with his Civil War service, he wore a full beard. He dressed in simple, sometimes ill-fitting clothes. A relaxed, easy-going person, Hayes was considered a good conversationalist and sharp observer of human nature. He enjoyed talking to people and hearing different viewpoints. He respected the opposition as a politician and welcomed constructive criticism. Although not regarded as a great orator, his speeches were well-planned and reasoned.

Born on October 4, 1822 in Delaware, Ohio, he carried his childhood nickname, Rud, with him throughout his life. His father, Rutherford Hayes, Jr., was a farmer, and his mother Sophia's maiden name of Birchard became his middle name. Unfortunately, his father died ten weeks before his birth. Rutherford had an older sister named Fanny along with two other siblings who both passed away before reaching adulthood. Fanny was his childhood protector and playmate. The two would frequently stage dramas and recite poems together as well as enjoy activities such as swimming, fishing, sailing and rifle shooting. The siblings were like-minded in terms of temperament. Each possessed a knack for irreverent criticism and had a caustic wit, which could lead to squabbling in their youth. Despite this, Rud and Fanny were very devoted to one another throughout their lives.

Fanny married William Augustus Platt on September 2, 1839 in Columbus, Ohio. He had been trained in watch making and went on to establish a successful jewelry store in Columbus. Not confined to one area of business, however, Platt would eventually become President of three prosperous businesses - a door company, the first gas corporation, and the Ohio Tool Company. He was also involved in real estate and acquired a large number of land holdings. After suffering from pneumonia and delirium for almost a month following the birth and then subsequent loss of twin girls, Fanny passed away on July 16, 1856. Devastated by the death, Rud wrote in his diary, "My dear only sister, my beloved Fanny, is dead! The dearest friend of childhood, the confidante of all my life, the one I loved best, is gone." Passing away at the age of just 36, Fanny's influence and affection would remain a constant memory throughout Rud's life.

Graduating from Ohio's Kenyon College in Gambier, Hayes was a Phi Beta Kappa at the top of his class in 1842. He then studied law at Harvard, receiving his degree in 1845. Admitted to the Ohio Bar, he established a successful legal practice in Cincinnati. A number of Presidents had been lawyers before Hayes but he was the first to actually graduate from a law school. The rest were self-taught or apprenticed.

Lucy Ware Webb was the daughter of James Webb. a Chillicothe, Ohio physician. An ardent abolitionist, he was notified that he had inherited 18 slaves and returned to his family home in Lexington, Kentucky to set them free. When Dr. Webb arrived, he was shocked to discover that members of his family were suffering from cholera. He attempted unsuccessfully to treat them. Not only did both his parents and brother die but he did as well. His widow, Maria Cook Webb, rejected the suggestion that she sell the slaves to support her now-fatherless children. She declared, "I'd rather take in washing for others if I have to raise money to support my family." (21)

Lucy W. Webb as a teenager (Courtesy Library of Congress)

Rud first met Lucy at Ohio Wesleyan University when she was just 15 years old. Her brothers were studying there and Lucy was taking college prep courses. Hayes remembered what he called the "bright-eyed" and "clever" young girl. A petite 5'4", she weighed just 100 pounds. Her black hair was parted in the middle and coiled into a tight bun. She had warm brown eyes, a spontaneous charm, charitable nature, self-deprecating sense of humor, and instinctive empathy. It was only natural that Rud would be struck by her.

The romantic sparks flew several years later when they met again after Lucy had recently graduated from Cincinnati Wesleyan Women's College with a Liberal Arts degree. They both happened to be guests at a wedding. At the reception afterwards, it was announced that one of the pieces of wedding cake had a gold ring hidden in it. Hayes turned out to be the lucky winner and chose to present it to Lucy as a gift. When they were engaged the following summer, Lucy commemorated the occasion by giving the ring back to her fiancé and placing it on his finger. He would wear it for the rest of his life. (22)

In 1851, Rud confessed in his diary, "I guess I am a great deal in love with Lucy. ... Her low sweet voice ... her soft rich eyes." He also praised her intelligence and character by saying, "She sees at a glance what others study upon, but will not, perhaps study what she is unable to see at a flash. She is a genuine woman, right from instinct and impulse rather than judgment and reflection." (23) They married in Cincinnati in a simple ceremony at the home of Lucy's widowed mother, Maria Cook Webb, on December 30, 1852. Rud was thirty and Lucy twenty-one at the time. They spent a month-long honeymoon at the home of Rud's sister Fanny in Columbus, Ohio, not the most romantic spot you could imagine. The couple briefly lived with Lucy's mother before buying a home of their own in Cincinnati.

Lucy and Rud's Wedding Portrait (Courtesy Wikimedia Commons)

Historian John W. Burgess commented that "They made such a perfect couple that whoever saw them together could not think of speaking of them apart." (24)

On November 4, 1853, they had their first child, Birchard Austin. Two days later, Rud described his feelings in his diary:

> "Lucy gave birth to our first child - a son. I hoped, and had a presentiment almost, that the little one

would be a boy. How I love Lucy, the mother of my boy! Sweetheart and wife, she had been before, loved tenderly and strongly as such, but the new feeling is more "home-felt," quiet, substantial, and satisfying. For the "lad" my feeling has yet to grow a great deal. I prize him and rejoiced to have him, and when I take him in my arms begin to feel a father's love and interest, hope and pride, enough to know what the feeling will be if not what it is. I think what is to be his future, his life. How strange a mystery all this is! This to me is the beginning of a new life. A happy one, I believe."(25)

Influenced by Lucy's strong abolitionist feelings when he was practicing law, Rutherford defended runaway slaves who crossed the Ohio River from Kentucky, a slave state. Ohio had many cases tried in its courts, including the previously mentioned Rosetta Armstead trial. The Cincinnati City Council named Hayes City Solicitor to fill a vacancy and he served a two-year term in 1859. He became associated with the newly-formed Republican Party.

Rud questioned whether the North and South could co-exist because of the irreconcilable differences regarding the issue of slavery saying:

> "The experiment of united free states and slaveholding states in one nation is perhaps a failure. Freedom and slavery can, perhaps, not exist side by side in the same popular government."

As the southern states began to talk of seceding, Hayes was ambivalent about the idea of fighting a Civil War to preserve the Union. He thought that it might be best to just "let them go." He explained his thinking this way:

> "Disunion and civil war are at hand; and yet I fear disunion and war less than compromise. We can recover from them. The free States alone, if we must go on alone, will make a glorious nation."

When the news of the shelling of Fort Sumter reached the home of the Hayes' family in Cincinnati, Ohio, Lucy's expressed a solid enthusiasm for military action. She even declared that if she had been there with a garrison of women, there would have been no surrender. "It is a hard thing to be a woman and witness so much and yet not do anything." (26) Her three little boys marched around the house beating their tin drums and shooting make-believe rifles. Birchard Austin was seven years old, Webb Cook five, and Rutherford Platt nearly three at the time.

A wave of patriotism engulfed the North. Lucy called it a "holy and just cause" and wrote in an 1861 letter, "The northern heart is truly fired. The enthusiasm that prevails in our city is perfectly irresistible. Those who favor secession or even sympathy with the South find it prudent to be quiet." (27) For a few weeks after the Sumter incident, Rutherford tried to concentrate on his law practice, but before the end of May, he decided "to go into the service for the war." Rud had changed his mind, concluding he had a patriotic duty to defend his country. By the end of December of 1861, he put out this cry to arms that was reported in the Boston Globe - "We are at the same high call here today – freedom, freedom for all. We all know this is the essence of this contest."

At the start of the war, Rud was a 40-year-old married man with three children and no prior military experience. He could have chosen to leave the fighting to younger men without family responsibilities. Rud expressed his dedication to the struggle, though, in this diary entry on May 15, 1861:

> "This is a just and necessary war and it demands the whole power of the country. I would prefer to go into it if I knew I was to die or be killed in the course of it than to live through and after it without taking any part in it."

After several weeks of communication with Governor William Dennison and other influential Ohioans, he received a commission as a Major of the newly-formed Burnet Rifles, a "volunteer home company" that was part of the 23rd Ohio Volunteer Infantry.

Following six weeks of intensive training at Camp Jackson, near Columbus, Ohio, the 23rd Infantry left for Clarksburg in western Virginia, part of the area that officially become West Virginia in 1863. Lucy, who had journeyed to Columbus to spend the last days near Rutherford, tried to conceal her tears as the train bearing the Regiment pulled out of the High Street station. Then, seeking solace for her loneliness, Lucy, her mother, and the three Hayes children left for a visit with her aunt, Margaret Boggs, who lived north of Chillicothe, Ohio. On the first of September, they returned to Cincinnati. With headaches that began increasing in her fifth month of pregnancy, Lucy found it pleasant to be "quietly at home" again.
(28)

As Rud knew, it would have been contrary to Lucy's nature to have hidden her worries. She wrote that the boys missed their father and also their uncle, Dr. Joseph Webb, who had been assigned to the 23rd as a surgeon. Showing her characteristic compassion, she asked Rud in a letter, "You know my great desire is that you and Joe constantly feel for the soldiers. Do what you can to lighten their hardships." Expressing her abhorrence of slavery, Lucy also admonished her husband, "Please do not allow the Regiment to be disgraced by returning any escaped slaves to the South." (29)

The unit also included fellow future President William McKinley, who noted that Hayes' demeanor would change markedly in battle, "From the sunny, agreeable, the kind, the generous, the gentle gentleman he was, once the battle was on to intense and ferocious." (30)

Hayes proved to be a trusted officer, earning the respect of both his troops and his superiors. Seven U.S. presidents served in the Civil War but Hayes was the only one who was wounded in action. In addition to having horses shot out from under him a number of times, he suffered five battle injuries including a knee wound from a bullet at Pearisburg in 1862, a gunshot wound which fractured his left arm during the Battle of South Mountain in 1862, a hit from a spent musket ball at the Second Battle of Kernstown in 1964, a severe ankle injury when he was thrown from a horse and a short-distance blow to the head by a spent round at the Battle of Cedar Creek in 1864.

General Ulysses S. Grant wrote of Hayes, "His conduct on the field was marked by conspicuous gallantry as well as the display of qualities of a higher order than that of mere personal daring." By the end of the war, Hayes had been honored with the title of Brevet Major General. The "Brevet" title was given as an indicator of outstanding service.

Lucy and Rud wrote letters to each other during the entirety of their relationship, and much of their correspondence took place during the Civil War. They expressed their love for each other and a deep appreciation of their relationship. He admitted:

> "I feel that you will not only be the making of my happiness, but also of my fortunes or success in life. The truth is I never did half try to be anything, or to do anything. Only now I believe I shall have purpose and steadiness to keep ever doing, looking to your happiness and approval as my best reward."

On December 21, 1861, Lucy gave birth to her fourth son, whom the older boys affectionately named "little Joseph." When the news reached Rud, he admitted how much he had worried. He wrote, "I love you so much and have felt so anxious about you. It is best it was not a daughter. These are no times for women."

In her first letter to Rutherford after the baby was born, Lucy wrote, "How long the time seems since we parted - almost six months - the first time in nine happy years." Before she had finished writing, a Sergeant who was on leave from Hayes' regiment stopped to collect the letter. A few days earlier, this same soldier, in a state of intoxication, pushed his way past her protesting nurse to personally deliver a message from Rud. With typical consideration, Lucy asked her husband not to reprimand the soldier because "getting home had quite overcome him."

Lucy was pleased whenever soldiers from the regiment stopped in Cincinnati to deliver messages from Rud. She indicated that they would always come with words of praise for his leadership. A visit from Hayes' Commanding Officer went well as he expressed admiration for him and candidly discussed army promotions with her. She wrote her husband's uncle, Sardis Birchard, that since both soldiers and officers liked Rud so much, "his talent for governing is fixed." Lucy's support and encouragement would prove invaluable to Rud throughout his career.

In February, Rutherford's turn for a furlough allowed him to spend time with the family. Arrangements were made at this time for Lucy and the children to move to Fremont, Ohio where they would live after the war in a house Sardis had built in Spiegel Grove. Lucy wished she could do something to ease the suffering of the wounded and dying. She often reminded her brothers Joseph and James, both of whom now served with the medical corps, that they should be kind and tender in their treatment of the wounded. She had an opportunity in May to help four disabled soldiers and their doctor-escort who were stranded for the night in Cincinnati. Lucy and her mother lodged them in their home and had coffee ready the next morning before they boarded the train for Chicago. She told Rud, "I thought of you in a strange country wounded and trying to get home but if anyone was kind to you would I not feel thankful."

Coincidentally, Rutherford did find himself in a similar position shortly thereafter. As commander of a company sent to relieve soldiers occupying an advanced position near the Perisburg railroad junction, he came under heavy enemy fire. To counteract a false report that he suffered a life-threating wound, he wired Lucy, "My wound was merely a scratch on the knee which did me no harm."

Having seen the account of the action in the newspaper, Lucy appreciated the prompt dispatch from Rutherford. She wrote, "The lightness of heart that took the place of the heavy load is indescribable. Now I feel you will let me know whatever happens." She said that "her heart glowed with pride" as she read the story of the engagement. However, she mourned those who had fallen and reminded her husband, "Would not the sad intelligence to relatives be lightened by words of praise and condolence from their leader?"

At times, Lucy felt that she could not endure separation. She wrote, "And yet with all my heart's longing I would not call you home. It is your right. Your duty. So believing, I look to the happy future when we shall be together." She wondered if he tired of reading her letters for "writing is not my forte but loving is." It was reported that he read and reread letters from Lucy many times over. He responded to her musing, "Darling wife, how this painful separation is made a blessing by the fine character it develops or brings to view. How I love you more and more!" On the morning of September 14, 1862, Ohio brigades tried to seize a fortified hill in the South Mountain Range, near Sharpsburg, Maryland. The leading regiment commanded by Hayes soon encountered a heavy concentration of enemy forces, and in the furious fighting a musket ball struck Hayes' left arm. Although painfully wounded, he continued to direct the action until his men insisted upon carrying him from the field. Shortly afterward, the remainder of the Brigade came up and a united charge drove the enemy from the hill. Dr. Joe Webb dressed Hayes' wound in the field hospital and later he was taken to

Middletown, Maryland where he was cared for in the home of Jacob Rudy. It was said that the treatment by Dr. Webb probably prevented amputation of Rud's arm.

The morning after the battle, Rud dictated dispatches concerning his injury to his wife, brother-in-law William Platt, and a close friend named John Herron. Later Lucy learned that the orderly had money for only two messages and the telegrapher transmitted those addressed to the men rather than her. She was understandably infuriated.

A few days later, Lucy, visiting near Chillicothe, received the following telegram from her husband: "I am here, come to me. I shall not lose my arm." The telegram bore a Washington byline. Leaving the children with relatives and entrusting her mother to find a wet nurse for the baby, Lucy caught the early morning stagecoach to Columbus. Platt met her at the stage office and insisted upon accompanying her to Washington. Lucy forgot the passes that would permit them to enter the military area, but evaded sentries at the Harrisburg railroad station by pretending to be with another party. Finally, a week after Hayes had been wounded, they arrived in Washington. Surprised not to find Rutherford at the Kirkwood House where he said he would be in case of accident, Lucy began making rounds of the hospitals. Personnel at the Patent Office, which had been turned into a military hospital, repulsed Lucy in what she described as a very "cruel and unfeeling manner," nor did she have any success in efforts to secure information from the Surgeon General's Office in the Capitol Building. After considerable difficulty, Platt located the original draft of the telegram on which Middletown had been marked out and Washington substituted.

At Lucy's insistence, they returned to the Patent Office, hoping for more information about Rutherford. Among the wounded soldiers on the steps, Lucy noticed several with "23" on their caps and called out "Twenty-third Ohio." Immediately, one shouted, "Why, this is Mrs. Hayes." Much to her relief, they told her that Rud had been taken to a house on the main street of Middletown to recuperate from his wound. (31)

By noon, Lucy Hayes and William Platt were on their way to Frederick, Maryland, as close as the railroad could take them to Middletown. Lucy stood in the aisle most of the three hours on the hot and dusty ride over a war-torn roadbed. When they finally arrived in Frederick, they found Dr. Webb, who had ridden over from Middletown every evening hoping they would arrive. While the men hitched the horse to a rented carriage, Lucy sat on the steps of the station looking rather forlorn. According to Lucy, "With my bundle in my hand, I was approached by a rather suspicious-looking man who had been staring at me saying, 'Haven't you any place to stay tonight?' I said, 'Yes, I am going on' and then quickly turned away." Fortunately, the buggy pulled up at that moment and Lucy, Platt, and Dr. Joe crowded into the single seat of the carriage. (32)

When they reached the Rudy house in Middletown, Rud greeted Lucy joking, "Well, you thought you would visit Washington and Baltimore." Lucy's sense of humor may have been strained because she answered rather sarcastically "I am happy to see you, too." (33)

Lucy spent her time in Middletown looking after her husband and visiting wounded soldiers in local homes and makeshift hospitals. About two weeks after her arrival, Rud Lucy, and six or seven wounded soldiers of the Twenty-third began the long journey back to Ohio. When they had to change trains, Lucy Hayes, finding no seats in the coach section, led the way into the Pullman car which was occupied by the wealthy and fashionable crowd returning from Saratoga. Oblivious to resentful glances, Lucy helped her "boys" into empty seats. When a messenger came through the car paging Colonel Hayes, the "society folk" suddenly became interested in the group and offered them food. Lucy disdainfully declined. As a cousin recalled, "Even reminiscently, years afterward, as she told the story, she became angry." (34)

It was no accident that she was affectionately called "Mother Lucy" by the troops she looked after. Many of them were smitten with her. A 20-year-old soldier named William McKinley wrote how he spent hours tending a campfire just because Lucy sat nearby and it meant he could be near her. (35) McKinley would later become the 25th President.

When the Hayes family discussed events of the Civil War, they remembered most vividly the months they spent together in army camps along the Kanawha River. After January 1863, Hayes served as commander of the First Brigade of the Second Kanawha Division, which was responsible for guarding West Virginia from enemy attacks. Except for occasional danger from Confederate raids and concern over forays into enemy territory, it provided a relatively safe haven for families of Union officers. Toward the end of the month, Lucy and the two older boys, Birch and Webb went to Camp Reynolds, a log cabin village on the Kanawha, near Gauley Bridge. As described by Hayes, "Mother and sons rowed skiffs, built dams, sailed little ships, played cards, and enjoyed the camp life generally."

It worried Rutherford, however, to have Lucy and the children ride any distance from the camp, particularly after one occasion when he found Union picket lines removed and had to dash back with Rebels in hot pursuit. When the Brigade abandoned Camp Reynolds and moved to Camp White, across the river from Charleston, Lucy and the boys returned to Ohio.

Referring to the selection of a former army officer for Superior Court Judge, Lucy wrote that she did not believe a soldier should leave his post for public office. This was expressing a sentiment that Rutherford made famous later when he refused to take time out from the military to canvas for a seat in Congress. A further item in her letter described the distress she felt when a relative, a surgeon in General Braxton Bragg's Confederate army, who had been set free following his capture in the Battle of Murfreesboro, stopped to visit them on his way South. It was a very short visit with the usually hospitable Lucy. She defiantly explained, "Love your enemies is not prominent in my character!"

In 1863, Lucy Hayes, her four sons, and her mother Maria traveled to Camp White on the river steamboat "Market Boy." After a few days, little Joseph became ill with dysentery and died on June 24. Hayes had seen so little of the eighteen-month-old baby that he claimed he "did not realize a loss but his mother, and still more his grandmother lost their little dear companion, and are very much afflicted." In later years, Lucy said the bitterest hour of her life was when she watched the steamer with the "lonely little body" depart for Cincinnati.

Early in the autumn, Rutherford, apprehensive that the Brigade might be ordered east, asked Lucy to return to Camp White. She left Webb and Ruddy with their grandmother in Chillicothe and Birchard with his uncle in Fremont. Lucy described in a letter how the officers and their wives sat around the campfire on the October nights listening to the Regimental band or watching the soldiers square-dance with each other to the merry sound of the fiddle.

Lucy deserved the popularity she enjoyed with the soldiers. She nursed them when they were ill, sewed and mended their uniforms, and listened to their troubles. She would sometimes even assist her brothers in caring for the sick and wounded. One story that reflected her kindness appeared in the Ohio State Journal:

> "James Parker of Trumbull County was a jolly good-natured 'boy' soldier. He expressed concern to his comrades because there was no one to mend his shirt and sew on pockets. 'Why Jim,' they said 'why don't you take it to the woman who does sewing for the Regiment, and get her to fix it.' When he asked where he could find the woman, they told him she was in the Colonel's tent.
>
> Parker walked over to the tent, saluted Colonel Hayes and explained what he wanted. Rud, with a merry twinkle in his eyes called Mrs. Hayes over and she promised to fix the shirt. When Parker returned to his comrades and told them that he had left clothing 'with the woman' to be fixed, they weren't sure whether the joke was on him or themselves. Later in the day, when Parker appeared with his shirt

neatly mended with two ample pockets in it, he was the hero of the company." (35)

Later in April, the 23rd Regiment broke camp and started on the campaign of 1864. For the first few days, the troops marched along the Kanawha River. Lucy and several of the wives rented a small boat and steamed slowly up the river, cheering and waving to the troops as they kept pace with them. As a veteran recalled, "Mrs. Hayes stood aft and waved us an encouraging adieu, and the mountains round rang with the cheers of the brave boys." (36)

When his soldiers rested between incursions into enemy-held territory in Virginia, Rutherford wrote that the new flag Lucy had sent was flying before headquarters. Provoked, Lucy reminded him that "The flag was meant for the soldiers and not the staff. To let them know how near they are to me. That not a day passes that our gallant soldiers are not remembered by me." Anxious as always to please his wife, Rud arranged to have the flag from Lucy presented to the men of the Regiment at dress parade.

During the time Hayes' Brigade took part in the dangerous raids into rebel territory, the family in Chillicothe spoke of little else but the war. Lucy wrote that Webb talked only of the "glory of victory" but Birch thought of "desolate homes and hearts." Worried about the fate of a cousin, who died later in Andersonville prison and fearing that wounded soldiers of the 23rd Regiment might be taken to Danville prison, Lucy criticized President Lincoln for excessive kindness to the rebel prisoners. In reply, Rutherford scolded her for suggesting that Lincoln should or could protect Union prisoners by a policy of retaliation. "There are 'brutal Rebels' no doubt," he wrote, "but we have brutal officers and men, too. And there are plenty of humane Rebels."

With Rud's Brigade exposed to constant danger in the fierce fighting for possession of the Shenandoah Valley and uncomfortable because of her latest pregnancy, the final days of the summer were a dark period for Lucy. She wrote, "I hope it is true that the darkest hour is just before day." Rud continued to try to send dispatches assuring her of his safety after every major engagement.

In August, 1864, political supporters in Cincinnati nominated Rud for Congress from the Second District. Appreciative of the compliments and congratulations, Lucy wrote to Sardis, "Of course dear Uncle it is gratifying to know how he stands with our citizens and friends. I wonder if all women or wives have such an unbounded admiration for their better half." Rutherford measured up to the expectations of his wife and friends in this answer to the plea that he take time off to canvass: "An officer fit for duty who at this crisis would abandon his post to electioneer for a seat in Congress ought to be scalped." (37) Rather than actively campaigning, Hayes simply wrote several letters explaining his political philosophy. He wound up defeating incumbent Democrat Alexander Long by 2,400 votes. Hayes' concept of duty, his war record, and reputation for integrity helped him win the election to Congress.

Rutherford and Lucy's fifth son was born on September 29, 1864. When Lucy was able to write her husband, she described the baby as a "fine child" gushing, "No little stranger was ever so warmly welcomed by uncles and cousins." They named the baby George Crook after Rutherford's Army commander. At a meeting of the

Ohio Commandery of the Military Order of the Loyal Legion of the United States on March 6th, 1889, Hayes would speak to his fellow Civil War veterans in an after-dinner speech about how he was reported as killed in action at Cedar Creek. They responded with hearty laughter and applause. Here's how he described what happened after the Cincinnati paper printed the erroneous story:

> "The next morning, the carrier took the daily paper to my wife as usual. It was carried into the room in which she was lying in bed and was laid upon the bed, as she was in the habit of reading it. Her uncle saw the paper coming, and hurried into the room, and before she could take it up, he grabbed it and quietly put it to one side, a little disturbed. He had heard what was in it, that a list of the dead was there, and a little complimentary obituary notice, which it is pleasant to have. It might be pleasant under some circumstances, but he concluded it would not be regarded so at the time, so he drew the paper away, and just at that moment it so happened that the telegraph boy came with the dispatch from the Captain of my command, giving the message I had recited. When that was read, the relief came.
>
> Well, that Captain was a man of sense, a good man to have about when anything was going on. He had sat right down at the instrument and telegraphed to my wife, at Chillicothe, Ohio: "The report that your husband was killed this morning is untrue. He was wounded, not dangerously, and is safe." (38)

When not living in Army camps, Lucy followed the movements of troops through accounts in the newspapers and exchanges of letters. While Rud bravely carried out his part as a soldier, Lucy faced the challenge of being a wartime wife and mother with equal courage and conviction.

Ch. 3 - The Emancipation Proclamation

Abraham Lincoln cast a long shadow in more ways than one. It wasn't just because of his 6-foot 4-inch, 180-pound gangly frame which caused him to tower over almost all his contemporaries. His iconic silk stovepipe hat would then add more than seven inches to his height. "Honest Abe's" course black hair was turning white at the temples when he was President. His eyes were gray with the left one slightly higher than the right. He had a distinctive wart on his right cheek above the corner of his mouth, a white scar on his thumb from an accident with an ax, plus a scar over his right eye from a fight with a gang of thieves. Lincoln's look was described by his law partner William Herndon as, "His cheekbones were high, sharp, and prominent. His eyebrows cropped out like a huge rock on the brow of a hill. His long, sallow face was wrinkled." (39)

Abraham Lincoln (Courtesy of National Archives)

John Nicolay, Lincoln's private secretary, claimed his features were too complex to be recorded accurately by photographers, painters, or sculptors:

> "Graphic art was powerless before a face that moved through a thousand delicate gradations of line and contour, light and shade, sparkle of the eye, and curve of the lip, in the long gamut of expression from grave to gay, and back again from the rollicking jollity of laughter to that far-away look." (40)

Unpretentious, plain-spoken, and genuinely interested in people and their problems, Lincoln would often sit in silence rubbing his chin while listening to others explain their point of view. His ready wit, down-home logic, and endless store of anecdotes readily engaged others. He was at his best in relaxed conversation. As one reporter wrote:

> "His custom of interspersing conversation with incidents, anecdotes, and witticisms are well calculated to impress his hearers with the kindheartedness of the man. And they are so adroitly and delicately mingled in the thread of his discourse that one hardly notices the digression." (41)

Lincoln, though, had a dark side. He wrestled with severe bouts of depression throughout his life. Upon meeting him for the first time, his long-time friend Joshua Speed recalled, "I looked up at him, and I thought then, as I think now, that I never saw so gloomy and melancholy a face in my life." (42) Lincoln himself noted:

"If what I feel was ever distributed to the whole human family, there would not be one cheerful face on earth. Whether I should ever be better, I cannot tell. I awfully forbode I shall not. To remain as I am is impossible. I must die or be better, it appears to me." (43)

Lincoln spoke with what is sometimes called a "frontier accent." He pronounced "get, there" as "git, thar." "Chair" came out sounding like "cheer." "Haven't" was "Haint."

As the Civil War battles raged on, the great question of what to do about slavery provoked increasingly angry discourse on Capitol Hill. In March of 1862, President Lincoln had requested that the legislature pass a resolution to provide federal aid to any state that was willing to adopt a plan for the gradual abolition of slavery. The idea went nowhere.

There was vitriol over the subject even within Lincoln's cabinet. According to Secretary of State William H. Seward, "The debates had grown so bitter that personal and even official relationships among members were ruptured, leading to a prolonged discontinuance of cabinet meetings." (44) The meetings were officially scheduled for every Tuesday and Friday but were being held less and less frequently. On the occasions when they were convened, there was often angry discussion about whether or not slavery was protected by or prohibited by the Constitution. Lincoln, for the most part, listened intently and didn't take an active role in the debates. He'd openly say that slavery was "a moral, a social, and a political wrong" but wasn't sure how to reverse it where it already existed.

Lincoln began mulling over a document that would later become known as the Emancipation Proclamation. He wrote a first draft of it in late July of 1862. As expected, some of his advisers supported it while others were hesitant. Seward urged the President to wait to announce emancipation until the Union won a victory on the battlefield and Lincoln took his advice.

On September 17, 1862, Union General George B. McClellan's Army of the Potomac halted the advance of Confederate forces commanded by General Robert E. Lee near Sharpsburg, Maryland in the Battle of Antietam. The first field army-level engagement of the Civil War to take place on Union soil, there was a combined tally of 22,717 dead, wounded, or missing. The battle was the deadliest 24-hour period of the entire Civil War. General Lee's army had driven the Union troops from the Confederate capital of Richmond and were massing to invade Maryland and then march up to Pennsylvania. The Rebels actually lost fewer soldiers than the Union army and the engagement left them in what many considered a stronger defensive position.

It was enough of a victory, though, for Lincoln to take action. Practically speaking, it would allow for the enrollment of nearly 200,000 badly needed former slaves in the Union Army. That proved to be a significant help in tilting the war in favor of the North. Despite the naysayers and doubters, Lincoln published an Executive Order called the Emancipation Proclamation. The document, issued on September 22, called on all Confederate states to rejoin the Union within 100 days - by January 1, 1863 - or their slaves would be declared "thenceforward, and forever free." He declared, "we must free the slaves or be ourselves subdued." Lincoln considered the signing of it to be the highlight of his career. With pen poised, he explained, "I never, in my life, felt more certain that I was doing right, than I do in signing this paper. If my name ever goes into history it will be for this act, and my whole soul is in it." (45) It was the very definition of commitment.

President Joseph R. Biden referred to those comments in his 21-minute Inaugural Address on January 20, 2021 after he was sworn in as the country's 46th President. Referencing Lincoln, he said, "Today, on this January day, my whole soul is in this. Bringing America together. Uniting our people. Uniting our nation. And I ask every American to join me in this cause." Later in the speech, he added, "We must end this uncivil war that pits red against blue, rural versus urban, conservative versus liberal. We can do this - if we open our souls instead of hardening our hearts. If we show a little tolerance and humility. If we're willing to stand in the other person's shoes." (46) Biden's speech could have been given in 1862. Lincoln would likely have welcomed him as a strong ally.

Here's the full text of Lincoln's history-making proclamation:

> "That on the first day of January, in the year of our Lord one thousand eight hundred and sixty-three, all persons held as slaves within any State or designated part of a State, the people whereof shall then be in rebellion against the United States, shall be then, thenceforward, and forever free; and the Executive Government of the United States, including the military and naval authority thereof, will recognize and maintain the freedom of such persons, and will do no act or acts to repress such persons, or any of

them, in any efforts they may make for their actual freedom.

That the Executive will, on the first day of January aforesaid, by proclamation, designate the States and parts of States, if any, in which the people thereof, respectively, shall then be in rebellion against the United States; and the fact that any State, or the people thereof, shall on that day be, in good faith, represented in the Congress of the United States by members chosen thereto at elections wherein a majority of the qualified voters of such State shall have participated, shall, in the absence of strong countervailing testimony, be deemed conclusive evidence that such State, and the people thereof, are not then in rebellion against the United States.

Now, therefore I, Abraham Lincoln, President of the United States, by virtue of the power in me vested as Commander-in-Chief, of the Army and Navy of the United States in time of actual armed rebellion against the authority and government of the United States, and as a fit and necessary war measure for suppressing said rebellion, do, on this first day of January, in the year of our Lord one thousand eight hundred and sixty-three, and in accordance with my purpose so to do publicly proclaimed for the full period of one hundred days, from the day first above mentioned, order and designate as the States and parts of States wherein the people thereof respectively, are this day in rebellion against the

United States, the following, to wit: Arkansas, Texas, Louisiana, (except the Parishes of St. Bernard, Plaquemines, Jefferson, St. John, St. Charles, St. James Ascension, Assumption, Terrebonne, Lafourche, St. Mary, St. Martin, and Orleans, including the City of New Orleans) Mississippi, Alabama, Florida, Georgia, South Carolina, North Carolina, and Virginia, (except the forty-eight counties designated as West Virginia, and also the counties of Berkley, Accomack, Northampton, Elizabeth City, York, Princess Ann, and Norfolk, including the cities of Norfolk and Portsmouth), and which excepted parts, are for the present, left precisely as if this proclamation were not issued.

And by virtue of the power, and for the purpose aforesaid, I do order and declare that all persons held as slaves within said designated States, and parts of States, are, and henceforward shall be free; and that the Executive government of the United States, including the military and naval authorities thereof, will recognize and maintain the freedom of said persons.

And I hereby enjoin upon the people so declared to be free to abstain from all violence, unless in necessary self-defense; and I recommend to them that, in all cases when allowed, they labor faithfully for reasonable wages.

> And I further declare and make known, that such persons of suitable condition, will be received into the armed service of the United States to garrison forts, positions, stations, and other places, and to man vessels of all sorts in said service. And upon this act, sincerely believed to be an act of justice, warranted by the Constitution, upon military necessity, I invoke the considerate judgment of mankind, and the gracious favor of Almighty God." (47)

The proclamation had enormous symbolic power. It announced freedom for enslaved people as one of the North's war aims, alongside preserving the Union itself.

"It is my greatest and most enduring contribution to the history of the war," Lincoln said of emancipation in February of 1865. "It is, in fact, the central act of my administration, and the great event of the 19th century." (48) Politically, it was a risk for Lincoln to issue the proclamation. It was a highly controversial issue, even in the North, where there were many who felt that the idea of "State's Rights" would be negatively affected. As the Union army advanced through the South, thousands of slaves were set free each day. Some believe that he issued the proclamation for idealistic and humanitarian reasons. Others claim he did it for strategic reasons to undermine the South's war efforts. He certainly hoped that the emancipation would lead to many slaves fleeing their places of work and thereby depleting the South's workforce. If slaves ran away, then the Confederacy's economy would suffer.

Although slaves were not used as soldiers by the Confederates, they provided significant support by digging trenches, building fortifications, serving as cooks, taking care of horses, working as assistants in field hospitals, etc. If they were left at home, they would take care of the farms and their crops. Lincoln realized that freeing the slaves would weaken the South and help the North, particularly if enough of them were willing to join the Union side in combat.

The preliminary proclamation was a warning that if the states that were in rebellion didn't free the slaves, Lincoln would issue "a fit and necessary war measure for preserving the union." (49) As it was becoming apparent that Lincoln would follow through on finalizing the Emancipation Proclamation, freed and enslaved Blacks were cautiously optimistic about the future. The Chicago Tribune printed the following on December 28, 1862:

> "Old Abe's Proclamation is beginning to work. The Negroes are counting the days and hours when the 1st of January shall come. They meet in little knots, and talk over the whole matter, and lay their plan for going. The day of Jubilee they think, has surely come."

Famed abolitionist, statesman, and writer Frederick Douglass wrote of the spirit of those who had gathered with him at the telegraph office to wait for the official announcement that the Emancipation Proclamation had been issued: "We were waiting and listening as for a bolt from the sky. We were watching by the dim light of the stars for the dawn of a new day. We were longing for the answer to the agonizing prayers of centuries." (50)

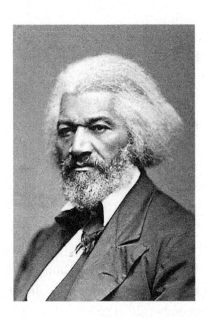
Frederick Douglass (Courtesy Library of Congress)

Douglass, originally born Frederick Augustus Washington Bailey said, "I have no accurate knowledge of my age, never having seen any authentic record containing it." Forced to live with his grandparents, Douglas only saw his mother a few times as she was enslaved on a plantation 12 miles way. He was just seven years old when she died. Although the precise date of his birth is unknown, he chose February 14 because he recalled that his mother would call him, "Little Valentine"

Douglass felt the proclamation was "the greatest event in our nation's history." He described it this way - "The scene was wild and grand. Joy and gladness exhausted all forms of expression, from shouts of praise to joys and tears." In later reflecting back on the event, he said:

"Can any colored man, or any white man friendly to the freedom of all men, ever forget the night which followed the first day of January 1863, when the world was to see if Abraham Lincoln would prove to be as good as his word? I shall never forget that memorable night, when in a distant city I waited and watched at a public meeting, with three thousand others not less anxious than myself, for the word of deliverance which we have heard read today. Nor shall I ever forget the outburst of joy and thanksgiving that rent the air when the lightning brought to us the emancipation proclamation. In that happy hour we forgot all delay, and forgot all tardiness, forgot that the president had bribed the rebels to lay down their arms by a promise to withhold the bolt which would smite the slave system with destruction; and we were thenceforward willing to allow the president all the latitude of time, phraseology, and every honorable device that statesmanship might require for the achievement of a great and beneficent measure of liberty and progress." (51)

According to Richard Striner in a New York Times editorial, "Almost all abolitionists and radical Republicans, even those who had condemned Lincoln's methods as being too cautious, were thrilled." The radical Republican Benjamin Wade proclaimed, "Now, hurrah for Old Abe and the PROCLAMATION!" (52)

A newspaper article on Emancipation Day Jan. 1, 1869 in Charleston, South Carolina's Charleston Daily News read:

"The colored fire companies and other colored organizations in the city celebrated Emancipation Day by a procession, oration, etc. There were 285 men and boy in the procession, of whom about two hundred were in uniform. A large number of colored people accompanied the procession through the principal streets to the Battery, where A.J. Rausier, Colored, Chairman of the Republican Executive Committee, delivered an oration, which seemed to delight his audience. He spoke of the events which had given glory to the day which they were celebrating, and of the principles which they illustrated. He endeavored to impress upon his hearers the value of the right of suffrage, one of the legitimate sequences of emancipation, and their duty to use it carefully and conscientiously. He dwelt at length on the subject of education and its special importance to his race, and advised his hearers, in the most earnest manner, to secure its blessings for themselves and their children."

The Emancipation Proclamation and subsequent amendments to the Constitution might have outlawed slavery, but certainly they did not outlaw racism, the belief that the innate characteristics of a person or group determine their capabilities and that one group is naturally superior to another.

When news of the proclamation spread, many southerners were incensed and newspapers reacted with horror. The Cincinnati Enquirer condemned Lincoln, calling the Proclamation a "complete overthrow of the Constitution he swore to protect and defend." Other words commonly used included "wicked" and "atrocious."

Confederate President Jefferson Davis called Lincoln's action "the most execrable measure recorded in the history of guilty man." (53) He claimed the proclamation would fail and that it was nothing more than a gesture of "impotent rage" for which Confederates should show "contempt." He also referred to the proclamation as "an attempt to subjugate the South by force of arms." Since the final Proclamation made provision for enlisting freed slaves in the army, Confederate General P.G.T. Beauregard called for the "execution of abolition prisoners" saying "Let the execution be made with the garrote." (54) A garrote is a gruesome hand-held weapon using chain, wire, or cord to strangle someone.

Despite the backlash from the southern states, Lincoln was defiant. When warned that the Confederate anger against the proclamation would have effect of doubling the size of their armies, he replied, "We'll double ours, then."

At the time, the situation facing the North did not look promising. The French and British were edging closer to recognizing the Confederacy and this would have been a great danger for the Union, especially if those countries were going to support the Rebels with money and troops. General Robert E. Lee and other Confederate leaders had also been able to inflict a string of defeats on the Union army.

The proclamation effectively outlawed the institution and practice of slavery in the Southern Secessionist States. Northern abolitionists welcomed this move but wanted the Emancipation to be proclaimed in all of the States of the Union. Lincoln deliberately issued a cautious Proclamation in order to appease the various political factions.

It didn't lead to a massive slave rebellion in the South, as some abolitionists had hoped, but slaves began to slowly escape in small groups. Towards the end of the Civil War many more slaves left their masters and many headed north via the Underground Railroad or relocated out west. Many joined the Union army or worked in northern industries. Some freed slaves faced continued discrimination in the North and even in the Union army. They almost all admired Lincoln, however, and they did all they could to help the Union defeat the South.

During the Civil War, Black Union soldiers refused their salaries for 18 months to protest being paid lower wages than White soldiers. When Black soldiers began signing up with the Union Army, they were paid $10 a month. White soldiers were paid at least $13, with officers earning more. Blacks were further angered when only they were charged a $3 monthly fee for clothing, lowering their pay to $7. As a result, the highest-paid Black soldier earned about half the lowest-paid White soldier's salary. To protest these conditions, Black regiments refused to accept their inferior wages. Finally, pressure from abolitionist congressmen coupled with the courage Black soldiers had shown in combat persuaded Congress to rectify the pay structure. In September of 1864, Black soldiers finally received equal pay that was retroactive to their enlistment date. For many, this meant they finally had enough money to send some home to their families.

But the Emancipation Proclamation did not end slavery, as it only applied to the Confederate states then at war against the Union and only to the portion of those states not already under Union control. To end slavery nation-wide would take constitutional amendments abolishing the institution.

There was some disagreement as to whether the President's Executive Order was even constitutional. Lincoln himself was unsure on this point. Executive Orders were not issued routinely by Presidents up to this point. Lincoln, therefore, began pushing for an official Constitutional Amendment to end slavery. He didn't want to run the risk of the Judiciary overruling him after the war, which was a distinct possibility with what was then the most conservative branch of the federal government. Lincoln also had to consider the fate of the slaves exempted from the Emancipation Proclamation, especially in the loyal border states. In particular, Kentucky and Delaware would continue to resist emancipation. Slavery would only end there with the ratification of the 13th Amendment in December of 1865.

So, while the Proclamation put the country on the road to the final end of slavery in the United States, it was far from an ideal solution. Slaves fleeing into Union lines to gain their freedom created a horrible humanitarian crisis, with thousands dying due to the often poor conditions in hastily established Federal Freedmen's camps.

The Emancipation Proclamation would pave the way for the permanent abolition via a Constitutional amendment. By the end of January of 1865, both houses of Congress passed the 13th Amendment, and it was ratified that December. The amendment states: "Neither slavery nor involuntary servitude, except as a punishment for crime whereof the party shall have been duly convicted, shall exist within the United States, or any place subject to their jurisdiction." (55) Despite the long history of slavery in the British colonies in North America, and the continued existence of slavery in America until 1865, the amendment was the first explicit mention of the institution of slavery in the U.S. Constitution.

On March 3, 1865, Congress, at the recommendation of President Lincoln, the created a federal government agency called The Bureau of Refugees, Freedmen, and Abandoned Lands, usually referred to as the Freedmen's Bureau, to direct "provisions, clothing, and fuel for the immediate and temporary shelter and supply of destitute and suffering refugees and freedmen and their wives and children." (56) During the Civil War, Union forces had confiscated vast areas of farmland owned by Southern plantation owners. Popularly known as the "40 acres and a Mule" provision, part of the Freedmen's Bureau Act authorized the bureau to rent or sell approximately 400,000 acres of this land to formerly enslaved persons. This was the first systematic attempt to provide a form of reparations to newly freed slaves and it was considered extremely radical and controversial.

This creative idea for massive land redistribution was the result of a discussion that Union General William T. Sherman and Secretary of War Edwin M. Stanton held four days before the issuance of what was called "William T. Sherman's Special Field Order No. 15" on January 16, 1865. The meeting was held with 20 Black ministers on January 12 on the second floor of a mansion on Macon Street in Savannah, Georgia where Sherman was headquartered following his famous March to the Sea.

The New York Daily Tribune printed a transcript of the discussion on Feb. 13, 1865, edition. Stanton said that "for the first time in the history of this nation, the representatives of the government had gone to these poor debased people to ask them what they wanted for themselves." Stanton had suggested to Senator John Sherman that they gather "the leaders of the local Negro community" and ask them something no one else had apparently thought to ask: "What do you want for your people following the war?"

The leader and spokesperson of the group was a 67-year-old Baptist minister named Garrison Frazier, who had been born in Granville, N.C., and was a slave until 1857, "when he purchased freedom for himself and wife for $1,000 in gold and silver," as the New York Daily Tribune reported. Reverend Frazier was the one who bore the responsibility of answering questions that Sherman and Stanton put to the group.

What did they tell Sherman and Stanton that Black people wanted? "Land!" was their clear answer. It was the way they could best take care of themselves. According to Reverend Frazier what they needed most, "is to have land, and turn it and till it by our own labor ... and we can soon maintain ourselves and have something to spare ... We want to be placed on land until we are able to buy it and make it our own." When asked whether the freed slaves would rather live scattered among the Whites or in colonies by themselves, Brother Frazier, as the transcript calls him, replied that, "I would prefer to live by ourselves, for there is a prejudice against us in the South that will take years to get over." (57)

Four days later, Sherman issued Special Field Order No. 15, after President Lincoln approved it. The reaction was immediate. Baptist minister Ulysses L. Houston, one of the group that had met with Sherman, led 1,000 Blacks to Skidaway Island, Georgia, where they established a self-governing community with Houston as the "Black Governor." By June, 40,000 freedmen had been settled on 400,000 acres of what some called "Sherman Land." Sherman later ordered that the Army, upon request, could lend the new settlers mules which is the practice known as giving "40 acres and a mule." (58)

In the summer of 1865, President Andrew Johnson would order all of this federally controlled land returned to its former White slave owners - the very people who had declared war on the United States. Now lacking land, most freedmen were forced to return to working on the same plantations where they had toiled for generations. They had little hope of achieving the same economic mobility enjoyed by White citizens. For decades, almost all southern Black people were forced to remain propertyless and mired in poverty. Had this policy been made permanent, former slaves would have had access to land ownership and would have had a chance to be self-sufficient economically. They would have been able to build, accrue, and pass on wealth. One of the principal promises of America has been the possibility of people being able to own property and businesses. Would it have made a been the key to making Reconstruction successful? According to W.E.B. Dubois, it would have been the game-changer:

> "Surprise and ridicule has often been voiced concerning the demand of Negroes for land. It has been regarded primarily as a method for punishing rebellion. Motives of this sort may have been on the minds of some Northern Whites, but so far as the

Negroes were concerned, their demand for a reasonable part of the land on which they had worked for a quarter of a millennium was absolutely justified, and to give them anything less was an economic farce. On the other hand, to have given each one of the million Negro free families a forty acre free-hold would have been the basis of real democracy in the United States that might have easily transformed the modern world."(59)

W.E.B. Dubois (Courtesy National Archives)

As one of the earliest and most influential spokesmen for Black liberation, William Edward Burghardt, known as "W.E.B.", DuBois pioneered many of the strategies of the American civil rights movement. He was one of the first leaders of the NAACP. One of the leading scholars and historians of his time, DuBois was a prolific writer with 21 books and countless journal articles to his credit. He received a Bachelor of Arts degree from Fisk University and then went on to earn a second Bachelor's degree, a Master's degree, and a Ph.D. from Harvard.

Headed by Maj. Gen. Oliver O. Howard, the Freedmen's Bureau might be called the first federal welfare agency. Despite inadequate funds and lack of trained personnel, the bureau built hospitals for, and gave direct medical assistance to, more than a million freedmen. More than 21 million rations were distributed to impoverished recipients.

Its greatest accomplishments were in education. More than 1,000 Black schools were built and over $400,000 spent to establish teacher-training institutions. Among the historically Black colleges and universities that received aid from the bureau were Atlanta University; Fisk University, named for General Clinton B. Fisk of the Tennessee Freedmen's Bureau who gave the school its original facilities in a former Union army barracks; and Howard University which was named for General Howard.

Ch. 4 - The War Ends

The Union Army was on the march. Ever since the pyrrhic victory in the Battle of Gettysburg in Pennsylvania, fought on July 1 through 3 of 1863, they had the clear momentum. There were an estimated 23,000 Union and 28,000 Rebel casualties at Gettysburg, the most costly battle of the Civil War. The Confederate forces were pushed all the way back to Virginia. General Robert E. Lee and the Army of Northern Virginia, the largest Rebel force, was forced to abandon the Capital of Richmond. General Ulysses S. Grant and his troops blocked their retreat at Appomattox. Lee's Army was running low on food and supplies.

Union cavalry forces under General Philip Sheridan outran Lee's army, blocking their retreat and taking 6,000 prisoners at Sayler's Creek, Virginia. Rebel desertions were mounting daily.

Lee sent a message to Grant announcing his willingness to surrender. The two Generals met in the parlor of the Wilmer McLean home at 1 p.m. on April 9, 1865.

Grant arrived in his muddy field uniform while Lee turned out in full dress attire, complete with sash and his famous gold-plated sword, commissioned in Paris by Louis Francois Devisme. It's believed the sword was used only for ceremonial purposes and never actually carried into battle.

Peers during the Mexican War, the two opposing Generals exchanged small talk to get reacquainted. Lee then asked for the terms of surrender which Grant hurriedly wrote out, having already agreed upon them with President Abraham Lincoln. All officers and men were to be pardoned, and they would be sent home with their private property, including the horses. The rank-and-file soldiers would turn in their rifles although officers were allowed to keep their side arms. As a humanitarian gesture, all the rebels would be provided with food.

Generals Ulysses S. Grant & Robert E. Lee (Courtesy National Archives)

The meeting lasted approximately an hour and a half. When it was finished, General Lee emerged from the house still wearing the sword which was never offered in surrender, despite rumors to the contrary, re-mounted his horse Traveler and set off for his lines. A band began to play in celebration but General Grant immediately stopped them declaring, "The war is over. The Rebels are our countrymen again, and the best sign of rejoicing after the victory will be to abstain from all demonstrations in the field." (60)

A lengthy period of scattered fighting continued as word of Lee's surrender spread through the South. A number of other Confederate forces still remained active, in particular General Joseph E. Johnston's Army of Tennessee, the second-largest Confederate force. On April 12 in North Carolina, Johnston and his men received news of Lee's surrender. The next day, Gen. William T. Sherman's Union cavalry captured Raleigh, pushing Johnston's forces westward. Jefferson Davis ordered Johnston to resume fighting. Realizing that defeat was certain, he refused. Under relentless pressure from Sherman, Johnston instead reached out to discuss peace terms. On April 26, Sherman and Johnston signed a peace agreement similar to the one signed by Grant and Lee. In the biggest surrender of the Civil War, Johnston gave up around 90,000 soldiers, virtually all remaining Confederate troops.

In 1864, President Lincoln ran for re-election with former Democrat Andrew Johnson as his Vice-Presidential candidate. The Republican Party used the temporary name of "The National Union Party" for the election. It was an attempt to begin to bring the country together in the midst of the war. This was a full 12 years before the Centennial Election would be held and the Republicans were just beginning to grapple with the issue of how to approach reunification. Choosing Johnson as Vice-President was one of the ways Lincoln signaled willingness to welcome the South back into the fold. He explicitly stated that goal in closing his second Inaugural Address:

> "With malice toward none with charity for all with firmness in the right as God gives us to see the right let us strive on to finish the work we are in to bind up the nation's wounds, to care for him who shall have

> borne the battle and for his widow and his orphan to do all which may achieve and cherish a just and lasting peace among ourselves and with all nations."
> (61)

Lincoln, unfortunately, knew that he lived in constant danger admitting, ""I long ago made up my mind that if anybody wants to kill me, he will do it. If I wore a shirt of mail and kept myself surrounded by a bodyguard, it would be all the same. There are a thousand ways of getting at a man if it is desirable that he should be killed." (62)

In a bizarre twist of fate, Edwin Booth, the older brother of Lincoln assassin John Wilkes Booth, saved the life of 21-year-old Robert Todd Lincoln, the President's only child to survive to adulthood, just months before the President was assassinated. Robert accidentally fell in the gap between a train and the station platform. Edwin, unlike his brother, was a Union sympathizer, had voted for Lincoln in the 1864 election, and was an acquaintance of Robert who described the incident this way in a letter to the editor of "The Century" magazine:

> "A group of passengers were late at night purchasing their sleeping car places from the conductor who stood on the station platform at the entrance of the car. The platform was about the height of the car floor, and there was of course a narrow space between the platform and the car body. There was some crowding, and I happened to be pressed by it against the car body while waiting my turn. In this situation the train began to move, and by the motion I was twisted off my feet, and had dropped

somewhat, with feet downward, into the open space, and was personally helpless, when my coat collar was vigorously seized and I was quickly pulled up and out to a secure footing on the platform. Upon turning to thank my rescuer I saw it was Edwin Booth, whose face was of course well known to me, and I expressed my gratitude to him, and in doing so, called him by name." (63)

On Good Friday, the night of April 14, 1865, while attending the comedy play "Our American Cousin" at Ford's Theatre, Lincoln was shot by John Wilkes Booth at point blank range at 10:13 p.m. during the third act of the show Doctors were on the scene to immediately attend to him and move him to a home across the street. He never regained consciousness and was pronounced dead at 7:22 a.m. the following day, sending shock waves throughout the nation. Vice-President Andrew Johnson was immediately sworn in as the country's 17th President.

When Booth learned that the Lincolns would be attending the theater that night, he put his plan into action. He also enlisted co-conspirators to kill Secretary of State William H. Seward and Vice President Andrew Johnson. These two assassinations were supposed to have happened as the actor pulled the trigger on Lincoln. Booth believed that the murders of the President and his two potential successors would likely throw the country into chaos.

Booth felt that Lincoln's presence in the theater gave him a unique opportunity to get close to the president. As the former had years of acting experience, he had actually performed there several times himself and was therefore familiar with the layout of the building.

He was also known to the staff and apparently used his connections to gain easier access to Lincoln's private box.

That evening, Lincoln and his wife were in their box above the stage with Army officer Henry Rathbone and his fiancé Clara Harris, the daughter of New York senator Ira Harris. The President and his group had arrived late to the theater. In response, the orchestra momentarily halted proceedings to play "Hail to the Chief," and the 1,700 patrons got to their feet to applaud.

The President had security at the event. John Frederick Parker, a police officer, had been assigned the duty of protecting the private box. During the play's intermission, however, the officer accompanied Lincoln's coachman and footman to a nearby saloon for some drinks. This left the box unguarded so that Booth was able to slip in easily and bar the door behind him to prevent anyone from escaping. Booth knew the play well, and he timed his attack to coincide with a particularly funny line uttered by actor Harry Hawk. Lincoln was reportedly laughing when Booth snuck up behind him and shot him behind his left ear. The actor used a single-shot .44-caliber derringer pistol, and the bullet passed through Lincoln's brain, fracturing both orbital plates. Rathbone turned to see Booth standing over the fallen President and immediately rushed him. However, the young army officer was stabbed in the left forearm in the struggle. Booth jumped the 12-foot drop from the box to the stage, breaking his left leg in the process of landing. The actor then held his bloody knife above his head and addressed the audience. At this point, most of the people in attendance thought the commotion was simply part of the performance. Booth called out the Virginia state motto of, "Sic semper tyrannis!" which means, "Thus always to tyrants!" (64)

The assassin then limped across the stage toward an exit door, stabbing orchestra leader William Withers Jr. on the way. After Booth escaped from the theater, he mounted a horse that he had left tied up in the alleyway. He rode off and spent the next couple of weeks in hiding.

At 8:00 a.m. on Saturday, while boarding a train, Ohio Governor Rutherford B. Hayes heard a report that Lincoln had succumbed to the attack. Pained and shocked, he wrote this letter to an Army Chaplain using, for the first time, a phrase "the darling of history" that he would repeat many times in the years to come.

> "The awful tragedy at Washington so shocked me that I hardly know how to feel or think about it. It is a great calamity. The fame of the President is safe. He is the darling of history ever more." (65)

Lucy's joy in the fall of Richmond and the surrender of Lee's army at Appomattox Courthouse on April 9, 1865 quickly turned to sorrow as she learned of the assassination of President Lincoln. She began a letter to Rud, "From such great joy how soon we were filled with sorrow and grief past utterance. I am sick and tired of this endless talk of Forgiveness - taking them back like brothers. Justice and Mercy should be together." Anticipating her husband's reaction, she added, "Now don't say to me Ruddy that I ought not to write so."

Attending Lincoln's funeral on April 19, the battle-hardened Ulysses Grant stood alone and wept openly. He later called Lincoln "incontestably the greatest man I have ever known." (66)

Frederick Douglass paid tribute to Lincoln by referring to him as, "not only a great President, but a great man – too great to be small in anything. In his company, I was never in any way reminded of my humble origin, or of my unpopular color." (67)

Lincoln was the first, although would not be the last, President to be assassinated. James Garfield, William McKinley, and John F. Kennedy would suffer the same fate. On April 26, the largest manhunt in American history ended before dawn in a Virginia tobacco barn. Booth was killed by single fatal shot in the back of the head fired by Union Sergeant Boston Corbett. It was just an inch below the spot where Booth had shot Lincoln.

On July 7, co-conspirators Lewis Powell, George Atzerdot, David Herold, and Mary Surratt were hung at Fort McNair for their involvement with Booth in the plot to assassinate high-ranking government officials. On Good Friday, Powell had attacked Secretary of State Seward with a knife causing serious injuries from which he was able to recover. He was accompanied by Herold who led him to Seward. Atzerdot was planning to assassinate Andrew Johnson. Surratt owned the boarding house in which the conspirators met. She became the first woman to be executed by the federal government. President Andrew Johnson was quoted in the Arkansas Democrat Gazette as saying while signing her death warrant that Surratt was "the one who kept the nest that hatched the egg." Jefferson Davis was captured with his entourage near Irwinville, Georgia, by a detachment of Union General James H. Wilson's cavalry on May 10. He never stood trial. It was feared that Davis would either prove to a jury that secession was legally permitted under the U.S. Constitution or he would be transformed into a martyr if convicted and executed. He was forced, however, to serve a two-year prison term at Fort Monroe, Virginia. Alexander H. Stephens, his Vice President, was arrested for treason at his home in Crawfordville, on May 11. He was imprisoned at Fort Warren, Boston Harbor, for five months. All other former Confederates were pardoned by President Andrew Johnson.

In the middle of May, Rutherford met Lucy at Marietta, Ohio and after stopping at his last post, New Creek, West Virginia, to send in his resignation from the military, they proceeded to Washington for a Grand Review of the Army celebration. On May 23 and 24, Rutherford and Lucy watched from the Congressional stand as Union legions marched in review along Pennsylvania Avenue. Lucy wrote her mother that she borrowed Rutherford's field glasses to watch President Andrew Johnson and General Grant, in the reviewing stand directly opposite the Hayes family. This is how Lucy described the proceedings:

> "While my heart filled with joy at the thought of our mighty country - its victorious army - the sad thoughts of thousands who would never gladden home with their presence made the joyful scene mingled with so much sadness that I could not shake it off."

Just a few weeks later, June 19, 1865, celebrated as Juneteenth, was another noteworthy day. That morning, Union Major General Gordon Granger arrived in Galveston to take command of the more than 2,000 federal troops in Texas, the most remote slave state, and enforce the emancipation of its slaves. Granger's troops marched throughout Galveston and read an order first at Union

Army Headquarters at the Osterman Building in the Strand Historic District. They next went to the 1861 Customs House and Courthouse before finally heading to the Negro Church on Broadway, since renamed Reedy Chapel-AME Church. The order announced the following:

> "The people of Texas are informed that, in accordance with a proclamation from the Executive of the United States, all slaves are free. This involves an absolute equality of personal rights and rights of property between former masters and slaves, and the connection heretofore existing between them becomes that between employer and hired labor. The freedmen are advised to remain quietly at their present homes and work for wages. They are informed that they will not be allowed to collect at military posts and that they will not be supported in idleness either there or elsewhere." (68)

Originally a holiday in Galveston Texas, Juneteenth was declared an official national holiday in 2021. Although this event is regarded as "the end of slavery," emancipation for those in the border states of Delaware and Kentucky, would actually not come until December 18, 1865, when ratification of the Thirteenth Amendment was announced.

In turn, the Civil War wasn't officially over until President Johnson signed Proclamation 157 on August 20 of 1866 proclaiming, "Said insurrection is at an end and that peace, order, tranquility, and civil authority now exist in and throughout the whole United States of America." (69) The war ended but the arduous process of trying to heal the nation was just beginning. In fact, you could say that the struggle moved from the battlefield to the streets. Overall, the effect of the Emancipation Proclamation wasn't completely felt until after the war was over and all slaves in America were set free as per the 13th, 14th, and 15th amendments. Together, the three are known as the Reconstruction Amendments:

- The 13th amendment made slavery unconstitutional and illegal. It was passed in 1865 with 100% Republican support in Congress. There were three states that actually did not ratify the amendment until the 20th Century - Delaware (February 12, 1901); Kentucky (March 18, 1976); and Mississippi (March 16, 1995.) The latter state didn't officially report the ratification to the Federal Register until protesters forced the issue in 2013.

- The 14th amendment guaranteed citizenship to all persons born in the United States and equal rights which could not be taken away without due process of the law. It was passed in 1868 with 94% Republican support.

- The 15th amendment prohibits deprivation of the right to vote to male citizens "by the United States or by any State on account of race, color, or previous condition of servitude." It was passed in 1870 with 100% Republican support.

Even after that, there would be more legislation to be passed and, unfortunately, more blood to be shed.

Ch. 5 - Reconstruction in the South

The country tried to find ways to heal its wounds during the period after the Civil War. It faced the dual challenge of integrating both the rebellious Confederate States and the former slave population into the cultural mainstream. It's hard to find evidence that either goal was accomplished.

Congress investigated just how much progress had been made by forming the Joint Committee on Reconstruction, also known as the Joint Committee of Fifteen. It was created on December 13, 1865 to "inquire into the condition of the States which formed the so-called Confederate States of America, and report whether they, or any of them, are entitled to be represented in either house of Congress." (70) The committee wound up drafting the Fourteenth Amendment to the Constitution and successfully recommending that the federal government refuse to readmit southern state representation in Congress until ratified.

Pennsylvania Representative Thaddeus Stevens and Senator William P. Fessenden of Maine served as co-chairmen of the committee. In all, 144 witnesses were called to testify. They concluded that Southern culture remained deeply racist and those Blacks who remained faced a dangerous situation. Typical of the witnesses was J. J. Gries, a former slaveholder from Alabama, who made the following grim prediction to the committee:

> "There is a kind of innate feeling, a lingering hope among many in the South that slavery will be regalvanized in some shape or other. They tried by their laws to make a worse slavery than there was

before, for the freedman has not the protection which the master from interest gave him before." (71)

Recognizing the volatile nature of the situation, Congress overrode President Johnson's veto and passed the Reconstruction Act in 1867. It placed 10 of the former Confederate states under military control with 20,000 federal troops deployed. The southern state governments were dominated by Republicans, elected largely by freedmen and their allies. Republicans nationally pressed for the granting of political rights to the newly-freed slaves. The federal government was the "custodian of freedom" as Senator Charles Sumner put it. With emancipation, former slaves began to exercise their rights as citizens. They participated in the political process by direct action such as staging sit-ins and marches, voting in elections, and running for office. Many Blacks moved to the South to work for Reconstruction. With the adoption of the 15th Amendment in 1870, a politically mobilized Black community joined with White allies in the southern states to elect the Republican Party to power, which brought about significant changes across the South.

By the end of that year, all the former Confederate states had been readmitted to the Union, and most were controlled by the Republican Party, thanks to the support of Black voters. In the same year, Hiram Rhodes Revels, a Republican from Natchez, Mississippi, became the first Black to sit in the U.S. Congress, when he was elected to the U.S. Senate. Although Black Republicans never were represented in political office in proportion to their electoral majority, Revels and a dozen other Black men served in Congress during Reconstruction. More than 2,000, in fact, served in state legislatures and many more held local offices.

A Black man with the unlikely name of Pinckney B.S. Pinchback became Governor of Louisiana in 1872. He was also a Senator and a member of the House. Douglas Wilder of Virginia was the second Black Governor in America. What was the year? It wasn't until 1990. The state Reconstruction administrations were unpopular with many White southerners who regarded them as "Occupation" governments. Some who were not willing to accept defeat continued to try to prevent Black political activity by any means. Under federal policies, the former Confederate states were required to uphold the abolition of slavery, swear loyalty to the Union, and pay off their war debt. Beyond those limitations, however, the states and their ruling class, traditionally dominated by White planters, were given a relatively free hand in fashioning their own governments. Many southerners particularly resented the presence of the federal troops. They wanted an end to the intervention of the federal government in "southern affairs," claiming the sanctity of "state's rights." The innocent-sounding claim of White southern politicians was that they wanted to rescue the South from corruption and interference from the northern states and the federal government.

"Carpetbagger" was a derogatory name applied by former Confederates to any person from the Northern United States who came to the South after the Civil War. It refers to a traveler who arrives in a new region with only a satchel, or carpetbag, of possessions, and who attempts to profit from or gain control. They were seen as attempting to exploit the local populace. The term broadly included both individuals who sought to promote

Republican politics, including the right of Blacks to vote and hold office, as well as those who saw business and political opportunities because of the chaotic state of the local economies following the war. "Scalawag," another pejorative term, was used to describe native White southerners who supported Reconstruction.

Although the Union victory in theory had given some four million slaves their freedom, many states severely restricted that freedom. In late 1865, Mississippi enacted the first official Black Code, requiring Blacks to have written evidence of employment for the coming year each January. If they left before the end of the contract, they would be forced to forfeit earlier wages and were subject to arrest. Black Codes were eventually also enacted by the legislatures of South Carolina, Alabama, Georgia, Louisiana, Virginia, Florida, Tennessee, and North Carolina. These restrictive laws limited the freedom of Blacks and ensured their availability as a cheap labor force. There were some minimal protections for former slaves contained in the Black Codes. Owners were, at least, prohibited from murdering their former slaves. They were also granted the right to buy and own property, marry, make contracts, and testify in court in cases involving people of their own race. Basically, extensions and modifications of the state laws of pre-war times, the codes restricted activity. They prohibited former slaves from moving from one plantation to another, or even visiting another plantation without written permission from the owner.

The Black Codes made it illegal for freedmen to learn to read and write and also for anyone to teach them these skills. Perhaps of greatest importance regarding the institutionalization of poverty is that under the law, slaves were explicitly prohibited from acquiring any other useful, marketable skill. Black people could get arrested for almost anything and were given very limited access to the courts. If they were granted access, they generally were denied the right to testify against a White person. Black codes could penalize someone for changing jobs or even require working without being paid.

If they refused to sign a labor contract, freedmen risked being arrested, fined and forced into unpaid labor. Some states limited the type of property that Blacks could own, while virtually all the former Confederate states passed strict vagrancy laws that required a Black person to have a job that was officially recognized by the legislators. If not, they were imprisoned and then leased out to people to do manual labor. There were even so-called "anti-enticement" measures designed to punish anyone who offered higher wages to a Black laborer already under a contract. This practice is sometimes referred to as "Slavery by another name."

Passed by a political system in which Blacks effectively had no voice, the Black Codes were enforced by all-White local and state police and forces often made up of Confederate war veterans. The Black Codes were also enacted on a local level where laws detailed when, where, and how formerly enslaved people could work and for how much compensation. They were a legal way to put Black citizens into indentured servitude, to take away voting rights, to control where they lived, and limit how they traveled.

Slavery was still permitted "as a punishment for crime." All the southern states had to do was find a reason to arrest their former slaves, and they could legally throw them right back on the plantation. A Black person could be jailed for anything from using obscene language to selling cotton after sunset. If he was as much as caught using a swear word, he could be charged, leased out as a slave laborer, and put to work in chain gangs and work camps on farms, mines, and quarries. By 1898, a full 73% of Alabama's state revenue came from leasing out convicts as slaves. They were treated terribly. They were beaten so brutally that, in one year, one of every four convicts died while working. Work camps kept secret, unmarked graves to hide the evidence of people they'd beaten to death. Estimates are that those graves hold the mutilated bodies of at least 9,000 people.

A judge in Alabama declared openly that he and his southern brethren were going to keep slave labor alive in the South admitting, "There is really no difference whether we hold them as absolute slaves or obtain their labor by some other method." (72)

Convict lease programs in the South allowed local plantations to rent inexpensive prison labor. While many of these arrangements have been phased out, prison labor continues in the U.S. under a variety of justifications. Prison labor programs vary widely. Some are uncompensated prison maintenance tasks, some are for local government maintenance chores, some for local businesses, and others resemble internships. Modern rationales for prison labor programs often include reduction of recidivism and to help in becoming reacclimated to society. The idea is that such labor programs will make it easier for the prisoner upon release to find gainful employment rather than relapse to criminality. However, most of the work offered is so menial as to be unlikely to improve anyone's employment prospects. Most prison labor programs do now compensate prisoners, but generally with very low wages, often well below the federal minimum wage.

Southern business owners sought to reproduce the profitable arrangement of slavery with a system called "peonage," in which disproportionately Black workers were entrapped by loans and compelled to work indefinitely due to the resulting debt. The term "peon" refers to someone who performs menial tasks. The practice continued well through Reconstruction and ensnared a large proportion of Blacks in the South. These workers remained destitute and persecuted, forced to work dangerous jobs and further confined legally by the racist state laws. Peonage differed from chattel slavery because it was not strictly hereditary and did not allow the sale of people. However, a person's debt, and by extension that person, could still be sold, and the system was tantamount to slavery.

With the Peonage Act of 1867, Congress abolished "the holding of any person to service or labor under the system known as peonage." It specifically banned "the voluntary or involuntary service or labor of any persons as peons, in liquidation of any debt or obligation, or otherwise." (73)

Andrew Johnson, Lincoln's successor, didn't believe that Blacks should have a role in determining how Reconstruction should proceed. He called on the Governors to convene state conventions to establish all-White governments. They, frankly, looked very much like the old Confederate governments that they replaced.

Republicans by and large felt the war had been fought for equal rights and wanted to see the powers of the national government expanded. The Civil Rights Act of 1866 defined citizens as those born in the United States regardless of race. President Johnson vetoed the bill using the classic racist claim that protecting the rights of Blacks was the same as discriminating against Whites. Again, Congress overrode his veto with a 2/3 majority and the bill became law on April 9. It ostensibly guaranteed Black Americans equal protection under the law, although not the right to vote. Here's the text of the Act:

Section 1

Title 1- No citizen of the United States of America shall be denied the right to vote because of their race, color, economic status or education level.

Title 2- Access to any public facility should not be denied to any person by state and local governments.

Title 3- The discrimination of any person based on their race, color or national origin is hereby illegal and is punishable by a minimum two years in prison.

Section 2

Title 1- The Bureau of Civil Rights Affairs is hereby created to investigate and prosecute breaches of the Civil Rights Act of 1866. (74)

The act also authorized the second Freedmen's Bureau Bill. Andrew Johnson vetoed these bills, but Congress once again overrode his vetoes. The new bill extended the agency's life for two more years and also gave the Army the responsibility of protecting the civil rights of Blacks in the South. The Civil Rights Act and Freedmen's Bureau Bill were tied together because, at least in theory, the Bureau would enable local enforcement of the act. This is an excerpt from a front-page article in the Charleston Mercury which was published on Nov. 5, 1868 in Charleston, South Carolina. It paints the South as the innocent victim of an evil alliance between Northern Radicals and the Black race:

> "Left to themselves, the two races in the South would easily find their interest in the mutual friendliness and dependency. But it will not suit the 'interests' of the Radicals of the North, who desire the party support of the Negroes; nor the 'interests' of the carpet-baggers – scalawags – and insolent, white-man-hating Yankee negro. These are all intent on money, rule and consequence. Their sole reliance for ruling and plundering the white race, is in the arms of the Government of the United States. But for this power, there would not be a single effort made to rule us. Their chief instrumentality, is in the organization of the negroes, by secret leagues and oaths, by which the passions and lusts of the negroes are excited, and their grand schemes of confiscation and robbery, by the forms of law, are alluringly displayed."

The final section of the article seems reminiscent of today's conspiracy theories designed to stoke fear. The fact that there is no truth to anything being said is beside the point. What matters is the visceral reaction it's designed to produce.

> "It is clearly not only the right, but the duty of the White man, to counteract as far as possible, these appeals to interest, by which the negro stands arrayed against him. He cannot prevent the secret leagues.

He cannot prevent the hate and lust they inspire; or the expectations of gain and plunder they present. But he can appeal to the "interest" of the negro in another form. He can have nothing to do with any Radical. He can refuse to employ him. He can say to him, since you think proper to join in a league against me, to rule me, to take my property, and go to those with whom you are associated in your robber schemes, for employment. You shall not in the shape of wages, by any voluntary act of mine, have one dollar of that property, you have conspired to appropriate. When you propose to play the robber and tyrant over me, do not expect to be supported by me, the better to enable you to accomplish your villainies. An employer and employee in the peaceable pursuits of industry, are friends. They mutually help each other. You are an enemy, seeking to use me to destroy me. You are plotting war.

But, whilst it is the policy of the white race to appeal to the interest of the negro in his employment, to prevent his being a tool of mischief against him, the instrumentality of reason or persuasion ought to be omitted. He is a poor ignorant creature, rapidly relapsing into barbarism. He is amongst us. He has been of us. His welfare is largely identified with ours. There is no natural antagonism, in the natural inequality which God has put between the races. We can have no interest in a conflict with him, or in his extermination. The whole drift of the Radical policy, is to drive him on these rocks of perdition. Co-equality with the white race, will be with him as it has been with the Indian – with all the colored races, forced into competition with the white race. His ruling the white race is a cruel farce, which the grinning bayonets of the United States cannot prevent relapsing into tragedy. In the meantime, let the white race use all the moral and peculiar power they possess, by appeals to his interest, to save the negro from themselves."

Andrew Johnson was stocky, standing 5 feet 10 inches tall with a swarthy complexion, thick dark hair graying on the sides, a broad forehead, deeply set black eyes with bushy eyebrows, a square jaw, cleft chin, and a large nose. He suffered from kidney stones throughout his term as President. He dressed neatly, usually in black.

Andrew Johnson (Courtesy National Archives)

Although he was a racist, Johnson did have some redeeming qualities. He spoke directly, was generally reserved, and went out of his way to maintain old friendships. He often loaned money to people who needed it. According to one of his Tennessee neighbors, "I found him kind and helpful, especially to poor young men and he was entirely without condescension." Because of his own humble roots, he identified with the underdog. He preferred the company of old friends to Washington society. He was considered a gifted orator.

Balancing the ticket by choosing Johnson, a southern Democrat from Tennessee, as running mate for Lincoln may have seemed like a good idea to Republican Party officials at the time. The duo won the election. But, once Lincoln was assassinated, it back-fired in many ways Johnson had a political outlook that was diametrically opposed to Lincoln's on many issues. President Johnson became an increasingly unpopular figure. On February 24, 1868, the United States House of Representatives resolved to impeach the 17th President for "high crimes and misdemeanors," which were detailed in 11 articles of impeachment. The primary charge against him was that he had violated the Tenure of Office Act, passed by Congress in March 1867, over his veto. Specifically, he had removed from office Edwin M. Stanton, the Secretary of War, whom the act was largely designed to protect, and attempted to replace him with Brevet Major General Lorenzo Thomas.

Johnson was impeached by the House of Representatives on February 24, 1868 and tried by the Senate in a proceeding that lasted from March to May of 1868. In the end, the Senate voted to acquit Johnson by a margin of 35 guilty to 19 not guilty - one vote short of the 2/3 needed to convict.

Johnson was not nominated for a second term as President. He then refused to attend Ulysses S. Grant's Inauguration at the U.S. Capitol in 1869. Johnson, instead, claimed he "needed to stay at the White House to sign last minute legislation." Grant and Johnson were enemies, and Grant had previously said he would not ride in a carriage to the Capitol with Johnson who was still fuming about his impeachment.

Actually, it may have been a good thing that Johnson stayed in the confines of the White House that day. Grant's Inaugural Ball turned into an "Inaugural Brawl." Held in the Treasury Department building, it was massively overcrowded which led to thefts and subsequent fisticuffs at the coat check.

To avoid a repeat four years later at his second Inaugural Ball, a large, temporary but lavish outdoor structure was built in Judiciary Square. Organizers spared only one expense but it turned out to be something important. They didn't provide for any heat. This oversight, combined with the fact that the day's high temperature was 20 degrees, exposed one of history's more unfortunate party-planning decisions.

At least 100 canaries had been brought in to add some cheery chirping to the ambiance, and they were suspended in cages over the frigid dance floor, where 3,000 guests shivered in overcoats and hats. A Washington Evening Star article the next day said the birds were "too cold to sing," which was a bit of an understatement. By the time the Grant family arrived at 11:30 p.m., canaries had begun to fall over dead. Some called them "the first martyrs to Grant's second term."

The Enforcement Acts of 1870–1871 and the Civil Rights Act of 1875, in combating the violence and intimidation of White supremacy, were also part of the effort to end slave-like conditions for southern Blacks. The Civil Rights Act, in particular, attempted to circumvent racism in local jurisdictions by allowing Blacks access to the federal courts. However, the effect of these laws waned as political will diminished and the federal government gradually lost authority in the South.

Most former slaves had hoped for better lives and new occupations after their emancipation. They had no money, no education, and no experience doing anything other than working on a plantation. Many ended up signing labor contracts with their former masters and were put back to work on the same farms. There, landowners kept slave-condition gang labor alive with Whites overseeing Black workers. Pay wasn't much better than it was during slavery. In fact, it was often worse. Records of black wages weren't kept until 1910. Even then, the average Black made no more than one-third the salary of the average White man. If you turned down the slave-labor job you were being offered, you could be forced to work. If a Black person was caught without a job, he could be charged with vagrancy. He'd typically be forced to spend the next three months working for pay that, even at the time, was described as "slave wages."

Trying to escape just made things worse. If a vagrant tried to run, he would be tied to a ball and chain and forced to keep working for no pay at all. So-called "apprentices" were also used to flout the law. Plantation owners would lure their former slaves back by promising to teach them everything the plantation owners knew and prepare them to succeed on their own. However, the owners would just put the freedmen right back in their old slave jobs. The former slaves would now be under contracts forcing them to work for their old masters, and the freed slaves could get in legal trouble for breaking these contracts. If they got real jobs, even the people who hired them could be sued by the slave owners for "enticing" their apprentices away.

In South Carolina, a law prohibited Blacks from holding any occupation other than farmer or servant unless they paid an annual tax of $10 to $100. In addition to legal restrictions, there was certainly violence. An 1871 report to Congress said that in just nine counties in South Carolina that year, there were 35 lynchings, 262 severe beatings of Black men and women, and over 100 homes burned to the ground.

The system of sharecropping replaced slavery in many areas of the South. Landowners would provide housing, tools, seeds, etc. The sharecroppers would receive anywhere from a third to a half of the crop's value at a price set by the landowner. It gave the landowners a steady work force that couldn't easily leave because they earned little money and couldn't make the investment in land and farms themselves. It was like a quasi-slavery that tied workers to land they didn't own.

The following is an example of a written Black Code from a Parish outside of Baton Rouge in Louisiana. They essentially just replaced the word "Slave" with the word "Negro." It was as if the Civil War never happened at all:

- Be it ordained by the Police Jury of the Parish of St. Landry that no Negro shall be allowed to pass within the limits of said parish without special permit in writing from his employer.

- Every Negro is required to be in the regular service of some White person, or former owner, who shall be held responsible for the conduct of said Negro.

- No Negro shall be permitted to preach, exhort, or otherwise declaim to congregations of colored people, without a special permission in writing from the President of the Police Jury. (75)

As Reconstruction went on, violence continued to increase in the South. In 1868, White supremacists tried to prevent Republicans from winning an election in Louisiana. Over a few days, they killed some two hundred freedmen in St. Landry Parish in the Opelousas massacre. Other violence erupted as well. From April to October of that year, there were 1,081 political murders in Louisiana. Most of the victims were freedmen.

In September, thousands of armed White militia, supporters of the Democratic gubernatorial candidate John McEnery, fought against New Orleans police and state militia in what was called the Battle of Liberty Place. They took over the state government offices in New Orleans and occupied the capital and armory. They turned Republican governor William Pitt Kellogg out of office, and retreated only in the face of the arrival of federal troops sent by President Ulysses S. Grant.

Similarly, in Mississippi, the Red Shirts formed as a prominent paramilitary group that enforced Democratic voting by intimidation and murder. Chapters of paramilitary Red Shirts arose and were active in North Carolina and South Carolina as well. They disrupted Republican meetings, killed leaders and officeholders, intimidated voters at the polls, or kept them away altogether.

Many racists in the South called themselves "Redeemers," a positive-sounding terms borrowed from Christian theology. The period after the Civil War represented the birth of a new activist southern society on a self-righteous crusade to legislate morality. Saying that "God wants it that way" gives a sense of authority to any cause, right or wrong.

The Redeemers emphasized opposition to the Republican governments, which they considered to be corrupt. The crippling national economic problems and reliance on cotton meant that the South was struggling financially. Redeemers denounced taxes higher than what they had paid before the war and sought to reduce state debts. Once in power, they typically cut government spending, shortened legislative sessions, lowered politicians' salaries, scaled back public aid to railroads and corporations, and reduced support for the new systems of public education and welfare institutions.

Thomas Nast cartoon (courtesy of Library of Congress)

The worst incidence of racial violence during the Reconstruction Era occurred in Colfax, Louisiana. It involved the White League, also known as the White Man's League, which was based in Grant Parish where Colfax was located. They attacked the Federal Courthouse in a bloody battle on Easter Sunday, April 13, 1873. According to the League's founding document, the principal problem of Reconstruction was that "the right of suffrage was given to the Negroes too hastily." According to the League's platform, Blacks were trying to "drive the White man from this state and convert Louisiana into a second Haiti." The White League called for "the White men of Louisiana to unite in defense of their families and civilization." (76)

The League pledged to defend "our hereditary civilization and Christianity menaced by a stupid Africanization" and called "to the men of our race to unite with us against that supreme danger." (77)

It is believed that as many as 150 people were murdered in Colfax. It was the most serious instance of racial violence during Reconstruction in Louisiana but hardly the first. Every election in the state since the end of the war had been marked by rampant violence and pervasive fraud. The massacre occurred in the wake of the disputed 1872 election for Governor of Louisiana. The State Returning Board, which ruled on vote validity, initially declared John McEnery and his Democratic slate the winners. Then, the board split, with a faction giving the election to Republican William P. Kellogg. A Republican federal judge in New Orleans ruled that the Republican-majority legislature be seated.

Confederate Veteran Christopher Columbus Nash, the Parish Judge and Sheriff, called for armed Whites to capture the courthouse on

April 1. Judge William R. Rutland, Bill Cruikshank, and Jim Hadnot led the recruiting effort in surrounding parishes. Local Black Republicans Lewis Meekins and William Ward recruited a group of armed Black men to defend the courthouse. Gunfire erupted on April 2 and again on April 5, but the shotguns were inaccurate and did no harm. The two sides arranged for peace negotiations which ended when a White man shot and killed a Black bystander. Another armed battle on April 6 ended with Whites fleeing from armed Blacks. With all the unrest in the community, Black women and children joined the men at the courthouse for protection.

William Ward, the Commanding Officer of Company A, 6th Infantry Regiment, Louisiana State Militia, headquartered in Grant Parish, had been elected State Representative from the Parish on the Republican ticket. He wrote to Governor Kellogg seeking U.S. troops for reinforcement and gave the letter to William Smith Calhoun for delivery. Calhoun took a steamboat down the Red River but was captured by Democratic organizers. They ordered Calhoun to turn back and tell Blacks to leave the courthouse immediately.

Although threatened by parties of armed Whites commanded by Nash, the Black defenders refused to leave. To recruit men during the rising political tensions, Nash had encouraged rumors that Blacks were preparing to kill all the White men and abduct the White women in Colfax. Such news attracted more insurgents, almost all of whom were experienced Confederate veterans, from the region to Grant Parish to join Nash. They acquired a small cannon that could fire iron slugs. As Klansman Dave Paul shouted, "Boys, this is a struggle for White supremacy." (78)

Nash didn't move his forces, which consisted of 300 armed White men mostly on horseback, toward the courthouse until noon on Sunday, April 13. Nash reportedly ordered the defenders of the courthouse to leave. When that failed, Nash gave women and children camped outside the courthouse thirty minutes to clear out. After they left, the shooting began. The fighting continued for several hours with few casualties. When Nash's paramilitary maneuvered the cannon behind the building, some of the defenders panicked and left the courthouse. About 60 defenders ran into nearby woods and jumped into the river. Nash sent men on horseback after the fleeing Black Republicans, and his paramilitary group killed most of them on the spot. Soon Nash's forces directed a Black captive to set the courthouse roof on fire. The defenders displayed white flags for surrender. One was made from a shirt while the other was from a page of a book. The shooting stopped.

Nash's group approached and called for those surrendering to throw down their weapons and come outside. Hadnot was shot and wounded by someone from the courthouse. It's believed the men inside were stacking guns when the men approached and Hadnot was shot from behind by an overexcited member of his own force. He died later, after being taken downstream by a passing steamboat.

In the aftermath of Hadnot's shooting, the White paramilitary group reacted with mass murders of the Black men trying to hide in the courthouse. They rode down and killed those attempting to flee. They dumped some bodies in the Red River. About 50 Blacks survived the afternoon and were taken prisoner. Later that night they were summarily killed by their captors, who had been drinking.

Only one Black from the group, Levi Nelson, survived. He was shot by Cruikshank but managed to crawl away unnoticed. He later served as one of the federal government's chief witnesses against those who were indicted for the attacks.

On April 14, some of Governor Kellogg's State Militia arrived from New Orleans. Several days later, two companies of federal troops searched for White paramilitary members, but many had already fled to Texas or disappeared in the hills. A military report to Congress identified 81 Black men by name who had been killed and also estimated that between 15 and 20 unidentifiable bodies had been thrown into the Red River with another 18 secretly buried for a total of "at least 105." A state historical marker from 1950 noted fatalities as three Whites and 150 Blacks.

James Roswell Beckwith, the U.S. Attorney based in New Orleans, sent an urgent telegram about the massacre to the Attorney General in Washington. Various government forces spent weeks trying to round up members of the White paramilitaries and a total of 97 men were indicted. In the end, Beckwith charged nine people and brought them to trial for violations of the Enforcement Act of 1870.

The men were charged with one murder, and charges related to a conspiracy against the rights of freedmen. There were two additional trials in 1874 that gained national attention. William Burnham Woods presided over the first trial and was sympathetic to the prosecution. Had the men been convicted, they would not have been able to appeal their decision to any appellate court according to the laws of the time. However, Beckworth was unable to secure a conviction. One man was acquitted and a mistrial was declared in the cases of the other eight. In the second trial, three men were found guilty of sixteen charges. However, the presiding judge, Joseph Bradley of the United States Supreme Court who was riding circuit, dismissed the convictions, ruling that the charges failed to prove a racial rationale for the massacre. He ordered that the men be released on bail and they promptly disappeared.

When the federal government appealed the case, it was heard by the US Supreme Court as "United States v. Cruikshank" in 1875. The Supreme Court ruled that the Enforcement Act of 1870, based on the Bill of Rights and 14th Amendment, applied only to actions committed by the state and that it did not apply to actions committed by individuals. This meant that the federal government could not prosecute cases such as the Colfax killings. The court said plaintiffs who believed their rights were violated had to seek protection from the state. Louisiana did not prosecute any of the perpetrators of the Colfax massacre. Most southern states would not prosecute White men for attacks against freedmen.

The publicity about the Colfax Massacre and subsequent Supreme Court ruling encouraged the growth of White supremacist organizations. The Ku Klux Klan is the most well-known of these groups formed in the years after the Civil War. Established on December 24, 1865 by six former Confederate soldiers from Pulaski, Tennessee as a fraternal organization, the KKK turned into a vicious hate group. According to "The Cyclopaedia of Fraternities:"

> "Beginning in April, 1867, there was a gradual transformation. The members had conjured up a veritable Frankenstein. They had played with an engine of power and mystery, though organized on

entirely innocent lines, and found themselves overcome by a belief that something must lie behind it all – that there was, after all, a serious purpose, a work for the Klan to do."(79)

It is believed the name was created by combining the Greek word for circle, which is "kyklos," with "clan." The "c" was later changed to a "k." Members often greet one another with the hand signal for "OK" which form a "k" with three fingers or by asking "AYAK" which stands for "Are You a Klansman?" If the other person answers "AKIA," that means "A Klansman I Am." The KKK grew into a secret society terrorizing Black communities and permeating White southern culture, with members at the highest levels of government and in the lowest echelons of criminal back alleys.

While the Klan was an underground organization, other groups such as the White League, Red Shirts, and Knights of the White Camelia were public and open about their racism. The Klansmen would wear hoods because they mostly came from small, rural towns where they could be easily recognized. The all-White groups wanted to take back what they saw as their rightful place in society and used violence to threaten and intimidate minority groups and their supporters. Law enforcement groups were ineffective in combating domestic terror organizations because they contained their members, were sympathetic to their cause, or were simply afraid of retaliation. The attempt at establishing post-war progressive governments failed in the South. Racism was just too firmly entrenched in America. There were many other small and lesser-known hate groups, of course. What they all had in common was their belief that the only way to return things to the way they were was through violence.

In 1874, racists in the city of Vicksburg, Mississippi were determined to suppress Black voting in that year's election. Roving White armed patrols prevented Blacks from voting. Democrats succeeded in defeating all Republican city officials in the August election. By December, the emboldened party forced the Black County Sheriff Peter Crosby to flee to the state capital. Blacks who rallied to the city to aid the sheriff also had to flee in the face of overwhelming White forces, as armed White supremacists flooded the city. Over the next few days, armed gangs murdered an estimated 300 Blacks in what became known as the Vicksburg riots.

U.S. President Ulysses S. Grant sent a company of troops to Vicksburg in January 1875 to quell the violence and allow the sheriff's safe return. Crosby, however, was assassinated by his own White deputy on June 7, 1875.

White paramilitary organizations such as the Red Shirts arose to serve as "the military arm of the Democratic Party." They sometimes invited newspaper coverage of their parades and activities, and their stated goals were to throw out Republicans. They were well-armed, with private financing for the purchase of weapons as they took on more power.

Planters, landlords and merchants used economic coercion against Black sharecroppers and farmers. The Red Shirts used violence, including whippings and murders, and intimidation at the polls. They were joined in the violence by White paramilitary groups known as "rifle clubs," who frequently provoked riots at Republican rallies, shooting dozens of Blacks in the ensuing conflicts and who would often act as vigilante mobs in the years following the Civil War. By 1876, an estimated 20,000 men in South Carolina were members of these clubs.

The violence went unchecked and the plan worked as intended. During Mississippi's 1875 statewide election, five counties with large black majorities polled only 12, 7, 4, 2, and 0 Republican votes, respectively. A Republican dominance by 30,000 votes in the 1874 national and city elections was reversed in 1875, with polls showing a Democratic majority of 30,000 in statewide elections. The success of the White Democrats in Mississippi influenced the growth of Red Shirt chapters in North and South Carolina as well, which also had thousands of White men involved in rifle clubs. The Red Shirts were instrumental in suppressing votes in majority-Black counties in South Carolina. Historians estimate that they committed 150 murders in the weeks leading up to the 1876 election in South Carolina.

White southerners showed a steadfast commitment to ensuring "slavery by another name" and the survival of plantation agriculture in the postwar years. In the North, support for Reconstruction policies had diminished by 1876, setting the stage for the Republican and Democratic Conventions to choose their Presidential candidates.

Things were about to get a lot worse. The "Civil War" might have been over. The "Uncivil War" was about to be unleashed.

Ch. 6 - The Republican Convention

Rud's first term in the House of Representatives was not memorable. He kept a low profile and sorely missed his family. This is apparent in the letter he wrote to Lucy on June 17, 1866:

> "I feel the desire to be with you all the time. Oh, an occasional absence of a week or two is a good thing to give one the happiness of meeting again, but this living apart is in all ways bad. We have had our share of separate life during the four years of war. There is nothing in the small ambition of Congressional life, or in the gratified vanity which it sometimes affords, to compensate for separation from you. We must manage to live together hereafter. I can't stand this and will not."

In 1867, he resigned from Congress and life in Washington and chose to return home to run for Governor of Ohio. The Republican Party had nominated him in part because of his stance on Reconstruction. The opposition candidate was Democrat Allen G. Thurman. The key issue of the campaign was whether Ohio Blacks should be given the right to vote. Supporting suffrage, Hayes was successful in his campaign for governor. Hayes thought he had lost the vote as he went to sleep on election night. He was shocked upon waking to find that he had actually squeaked out a 2,983-vote victory out of the total of 484,603 votes.

Rud was, however, disappointed that an amendment for Black suffrage was not passed by the state legislature. He went on to win reelection against George H. Pendleton in 1869. This time, the legislature turned Republican. Ohio ratified the 15th amendment to the Constitution, which guaranteed Blacks the right to vote.

Hayes helped reform the state's mental hospitals, schools, and prison system. Recognizing that President Ulysses S. Grant fought for civil rights for Blacks in the South, he fully backed Grant's bid for a second term in the White House. Although the Republican Party wanted Rud to run for a third term in 1871, he retired from politics and returned to his home in Fremont, Ohio. Lucy always took an active interest in her husband's political career. When he served in congress, she worked for the welfare of children and veterans. During his time as Governor of Ohio beginning in 1867, she secured funding for an orphanage for the children of Civil War veterans.

Rutherford B. Hayes adamantly believed the nation needed to turn away from force and embrace education as the solution to the continuing refusal of Southerners to accept Reconstruction. From his home in Fremont where he was enjoying retirement, he wrote this to Texas Congressman and his old college roommate Guy Bryan:

> "The most important thing in Texas, as everywhere else, is education for all. I recognize fully the evil of rule by ignorance. But the remedy is not, I am sure to be found in the abandonment of the American principle that all must share in government. The Whites of the South must do as we do, forget the past and learn to lead the ignorant masses around them."
> (80)

Rud's retirement from politics was brief. Republicans convinced him to run for governor in 1875 against Democratic candidate William Allen. After accepting the Republican gubernatorial nomination for that third term, Hayes wrote to Bryan:

> "As to Southern affairs 'the let-alone policy' seems now to be the true course. The future depends largely on the moderation and good sense of Southern men in the next House of Representatives. I think we are one people at last for all time." (81)

As he was campaigning, Hayes noted in his diary that "I do not sympathize with a large share of the party leaders. I doubt the ultra measures relating to the South." He did not consider himself to be a radical liberal. Not the kind of man who would take what he referred to as "ultra" measures. Once again, he was successful in capturing the governorship. It was the first time that an Ohio governor had been elected to a third term. This time, his victory margin was 5,544 votes. His "middle-of-the-road" philosophy was paying off. Here's how he described it:

> "We are in a period when old questions are settled and the new are not yet brought forward. Extreme party action, if continued in such a time, would ruin the party. Moderation is its only chance. The party out of power gains by all partisan conduct of those in power."

Hayes's strong record as Governor began to get him noticed by national Republicans. His unblemished public record and high moral tone offered a striking contrast to widely publicized accusations of corruption in the administration of President Grant. Still, the economic depression and disenchantment with Reconstruction policies in the South appeared to give the Democratic Party the advantage going into the 1876 nominating conventions.

As the 1876 Presidential election approached, Hayes was identified as a possible candidate for the Republican nomination. He was regarded as an honest and solid citizen, a veteran of a decade of state and congressional politics. He was described by a congressman as "Not a leading debater or manager in party tactics but always sensible, industrious, and true to his convictions." Throughout his political career, Rud personally identified with the Republican Party's moderate wing but often voted with the radicals for the sake of unity.

In early May, many newspapers published a letter from Guy Bryan in which he claimed that Hayes would even be acceptable to southern Democrats. He wrote:

> "Although I am and have long been from principle, a Democrat, and expect to support and vote the Democratic ticket at the next Presidential election, yet, I hope Gov. Hayes will receive the nomination of the Republican party. For if your party should be successful, there is no distinguished member of it I would rather see President than Rutherford B. Hayes, for I know him well, and I believe that he is honest, that he is capable, and that he will be faithful to the Constitution. Having been in Congress four years, and Governor of Ohio the third time, he has

experience, and is a Statesman of incorruptible integrity-besides being a sound lawyer and patriot. One who, if elected, would be President for the whole country, and not for a section. What the South most needs is good local government, and one in the Presidential chair who will do all he can under the Constitutions, Federal and State, to promote it. I believe if elected Hayes will do this." (82)

The 1876 convention was held in Cincinnati on June 14-16. In keeping with long-standing political tradition, although it seems quaint now, neither Hayes nor the other leading candidates attended the convention. It was considered bad form to openly politic for the nomination. There were also no primaries back then. The Favorite Son candidate as Ohio's Governor, Hayes hated the thought of having to campaign saying, "Nothing brings out the lower traits of human nature like office-seeking." (83)

Frederick Douglass, the charismatic Black orator and abolitionist, was the first speaker. There had been a disagreeable incident at a Cincinnati hotel in which Black delegates to the convention had been denied rooms on the basis of race. Douglass worried that the Republican party as a whole was showing signs of abandoning its commitment to racial equality and needed a wake-up call. It seemed, said Douglass, that the Republican party had come to the conclusion that it could "get along without the vote of the Black man of the South." He challenged the Convention attendees by saying:

> "Do you mean to make good to us the promises in your Constitution? You say you have emancipated us. You have and I thank you for it. You say you have

> enfranchised us. You have and I thank you for it. But what is your emancipation? What is your enfranchisement? What does it all amount to, if the Black man, after having been made free by the letter of your law, is unable to exercise that freedom, and, having been freed from the slaveholder's lash, he is to be subject to the slaveholder's shotgun?" (84)

The collective shrug that his speech engendered from the delegates was all the answer he required. It may have been a warning that the support for what so many died for in the Civil War was not as strong as most people believed.

The next morning the Convention heard from another eloquent speaker. Sarah J. Spencer, a leader of the Women's Suffrage movement, rose to address a gathering that contained no female delegates. Echoing Douglass's earlier complaint, Spencer noted that:

> "In 1872 the Republican party declared that it had emancipated four million human beings and established universal suffrage. Where were the ten millions of women citizens of this Republic? When will you make this high-sounding declaration true? We ask you for a plank that will place that mighty emblem of power, the ballot, in the hands of ten million American citizens - the wives and daughters of this fair Republic. In this bright new century, let me ask you to win to your side the women of the United States." (85)

During the speech, Spencer's emotional plea for gender equality was received with lukewarm applause from some but outright silence from most of the convention delegates. When she was finished, she was unceremoniously hissed by the crowd. The "gentlemen" of the press were even less polite. "The women-folk are dabbling in politics," sneered the Chicago Tribune. The New York Herald was particularly dismissive, describing her as "commonplace in appearance and speech" and "when she had spoken her little piece, without anything in it, she wafted back to the handiest seat, and that was the end of the incident."

So, maybe the "Liberal" Republican party was not so liberal, after all. Maybe it was tired and not ready for the epic struggles ahead for racial and gender equality. Maybe the unimaginable loss of life during the Civil War took more of a toll on the country than people were willing to admit. Maybe there was an enormous leadership void that no one could fill. Or, maybe unlikely things can happen, even in unlikely times. The name of 27-year-old feminist Susanna Madora Salter was placed in nomination for Mayor of Argonia, Kansas on April 4, 1887. It was a prank by a group of men that wanted to humiliate her along with those who were supporters of women's suffrage. The local Republican party and the Women's Christian Temperance Union visited her home and found out she would actually be willing to serve if elected. They threw their support behind her and she wound up securing 2/3 of the vote. She successfully served as America's first woman Mayor, despite the fact that she and other women were not allowed to vote. It turned out to be quite a bargain for the town as she was paid just $1 and her home became a popular tourist attraction. She lived to be 100 years old. (86)

The Cincinnati convention was the first truly open Republican convention in 16 years. Both Lincoln and Grant had enjoyed solid support in the last three elections. Six major candidates, along with several minor candidates, vied for the nomination. At the time, the Republican Party was split into two factions:

- **The Stalwarts**, the conservative faction, saw themselves as "stalwart" in opposition to efforts to reconcile with the South. They opposed all forms of civil service reform, preferring to keep in place the existing patronage system. Among their numbers were many Radical Republicans, Union war veterans and most of the Republican political bosses. The Stalwarts also backed protective tariffs.

- **The Half-Breeds**, a term of disparagement favored by the Stalwarts, was applied to the moderately liberal faction of the Republican Party. In the minds of the Stalwarts, the term "Half-Breed" was meant to suggest that they were only half Republican. The Half-Breeds backed lenient treatment of the South and supported civil service reform.

Maine's James G. Blaine, the acknowledged front-runner for the nomination, was leader of the Half-Breeds. Among the challengers to him were New York Senator Roscoe Conkling, Indiana Senator and former Governor Oliver H.P.T. Morton, the Secretary of the Treasury Benjamin Helm Bristow, Pennsylvania Governor John F. Hartranft, and Ohio's Hayes.

Speaker of the House James G. Blaine of Maine emerged as the frontrunner for the nomination. The avid supporters of the "Magnetic Man" who drew others to him earned the distinction of being called "Blainiacs." But, like Grant, and many of the other Republicans associated with his administration, he was tainted by scandal. He was accused of using his influence to help railroad interests in Little Rock, Arkansas. While he was considered innocent of any wrongdoing, it still harmed his electability.

The second-tier candidates were Morton, Bristow and Conkling. Morton was in poor health and had a controversial past on economic issues. Bristow of Kentucky was both a popular reformist and considered an economics expert. Bristow was well-known nationally since he was a member of Grant's cabinet. However, rumors spread that by working to uproot corruption, he was, in fact, being disloyal to Grant. Conkling was the leader of the Stalwarts, the establishment faction of the party, which was opposed to reform and he desired a continued domination over the South. He had been a leading spokesman for Grant and considered himself as heir. Unfortunately, the corruption of both Grant and of New York politics worked against him in an era calling for reform.

The third-tier of candidates included two Governors who had also been Civil War Generals - John Hartranft and Hayes. The latter had the firm support of his state and solid endorsements from influential Ohio Senator John Sherman, the brother of General William Tecumseh Sherman, and James Russell Lowell, a popular poet and ambassador. Noted orator Robert G. Ingersoll gave a stirring nominating speech for Blaine. It became known as the "Plumed Knight" address. Ingersoll used his allotted ten minutes, but the enthralled audience insisted that he be allowed to continue. Alluding to the centennial of the Revolution to be celebrated that year, Ingersoll intoned:

> "This is a year in which the people call for the man who has preserved in Congress what their soldiers won on the field. A man who has snatched the mask of Democracy from the hideous face of rebellion. Like an armed warrior, like a plumed knight, James G. Blaine marched down the halls of the American Congress and threw his shining lance full and fair against the brazen forehead of every traitor to his country and every maligner of his fair reputation. For the Republican party to desert that gallant man now is as though an army should desert their General upon the field of battle." (87)

The speech helped Blaine gain a large lead on the first ballot, but he had difficulty maintaining it. The radical Republican establishment, which favored a continued domination over the defeated South, rallied against him by the 7th ballot, and blocked a potential Blaine victory by endorsing a compromise candidate named Rutherford B. Hayes. On his behalf, ex-Governor Edward F. Noyes, Chairman of the Ohio delegation, gave a more low-key speech which seemed fitting. Noyes stressed Hays' service during the war, "when those who are invincible in peace and invisible in battle were uttering brave words to cheer their neighbors on." Noyes pointed out:

> "Hayes had carried Ohio against the State's three most prominent Democrats and would certainly do so again if he headed the ticket in November. Hayes is a scholar and a gentleman and the perfect

compromise nominee. Ohio Republicans would manfully support whomever the convention chose but we beg to submit that in Governor Hayes you have those qualities which are calculated best to compromise all difficulties, and to soften all antagonisms. He has no personal enmities. His private life is so pure that no man has ever dared to assail it. His public acts throughout all these years have been above suspicion even. Is it not worthwhile to see to it that a candidate is nominated against whom nothing can be said, and who is sure to succeed in the campaign?" (88)

It seemed that the momentum was in Blaine's favor. Just before the first ballot vote, however, the lights went out. It is still not known who or what caused the power malfunction. It has been charged that the gas supply was clandestinely cut off for the express purpose of forcing an adjournment. The convention was postponed until the next day. The other candidates met during the night and agreed that if Blaine did not become the nominee, they would band together and support Hayes.

Blaine led after the first ballot but had only 285 of the 378 delegates required to secure the nomination. The second, third, and fourth ballots saw the same mixed results. Hayes began to surge on the fifth ballot, securing third place behind Blaine and Bristow.

When Michigan was called on that fifth ballot, a veteran Republican, William A. Howard, a member of the House of Representatives, hobbled out into the aisle. Prior to declaring that Michigan would cast all of its 22 votes for Hayes, he said:

"There is one candidate before the convention who has already defeated three Democratic aspirants for the Presidency - Allen G. Thurman, George H. Pendleton, and William Allen - and that as he seemed to have a habit of defeating distinguished Democrats, it would be the part of wisdom to give him an opportunity to defeat yet another one." (89)

This announcement was received with tremendous applause. When the over-all ballot count was announced, it was found that the vote for Hayes had increased from 68 to 104. The sixth ballot saw Blaine rise to 308 but Hayes, continuing his surge, moved into second place. After the sixth ballot, the Bristow, Conkling, Morton, and Hartranft supporters withdrew their candidates' names, leaving Hayes as the sole alternative to Blaine. Roscoe Conkling had actually been so sure he'd get the nomination that he had already picked his Vice President and come up with a motto - "Conkling and Hayes is the Ticket that Pays!"

It became apparent that the seventh ballot would be the final one. The 53-year-old Hayes won by a narrow margin of 384 to 351 for Blaine. A total of 21 votes went to Brisos. Rud had finally secured the nomination. New York Senator William A. Wheeler was selected as his running mate. The Republicans felt they needed a New Yorker on the ticket to have any chance of carrying the Empire State and its cache of 35 electoral votes. After a few votes were cast on the first roll call, the convention named Wheeler by acclamation. When Hayes was told that Wheeler would be the Vice-Presidential candidate, he reportedly said, "I am ashamed to ask. Who is Wheeler?" (90) Presidents in the 19th Century had much less power and authority than they do now. The Presidential nominee having the ability to choose a running mate was not an idea whose time had come.

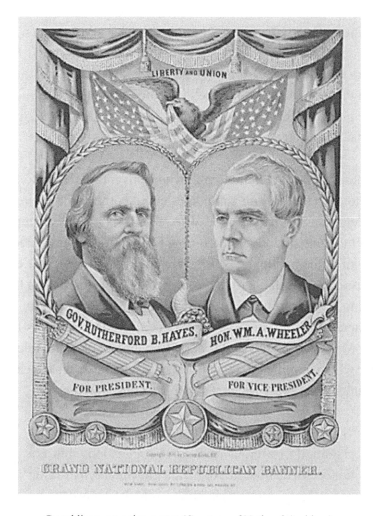

Republican campaign poster (Courtesy of National Archives)

The Republican party was pro-business but also the party of abolition and civil rights reform. The party platform stated that "the permanent pacification of the Southern section of the Union and the complete protection of all its citizens in the free enjoyment of all their rights, are duties to which the Republican party is sacredly pledged." It further criticized the Democratic Party for its lack of commitment to civil rights, arguing that the "party counts, as its chief hope of success, upon the electoral vote of a united South, secured through the efforts of those who were recently arrayed against the nation and we invoke the earnest attention of the country to the grave truth, that a success thus achieved would reopen sectional strife and imperil national honor and human rights." (91)

It was no surprise when the Republican Convention turned to Hayes when none of the leading candidates could command a majority of the delegates. He had a good war record, had loyally supported President Grant, and was a three-time Governor of a state necessary to prevail in the national election. He was considered a safe choice and was even acceptable to the reform wing of the party. As he was gathering his thoughts for the letter to the Republican Party of his acceptance of the nomination for President, Rud wrote to his friend, former Missouri Senator and Liberal Republican Party founder Carl Schurz who recommended that he begin using the term, "Local self-government" as a way to elicit support from southerners:

> "I now feel like saying something as to the South, not essentially different from your suggestions, but am not decided about it. I don't like the phrase, by reason of its Democratic associations, which you use "local self-government" in that connection. It seems to me to smack of the bowie-knife and revolver. Local self-government has nullified the Fifteenth Amendment in several states, and is in a fair way to nullify the Fourteenth and Thirteenth. But I do favor a policy of

reconciliation, based on the observance of all parts of the Constitution, the new as well as the old, and, therefore, suppose you and I are substantially agreed on the topic."

On June 23, Rud expressed humility when he wrote in his diary, "The nomination has been well-received. The best people, many of them heretofore dissatisfied with the Republican party, are especially hearty in my support. I must make it my constant effort to deserve this confidence."

Later that day, he wrote a follow-up letter to Ohio Senator John Sherman saying that he was already being pressured by the various forces within the party to adopt their positions but that he wanted to avoid getting pinned down and was seeking to commit to as little as possible:

> "The next thing in order for me is my letter of acceptance. I am advised to harden by some, and to soften by others the money plank, and so on. Perhaps I would do well to approve it as it stands. I shall hardly reply to the Committee before the end of the month, or till after the 4th. If you have any suggestions, you will oblige me by making them. My inclination is to say very little. The people are already organizing meetings, are ratifying, and the letter of acceptance may as well be a purely formal affair, may it not?"

In his letter accepting the nomination of the Republican Party, he took the unusual step of announcing that he would only serve one term. He explained the decision this way:

> "An Executive who is under no temptation to use the patronage of his office, to promote his own re-election, I desire to perform what I regard as a duty, in stating now my inflexible purpose, if elected, not to be a candidate for election to a second term." (92)

In terms of his southern policy, he stated the following in strong terms in his letter:

> "Let me assure my countrymen of the Southern States that if I shall be charged with the duty of organizing an Administration, it will be one which will regard and cherish their truest interests the interests of the White, and of the Colored people both, and equally; and which will put forth its best efforts in behalf of a civil policy, which will wipe out forever the distinction between the North and South in our common country." (93)

He did not, however, give any specifics as to how he would accomplish the objective of "wipe out forever the distinction between the North and South."

Hayes' service as a General during the Civil War was central to his identity. According to the Rutherford B. Hayes Presidential Center Executive Director Christie Weininger, "He saw firsthand the passions that were behind the sectionalism that caused the Civil

War. I think that always in the back of his mind was how to make this country feel united again." (94) Was Hayes a fire-breathing champion for change? Did he galvanize the nation with inspiring rhetoric? Was he a risk-taker vowing to do the right thing no matter how unpopular it was? Did he espouse grand causes that would produce immediate and dramatic improvements? Did he change history? The answer to these and so many other questions is a resounding "No!" Hayes described himself as "a radical in thought and principle and a conservative in method and conduct." In fairness to him, that's what every successful politician was at the time, including Lincoln. It wouldn't be fair to judge him by today's standards.

On the other hand, judge him by the standards of anyone at any time in history. Great leaders change the world. They have the courage to stand above others. They are willing to do what's unpopular, often at significant personal risk. Rud, on the other hand, took this meek approach, as he described in his diary:

> "Personally I do not resort to force, not even the force of law, to advance moral reforms. I prefer education, argument, persuasion, and above all the influence of example."

He, and the others of his time, remind you of H.T. Webster's character "Caspar Milquetoast," who featured in "The Timid Soul" comic strip series. Webster described Milquetoast as "the man who speaks softly and gets hit with a big stick." (95) Hayes, unfortunately, would soon wind up getting hit by one of the biggest sticks in American history.

Ch. 7 - The Democratic Convention

Born in New Lebanon, New York, on February 9, 1814, Samuel Jones Tilden was the fifth child of Elam and Polly Tilden. His father owned a store and held the job of Postmaster. He was an important political figure in the state, meeting regularly with elected officials and candidates. Among them was Martin Van Buren, a New York Congressman and Governor, a founding member of the Democratic Party in the late 1820s and a future President. The thin and frail-looking Tilden had a pale complexion, looking like he had never been outside. He had piercing blue eyes and a protruding nose. Sam's right eyelid noticeably drooped from a disease called Ptosis. He suffered numerous other health problems while growing up, and they may have been worsened by home remedies. His father and other family members were the makers of Tilden's Extract, a popular patent medicine of the 1800's and early 1900's derived from cannabis.

Samuel J. Tilden (Courtesy National Archives)

When he was just three years old, Sam was afflicted with an illness that caused him to relentlessly claw at his mouth. A "doctor" prescribed laudanum, a bitter narcotic painkiller that mixes alcohol with 10% powdered opium. Laudanum contains almost all of the opium alkaloids, including morphine and codeine. What could possibly go wrong if you feed a three-year-old a constant diet of opium? From that time on, Sam developed a weak stomach and poor digestive system. What was his father's response to this shocking development? It was to give Sam more "magic potions" and elixirs.

Sam didn't have a normal childhood. Must of the time, he was bedridden with his various ailments. They included, in alphabetical order, arthritis, catarrh, chills, colds, constipation, corrugated tongue, diarrhea, dryness of the mouth, fever, headaches, hoarseness, insomnia, lameness, neuralgia, palsy, rheumatism, pulsations in the back of the head, swellings, and tremulous hands. He went to coastal and mountain health resorts and spent an immense amount of money on medical specialists. To look at him, you'd never guess that he was the fearless hero who would go on to stand up to the toughest gang in New York – The Tweed Ring – and beat them.

Unable to attend school regularly, he received tutoring at home. In his early teens, Tilden attended an academy in Williamstown, Massachusetts, but returned home for health reasons. At age eighteen in 1832, he went to New York City to continue his schooling and to receive professional medical attention. Living with an aunt who owned a boarding house, Tilden ended up spending most of his time running her business as well as handling political errands for his father.

Sam's interest in politics led him to write an article on a highly controversial political topic - the veto of a bill by President Andrew Jackson that would have renewed the charter of the National Bank of the United States. Jackson believed that the bank concentrated too much power in the federal government and wealthy people of the North at the expense of states. Tilden's defense of Jackson's veto was published by the Democratic Party and distributed throughout New York State.

Using the pseudonym "Jacksonis Amicus," he also wrote a series of articles for the New York Times during the spring of 1837 in which he defended President Martin Van Buren's threat to veto bills that would abolish slavery in Washington, D.C. Democrats of the time believed that states, not the federal government, should decide whether or not to permit slavery.

He tried to attend Yale but wrote in a letter home that "it was impossible to eat the bread because it was too freshly baked." Another time he complained about the warm weather in New Haven, CT saying, "Yesterday it was scarcely cold." He quit, went to New York University, and withdrew. Tilden re-entered the law school of New York University in 1838 and went on to complete a three-year course. While at NYU, Tilden also worked as a law clerk in the office of attorney John W. Edmonds. Through private study, he was admitted to the bar in 1841 and began his law practice at the age of 27. He soon became a skilled corporate and railroad lawyer active in Democratic politics.

He frequently campaigned on behalf of Democratic candidates. Sam was a member of the New York Assembly in 1846 representing New York County's 18th District and was a member of the state constitutional conventions. A supporter of the Union cause in the Civil War, he was a leader of the Free-Soil element among New York Democrats. The group focused on opposing expanding slavery in the vast public lands in the West.

Sam also helped found the "Barnburners," an anti-slavery faction of the New York Democratic Party. The group sought to prevent the spread of slavery into the land acquired from Mexico in the Treaty of Guadalupe Hidalgo. He was an organizer of the 1848 Free Soil Convention, which nominated Martin Van Buren for President.

In the 1860 presidential election, Sam strongly opposed the candidacy of Republican presidential nominee Abraham Lincoln. He warned that Lincoln's election could lead to the secession of the South and a subsequent Civil War. Tilden initially opposed using force to prevent secession, but he then supported the Union after the outbreak of the Civil War. Sam served as the manager of Horatio Seymour's successful 1862 campaign for governor, and played a key role in securing the nomination of George B. McClellan at the 1864 Democratic National Convention. Tilden played a prominent role in the reorganization of the Democratic Party in the decade from 1865 to 1875, serving as New York State Party Chairman. Tilden's political activity during this period included a term in the New York state legislature, serving as a delegate in a state constitutional convention in 1846, and an unsuccessful bid for the position of Attorney General of New York in 1855. He turned his attention back to his law practice in 1855 and won recognition for his work on a voting fraud case. In 1857, he was involved in a high-profile murder trial. Meanwhile, he fought corruption and began advising railroad companies on legal ways to finance operations and reorganize their businesses to maximize profits. Tilden became so popular as a legal adviser to railroads that he made a fortune during the boom in railroad building from the 1850s to the 1870s.

A private, introverted, and cautious man, Tilden was gifted with significant intellectual ability. His law practice and investments brought him substantial wealth, with a fortune estimated at $7 million. When the Civil War broke out, Tilden expected the North to use its superior manpower and industrial might to crush the rebellion. When the war progressed more slowly, Sam turned his attention to maintaining the strength of the Democratic Party. Democrats were a decided minority in Congress during and immediately after the Civil War because many of their members were from Southern states that had seceded from the Union.

Tilden supported the policies of President Andrew Johnson, who favored the quick reinstatement of former Confederate states and little federal management of them. Johnson's program for Reconstruction was opposed by congressional Republicans, who wanted more difficult requirements for Confederate states to rejoin the Union as well as federal supervision of state governments and civil rights legislation that extended voting rights and legal protection for newly emancipated slaves. Tilden was also known as a "Bourbon Democrat," a liberal who supported free trade and the gold standard for currency. Sam became chairman of the New York Democratic Party in 1866 and was elected as a delegate to the state constitutional convention of 1867. Tilden's major activity during the Reconstruction era involved exposing and undermining the "Tweed Ring" in New York City. Led by an unethical city official and head of Tammany Hall, William M. Tweed carried the nickname of "Boss Tweed." The gang exerted absolute control over city politics and finances. It's estimated they defrauded New York City of anywhere from $30 million to $200 million. In 1872, Tilden worked with the state legislature to create laws that broke the power of the ring. He was also instrumental in the removal of several corrupt judges.

Using his skill as a lawyer, he fought appeals by members of the ring and used legal means for bringing those involved in criminal activities to trial, and then worked to win convictions and remove them from city positions. For evidence of fraud, Tilden developed a system that tracked how municipal funds were diverted into private bank accounts of members of the Tweed Ring. In addition to smashing the Tweed Ring, Tilden led reform efforts of the state judiciary.

Tilden was immensely popular in New York, where his work against the Tweed Ring was regularly reported in newspapers. He was elected the 25th Governor of New York in 1874 as a champion of reform. He swiftly improved the financial situation in the state during a period when the nation was experiencing an economic depression. He cut state taxes and expenditures and saved the state millions of dollars by eliminating fraud and wasteful spending. He took down the "Canal Ring," a group of politicians who had become wealthy by controlling construction and repair of the state's extensive system of canals. Sam's success as a reformer during the first half of the 1870s occurred at a time of much corruption in the federal government. Many government officials in the administration of President Ulysses S. Grant were implicated in scandals, as were members of Congress. During a period of significant economic hardship for the country, Congress voted and cashed in on a large, retroactive pay raise. Tilden's name was associated with integrity in politics. This was just what the Democratic Party wanted as a contrast to Grant's administration. In one of his most famous speeches, he declared at a state convention, "It is time to proclaim that whoever plunders the people, though he steals the livery of heaven to serve the devil in, is no Democrat." (96)

What Tilden had in honesty and dedication, he lacked in personal charisma. Robert Yahner, who oversaw New York City's National Arts Club, once Tilden's spacious Gramercy Park mansion, admitted the former Governor was known as "someone who was a bit lethargic" and added, "Quite frankly, a lot of people thought he was dull. Dull but dedicated." (97)

The Democrats held their convention on June 27-29, in St. Louis, Missouri. It was the first time a national convention was held west of the Mississippi. The Democratic platform pledged to replace the corruption of the Grant administration with honest, efficient government, ending what they called "the rapacity of carpetbag tyrannies" in the South. (98)

Meanwhile, the Democrats were hungry to reclaim the White House, which they had not won in 20 years. The economic collapse of 1873 caused the country's attention to sway from Reconstruction efforts in the South. By 1876, the Democrats were surging and the Republicans were in retreat. This set the stage for Tilden to be the favorite in the Presidential election.

In addition to Tilden, there were five others whose names were placed in nomination – Indiana Governor Thomas A.

Hendricks, Major General Winfield Scott Hancock, Former Ohio Governor William Allen, Delaware Senator Thomas F. Bayard, and former New Jersey Governor Joel Parker. Tilden was a popular choice along with Thomas A. Hendricks, a well-liked congressman from Indiana.

The Democratic platform called for "immediate reform" of the federal government and, to forestall Republican charges of sectionalism, committed itself to the "permanence of the Federal Union." It also called for civil service reform and restrictions on Chinese immigration to the United States. It proclaimed that:

> "Reform is necessary to secure the country from a corrupt centralism which, after inflicting upon ten states the rapacity of carpet-bag tyrannies, has honeycombed the offices of the federal government itself with incapacity, waste, and fraud, infected states and municipalities with the contagion of misrule, and locked fast the prosperity of an industrious people in the paralysis of hard times." (99)

New York Senator Francis Kernan entered Sam's name in nomination declaring:

> "The great issue upon which this election will be lost or won is the question of needed administrative reform. If we have a man who has laid his hand on dishonest officials, rooted out abuses, lowered taxes, and inaugurated reforms, and if we are wise enough to select him as our leader, we will sweep the Union."
> (100)

There was a deafening cheer for Tilden and then the voting began. Of the votes cast in the first ballot, Tilden received 417 out of a total of 739. Although Tilden had a majority of the votes, he had not yet received the requisite two-thirds, so a second ballot was ordered. The results were: Tilden 535, Hendricks 60, Hancock 59, Allen 54, Bayard 11, and Parker 18. Before the count was announced, the anxiety of many delegates to be on the winning side resulted in states announcing changes in their votes, with the result that the 62-year-old Tilden received all 738 votes and the unanimous nomination on the third ballot.

Tilden's arch-enemy was "Honest John" Kelly, the leader of New York's Tammany Hall, who could not stop him from obtaining the nomination. In fact, it was claimed that Tilden's nomination was met by the 5,000 convention attendees with more enthusiasm than any leader since Andrew Jackson. The focus on the convention then turned to the possibilities for the Vice Presidency. Among those mentioned were Hendricks, Representative Henry B. Payne of Ohio, former Governor John M. Palmer of Illinois, and Cyrus McCormick of Illinois. Thomas Hendricks was the only individual actually nominated for Vice President. The delegation from Ohio had thought of offering the name of distinguished son Henry B. Payne. However, the Ohio delegation declined to present his name because the feeling of unanimity toward Hendricks was so great and Payne actually seconded the nomination of Hendricks. When the roll call vote took place, Ohio cast eight blank ballots and **Hendricks was nominated by acclamation.**

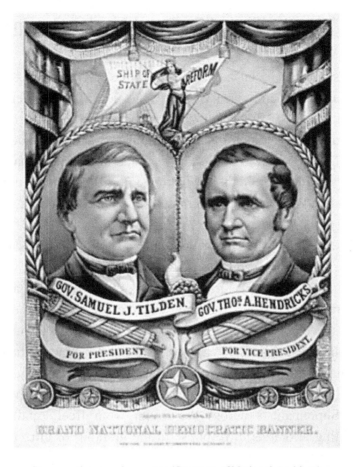

Democratic campaign poster (Courtesy of National Archives)

The Republican and Democratic parties were both looking for "new faces" that came from outside of Washington and were not tainted by scandal. They, understandably, chose two state Governors. Both ran on party platforms of anti-corruption. Ironically, in the coming Presidential election, there would be unprecedented corruption all around them from the top of the parties at the national level, through state officials, and all the way down to local election boards.

Ch. 8 - The 1876 Presidential Campaign

It was supposed to be a year to celebrate. After all, 1876 was America's 100th anniversary. The huge Philadelphia Centennial Exhibition was the first World's Fair ever held in the United States. It was a time to honor the progress that had been made in the country's first century. At a time when the total population was 46 million and Philadelphia's less than one million, almost ten million people attended, paying the admission price of fifty cents.

But all was not good. America was mired in a deep Depression, the worst in American history to that point. Unemployment was at a staggering 14%. It was first called "The Panic of 1873" and then "The Great Depression," until one would come along in the 1930's that was even worse, with 23% of the work force unemployed. Labor disputes, often violent, were erupting. Lincoln had been assassinated the previous year, sending shock waves throughout a country that was still reeling from the effects of the Civil War. White Supremacists across the South were freely and openly committing atrocities in response to the granting of citizenship to former slaves.

Then, in the days between the Republican and Democratic Conventions, General George Custer's forces were annihilated by the combined forces of the Sioux, Cheyenne, Lakota, and Arapaho tribes at the Battle of Little Big Horn. Five of the 7th Cavalry's twelve Companies were wiped out on June 25 and Custer, two of his brothers, his nephew and his brother-in-law were among those killed. The total U.S. casualty count was 268 dead and 55 critically wounded.

Looking at their resumes, you'd think the two Presidential candidates would be anything but boring. Hayes, after all, was a decorated war hero wounded five times in battle while Tilden earned his reputation as a resolute crime-fighter. What they both had going for them was honesty, unfortunately a rare commodity for the times.

Governor Tilden, a very private corporation lawyer without personal magnetism, was as low-key as they come. "He postpones too much and waits too long," the New York Tribune despairingly said of him. "He rides a waiting race." To 8th President Martin Van Buren, Tilden "was the most unambitious man I have ever known." (101)

In turn, the mild-mannered Hayes was called "offensive to no one" He described himself this way:

> "I have a talent for silence and brevity. I can keep silent when it seems best to do so, and when I speak I can, and do usually, quit when I am done. This talent, or these two talents, I have cultivated. Silence and concise, brief speaking have got me some laurels and, I suspect, lost me some. No odds. Do what is natural to you, and you are sure to get all the recognition you are entitled to."

It was the urgency of the time rather than the attractiveness of the candidates that drove voter enthusiasm. The old adage about "The office should seek the man, not man the office" applied. The election was preceded by months of illuminated parades, local ceremonies, grand public dinners, and eloquent oratory. Back then, the candidates, along with anyone else who took the podium, had to speak with enough power, unaided by microphones, that audiences in the thousands could hear them. Each party held massive midnight rallies and some leaders on both sides urged voters to come armed.

Both men considered themselves reformers, even while their parties used aggressive and often underhanded campaign tactics. Rampant voter fraud played a big part in the 1876 election. Everyone knew that the election would be tightly-contested. The few southern states still controlled by Republican governments, Florida, South Carolina, and Louisiana, were especially tense. The legacy of one Civil War and fears of another were on the ballot.

Although slavery had been outlawed and the Constitution amended to give the right to vote to freedmen, no law could change the rampant racism that remained. Strong opposition to civil rights reforms ran deep, and many state and local governments refused to recognize the equality the Constitution now guaranteed. The Presidential campaign of 1876 was as volatile as any in history. Democrats were unrelenting in their criticism of the Grant administration and Congress. Republicans called Tilden a sympathizer of the South and implied that his long association with railroad companies was a form of corruption that had made him rich. Tilden, meanwhile, did not run an energetic campaign. He continued to devote his energy to his role as Governor of New York.

The campaign of 1876 generated little actual disagreement on issues. Although Hayes and Tilden were heavily influenced by their parties and their passionate bases, they actually agreed on a lot. There was no Presidential debate back then but, if there had been, it would likely have been a ho-hum affair with low ratings. While their respective parties were exchanging insults, Hayes and Tilden were very polite to and respectful of each other. Their biggest area of disagreement might have been the pace of withdrawal of federal troops from the South. Tilden clearly promoted immediate and unconditional southern rule in the American South. Hayes spoke more in general terms. In his letter accepting the nomination, Hayes indicated his desire that the South enjoy "the blessings of honest and capable local government" but with guarantees that the states would guard the civil rights of the freedmen. When asked to be more specific during the months of campaigning, Hayes repeatedly responded, "I stand by what I said in my letter of acceptance."

With little of substance to focus on, each candidate let their respective camp turn to mudslinging. The Democrats aired the Republicans' dirty laundry, reminding voters of the scandals and corruption present during the Grant years. In response, the Republicans linked the Democratic Party with secession and with the outrages committed against Black and White Republicans in the South. Some Republican leaders went so far as to comment that every man who tried to rip the country apart was a Democrat, and to remind the public that Abraham Lincoln's assassin was a Democrat. What were the real election results? No one will ever know. In those days, a number of places didn't even have official ballots. People could just put the name of the candidate they were voting for on a piece of paper. There were many stories of Democratic ballots with all Republican names on it and vice-versa to try to trick voters. There were Republican election boards in Southern states that threw out a significant number of Democratic votes. Both Democrats and Republicans were accused of voting multiple times. There was massive voter suppression of Blacks by Democrats using lynchings, beatings, and other acts of violence.

When it was time to vote, the ritual was public back then. Voters who identified with a particular party would step forward clutching brightly-colored tickets, which signaled their allegiance, and place them in the ballot box in front of hundreds of onlookers. Those who had bribed voters could be certain they were getting their money's worth. Not until the 1890's would the secret ballot come along, dismaying many of those who witnessed earlier elections. The drama diminished, as did the more flagrant forms of election abuse.

The battle lines were clearly drawn. Left to themselves, it's likely that Hayes and Tilden would have kept the election campaign free from distortion of facts and bitter personal invective. Wild conspiracy theories were not relegated to 21st century politics.

Democrats charged that Hayes had pocketed money given to him by enlisted men to send to their families. Outraged, Hayes gathered testimony from officers who had served with him in West Virginia to refute those accusations. In retaliation for Republican claims about Tilden's record as a taxpayer during the war, some enterprising Democrats discovered that Hayes had filed no income tax returns for 1868 and 1869, his first term as Ohio's governor. This exposure deeply embarrassed Hayes. "If no returns were made in the two years 1868 and 1869," he complained to his diary, "it was because no returns were called for since my income was so low in those years."

Tilden was also subjected to more than his share of damaging rumors. There seemed to be no limit to the charges that he was a liar, swindler, perjurer, and counterfeiter. There was even an absurd allegation that he had been in league with the infamous Tweed. Some Republicans falsely claimed that Tilden had rampant syphilis that had impaired his mental capacity and even that he had shot his mother while drunk. A life-long bachelor, some Hayes backers conducted a campaign suggesting Tilden was homosexual. Tilden's opponents painted him as a diseased drunkard who planned to use federal funds to pay off the former Confederacy's debts.

In response to the question of why he wasn't a Republican, Tilden's admitted:

> "I was never a Republican, because those gentlemen, distinguished as they are, have only one real interest, and that is the making of special laws in order to protect their fortunes. I also know they have no compassion for the masses of the people in this country who are without money and who are, many of them, without food or houses. I have always thought that only as a Democrat, reflecting Jefferson and Jackson, could justice ever be done the people because, at this moment in history, ours is the only party which is even faintly responsive to the force of ideas."(102)

He sounds like a modern politician except for the part about "those gentlemen, distinguished as they are..." It would be hard to image someone today being that deferential.

An indicator of the vitriol and divisiveness between the two parties is this stump speech by Ingersoll, the orator who spoke at the Republican Convention, given many times during the campaign:

> "I am opposed to the Democratic party, and I will tell you why. Every state that seceded from the United States was a Democratic state. Every ordinance of

secession that was drawn was drawn by a Democrat. Every man that endeavored to tear the old flag from the heaven that it enriches was a Democrat. Every man that tried to destroy this nation was a Democrat. Every enemy this great republic has had for twenty years has been a Democrat. Every man that shot Union soldiers was a Democrat. Every man that denies to the Union prisoners even the worm-eaten crust of famine was a Democrat. Every man that loved slavery better than liberty was a Democrat. The man that assassinated Abraham Lincoln was a Democrat. Every man that raised bloodhounds to pursue human beings was a Democrat. Soldiers, every scar you have on your heroic bodies was given you by a Democrat." (103)

Referring back to the Civil War, a popular Republican slogan used during the convention and throughout the campaign was, "Not every Democrat was a Rebel but every Rebel was a Democrat."

Attacks on Tilden were led by the New York Times. The chief charges brought against him were that he had been a railroad "wrecker," that he had extorted excessive fees for legal services, that he had been a Rebel sympathizer, and that he was a sham eleventh-hour reformer who had gone into the fight against the Tweed Ring and the Canal Ring merely to pave his way to the Presidency.

In line with their basic campaign strategy, the Republicans alleged that Tilden had supported the Confederacy, the right of secession, and the continuation of slavery. This all stemmed from his opposition to Lincoln's election in 1860, fearing a Republican victory would bring disaster to the United States.

The solid Republican majority, including ex-slaves in the South protected by the presence of federal troops, that had reelected Civil War hero Ulysses S. Grant in 1872 was weakened by continuous charges of "Grantism," which became synonymous with corruption. The midterm elections of 1874 had produced an enormous 94-seat swing in House seats away from Republicans and towards Democrats. They overwhelmingly won the Lower Chamber, which consisted of 293 seats at the time. Grant had all but abandoned the idea of continuing Reconstruction, with federal courts undermining civil rights enforcement powers and Congress no longer interested in restoring them. By the time the 1876 election came around, the country was experiencing "Reconstruction Fatigue." Increasing calls for a return to normality sparked calls for the end of Reconstruction and the return of full control of state governments to local authorities. Political pundits felt the Democrats had their best hope of regaining the White House since before the Civil War.

The social, economic, and political unrest in 1876 created the ideal conditions for an election meltdown for Republicans. Even in those days, the phrase, "It's the economy, stupid" was applicable. The economic depression led to widespread job losses and business failures. Because of the bad economy, voters repudiated the Republican Party at the polls in local elections. But insult-slinging was just the tip of the iceberg during the election. The real iceberg was violence, intimidation, and bribery. It wasn't a free, fair election from the very beginning. Tilden would go on to win the popular vote only because Klansmen and other White supremacist organizations used violence to suppress the Black vote in many parts of the South. Tilden would likely never have carried the southern states such as Mississippi or Alabama without that suppression. In South Carolina, a majority Black state, armed White men belonging to "rifle clubs" and dressed in red shirts had harassed Republicans. The "Red Shirts" killed six Black men in a massacre in Hamburg. The militant group backed a former Confederate general for governor and threatened to kill Republican Governor Daniel Chamberlain.

On Election Day in Edgefield, South Carolina, more than 300 armed White supremacists on horseback "packed their horses so closely together that the only approach to the windows, back of which was the ballot box, was under the bellies of the beasts," the New York Times said. In Barnwell County, one newspaper reported that there were "riflemen wearing red shirts, riding to and fro, cursing and threatening the Negroes."

In one state with a Black majority, So. Carolina, and two with very large black minorities, Louisiana and Florida, Republicans still held power. Democrats used violence and intimidation to keep Blacks from the polls while claiming that Republicans weren't simply disallowing votes tainted by violence but also legitimate returns that favored the Democratic party. Some prominent militias were urged to make threatening appearances at party meetings and polling places, specifically targeting Black citizens. Continuing hard times, still vivid memories of Civil War sacrifices, and White southerners' determination to reestablish White supremacy in their region probably best explain the unusually high interest in the 1876 election. Nineteenth-century elections were primarily referenda on competing political parties, not their presidential candidates, because few, if any, voters ever personally saw or heard those candidates.

One of the most influential leaders of the Redeemer movement was former Confederate General S. W. Ferguson of Washington County, Mississippi. He described how in an overwhelmingly Republican county where Blacks outnumbered Whites by five to one, the decision by the Whites to use concentrated political violence had given them control of the election. Ferguson wrote that "We determined to carry the election at all hazards, and, in the event of any blood being shed in the Campaign, to kill every White radical in the country; we made no threats, but we let this be known as a fixed and settled thing." He claimed that White Republicans were not willing "to sacrifice themselves on the altar of rascality" and that Blacks did not turn out to vote when they saw the Republican leaders "cower and finally retire from the contest." (104)

Ferguson advised that armed White men needed to be posted at the polls to control the votes of Blacks, and if necessary to kill them. He famously told the South Carolinians, "Never threaten a man individually. If he deserves to be threatened, the necessity of the times require that he should die. A dead Radical is very harmless. A threatened Radical is often very troublesome, sometimes dangerous, always vindictive." (105)

In South Carolina the friends of gubernatorial candidate Wade Hampton hoped to emulate the White Mississippians. They sought advice from the leaders there on how to organize the redemption of their own state. One of the men they looked to for guidance was Ferguson, who offered assistance to Theodore G. Barker, of Charleston, Hampton's adjutant during the Civil War. Ferguson was originally from South Carolina and had moved to Mississippi after the Confederate surrenders.

Martin W. Gary, another former Confederate Brigadier General, obtained a copy of Ferguson's writings which provided useful guidance on how to use violence to help secure victory. Gary had taken on himself the organizing of a "Mississippi Plan" style of campaign for the 1876 Election in South Carolina. Gary had served under General Wade Hampton and refused to surrender with the rest of Lee's army at Appomattox. An attorney by trade, he became a militant opponent of Reconstruction in South Carolina and of civil rights for Blacks after the war. Gary saw the 1876 Election as "a struggle for supremacy between the races and not a mere contest for honest government as has been alleged." (106)

While Hampton campaigned for Governor in 1876 promising a return to White conservative control of the state, Gary drew up a scheme called "The Shotgun Policy." It was written in secret and distributed to Democratic clubs in all of the counties of South Carolina. It was considered a proud legacy by the Gary family and the General's widow archived it after her husband's death. Gary's plan required intelligence gathering about those whose votes were to be suppressed. He ordered that the names of all Black voters be collected throughout the state. Knowing who the enemy was would not be enough. Gary knew he needed to use the threat of violence to secure White supremacy in a state where more than half the population was Black. He instructed the Red Shirts to make sure Black citizens in South Carolina could not get out to vote. This is a listing of some points from his much-longer repugnant battle plan to capture the 1876 Gubernatorial and Presidential races in South Carolina:

1. That the Democratic Military Clubs are to be armed with rifles and pistols and such other arms as they may command. They are divided into two companies, one of the old men the other of the young; an experienced Captain or Commander to be placed over each of them. That each Company is to have a 1st and 2nd Lieutenant. That the number of ten privates is to be the unit of organization. That each Captain is to see that his men are well armed and provided with at least thirty rounds of ammunition. That the Captain of the young men is to provide a Baggage wagon, in which three days rations for the horses and three days rations for the men are to be stored on the day before the election in order that they may be prepared at a moment's notice to move to any point in the County when ordered by the Chairman of the Executive Committee.

2. Every Democrat must be at the polls by five o'clock in the morning of the election, carry his dinner with him and stay there until the votes are counted, unless the exigencies require him elsewhere.

3. Every Democrat must feel honor bound to control the vote of at least one Negro, by intimidation, purchase, keeping him away or as each individual may determine, how he may best accomplish it.

4. We must attend every Radical meeting that we hear of whether they meet at night or in the daytime. Democrats must go in as large numbers as they can get together, and well-armed, behave at first with great courtesy and assure the ignorant Negroes that you mean them no harm and so soon as their leaders or speakers begin to speak and make false statements of facts, tell them then and there to their faces, that they are liars, thieves and rascals, and are only trying to mislead the ignorant Negroes and if you get a chance get upon the platform and address the Negroes.

5. In speeches to Negroes you must remember that argument has no effect upon them: They can only be influenced by their fears, superstition and cupidity. Do not attempt to flatter and persuade them. Tell them plainly of our wrongs and grievances, perpetrated upon us, by their rascally leaders. Prove to them that we can carry the election without them and if they cooperate with us, it will benefit them more than it will us. Treat them so as to show them, you are the superior race, and that their natural position is that of subordination to the White man.

6. In the nomination of candidates we should nominate those who will give their time, their money, their brains, their energies and if necessary lay down their lives to carry this election. Any attempt to run independent candidates must be prevented at any risk.

7. The watch word of our Campaign should be "fight the Devil with fire." That we are in favor of local self-government, home rule by home folks and that we are determined to drive the carpetbaggers from this State at all hazards.

8. Every club must be uniformed in a red shirt and they must be sure and wear it upon all public meetings and particularly on the day of election.

9. Secrecy should shroud all of transactions. Let not your left hand know what your right does.

10. Where the Negroes are largely in the majority a corps of challengers should be organized, with appropriate questions. You gain time by this. (107)

Election Day went anything but smoothly in South Carolina. The heavily armed Redshirt supporters of former Confederate General Wade Hampton set the tone with paramilitary operations near polling places. In Greenville, Democrats set up a "Police Force" around the polls that admitted only Whites to vote. In the counties of Edgefield and Laurens, more Democratic votes would be cast than the total number of registered voters. Over-all in South Carolina, despite serious voter suppression, the official turnout was reported as 101% of eligible voters. That math is pretty suspicious.

The Democrats used "repeaters" - people who voted again and again. The national voter turnout was reported to be 81.8 percent, supposedly the highest ever for a Presidential election. That number, though, is highly suspect. Voter intimidation also was rampant in Louisiana where Black registered voters outnumbered Whites by 104,191 to 84,167. In spite of this majority, the Democrats somehow won the count in Louisiana by 7,000 votes. Charges of the suppression of Black voting were rampant in the Pelican State.

As soon as doubt emerged about the electoral votes in question, both parties set out to steal victory. Politicos flooded into the three disputed southern states to influence the "returning boards" that would determine each states' electoral votes. Backed by state officials, cash, and the US Army, Republicans began to disqualify Democratic votes. In Louisiana, the board dismissed nearly 10 percent of the state's ballots, 85 percent of which were cast for Tilden.

There were many documented stories of heavily-armed, marauding White supremacist Democrats canvassing the South, preventing countless Blacks from voting while calling themselves "election observers." Another of the many points of contention centered around the design of ballots. At the time, the political parties would print "tickets" to enable voters to support them in the open ballots. To aid illiterate voters, the parties would print symbols on the tickets. In this election, many Democratic ballots were printed with a drawing of Abraham Lincoln on them. In turn, there were fraudulent Republican ballots printed with a picture of a Donkey on them. The donkey had been introduced as a symbol of the party six years earlier, in 1870, by Thomas Nast in Harper's Weekly. In both cases, the intent was to trick illiterate people into voting for the opposite party. Northern Republicans possessed a weapon of greater potency. It's clear that fear of ex-Confederates recapturing control of the federal government in Washington, thereby betraying more than 300,000 dead Union soldiers, constituted the Republican Party's most important appeal in the North. That their candidate, unlike Tilden, had repeatedly demonstrated valor on the battlefield only added to their advantage. Yet memories of the war and more recent experience with Republicans' Reconstruction programs also best explain the breathtaking jump in White support for Democrats in the South that year. (108)

Tilden was not in favor of any form of violence. "We have just emerged from one Civil War," he said. "It will never do to engage in another; it would end in the destruction of free government." (109)

Black men, almost all of whom were Republican, had only recently won the right to vote. Women would not be allowed to vote until the 19th Amendment was passed in 1920, some 44 years later. No one knows which party benefited the most from the rampant voter suppression and fraud. It may have been that all the corruption from the Republicans and Democrats resulted in no net gain for either party. There was also a new party that had emerged - the Greenback Party – to offer a third option. It wound up receiving 1% of the popular vote but no electoral votes. They wanted the ability to print paper money, called greenbacks, that would not be backed by gold and would presumably help the economy. They were also extremely anti-monopoly. They nominated inventor and entrepreneur Peter Cooper who had developed and built the first American steam locomotive. His main appeal seemed to be that he was not a politician. Born in 1791, he was 85 years old, making him the oldest person who has ever run for President. His running mate was Samuel Fenton Cary, a former representative from Ohio. The party would also go on to run Presidential candidates in the 1880 and 1884 elections before fading away. The 1876 ballot count turned out to be even more of a mess than the voting process itself. After the long, nasty, contentious campaign, the voting was over, but the outcome was far from clear. The Democrats pointed to the popular vote and apparent Electoral College victory.

Both parties maintained that their candidate was the rightful winner of the White House. Rather than come together in unity, the country found itself further entrenched in partisanship. One of the ugliest, most contentious and most controversial presidential elections in U.S. history was far from over.

President Grant summed up the election by declaring, "No man worthy of the office of President should be willing to hold it if counted in, or placed there, by any fraud. Either party can afford to be disappointed in the result, but the country cannot afford to have the result tainted by the suspicion of illegal, or false returns." (110) The problem is that neither Grant nor anyone else knew what to do about it. As votes were counted, it appeared that New York Governor Samuel J. Tilden was going to be the 19th President of the United States. His 4,288,546 vote total surpassed Hayes' 4,034,311 votes by a margin of more than a quarter-million. However, since it's the Electoral College vote that matters and not the popular vote, that's where things got complicated. With 185 electoral votes needed to clinch the election, Tilden was almost there with 184 votes to his credit. Hayes had only 163.

The four states of Oregon, Louisiana, South Carolina, and Florida, with a combined vote total of 22, remained unresolved. Hayes would have to win each of those states to cross the finish line. Tilden would need just one more electoral vote.

Ch. 9 - The Centennial Election

The Electoral College system is a highly controversial process by which the United States selects the President every four years. The method is a patchwork of complexity and ambiguity. It's hard to image something more expertly designed to thrust the nation into periodic confusion. The Constitution established the Electoral College system as a hodgepodge of divided responsibilities between the federal and state governments. It's not a meaningless anachronism. It is genuinely unfair.

Consider the scenario that has now occurred a number of times, including the 1876 election. A candidate who receives a majority of the popular vote may not, under the Constitution, necessarily become President if that person fails to secure a majority of the electoral vote. The contradiction of this with the most elementary principle of democracy is obvious - the will of the people is denied.

How could anyone devise a system where Presidential candidates only visit, pay attention to, and make promises to voters in swing states? Those are not necessarily the largest or the most important states. They are simply those that appear to be toss-ups, that is they could be won by either candidate. Meanwhile, the states that are acknowledged to be non-competitive are largely ignored. California, for instance, now has a population of 40 million. The state is hardly given a passing thought by Presidential candidates since it is considered a lock for the Democrats. If Wyoming, with a tiny population of 596,000, were considered a swing state, the candidates would give it disproportionate attention to try to court its voters. Keeping things simple by having a winner by popular vote forces the candidates to pay attention to places that actually have a lot of people. That's what democracies are supposed to do. Pay attention to the people. Not just those in toss-up states.

Doing a little more math helps you quickly realize the inequity of the Electoral College process. California now gets 55 electoral votes. That's one electoral vote per 727,272 people. At the other extreme, Wyoming gets 3 electoral votes. That amounts to one electoral vote per 198,666 people. That means a Wyoming vote is worth 3.7 times as much as a California vote. The net effect is that smaller population states have greater representation in the Electoral College while larger states are underrepresented. One way to ensure equity would be for the states to have a proportional allocation of electoral votes to more accurately reflect the popular vote. Another way would be much simpler. Just have the popular vote.

The Founding Fathers, of course, understood the argument for a simple popular vote but intentionally decided on the Electoral College system so that smaller states would not be overlooked. They were "looking out for the little guy" which may be admirable but, in the process, made the "big guy" often irrelevant. Imagine trying to explain the logic to a fledgling democracy in a third-world country.

The creators of the Constitution saw two ways to accomplish the worthy goal of ensuring that the people are given direct input in choosing their leaders:

- The entire nation could elect the President and Vice President based on popular vote alone.

- The people of each state could elect their members of the U.S. Congress by direct popular election and, in turn, Congress would elect the President and Vice President themselves.

They feared the direct popular vote option, opting for a representative rather than true democracy. There were no organized national political parties yet, and no structure from which to choose and limit the number of candidates. They imagined an election with scores of political parties. There was no mass communication so they felt most people would only be familiar with local politicians. Also, travel and communication were slow and difficult at that time. A very good candidate could be popular regionally but remain unknown to the rest of the country. A large number of regional candidates would thus divide the vote and make it difficult, if not impossible, for a candidate to win a majority.

On the other hand, election by Congress would require the members to both accurately assess the desires of the people of their states and to vote accordingly. This could have led to elections that better reflected the opinions and political agendas of the members of Congress rather than the actual will of the people. As a compromise, the Electoral College system was developed.

The Founding Fathers' concerns with direct popular elections have mostly vanished now. The national political parties have been around for many years. Travel and mass communication are no longer problems. The public has access to every word spoken or written by every candidate every day.

Rutherford B. Hayes pledged in a diary entry that if he won the election, a high-priority item for him would be reforming the

Electoral College system. It was obsolete even then. "Before another Presidential election," he wrote, "this whole subject of the Presidential election ought to be thoroughly considered, and a radical change made. Something ought to be done immediately." But nothing was done immediately. Nothing was done later. Nothing has ever been done.

Established by Article II of the Constitution, the Electoral College process was modified by the 12th Amendment in 1804. When you vote for a Presidential candidate on the first Tuesday in November, you are in fact voting to instruct the electors from your state how to cast their votes when the Electoral College meets in December. Each state gets a number of electors equal to its number of members in the U.S. House of Representatives plus one for each of its two U.S. senators. State laws determine how electors are chosen, but they are generally selected by the political party committees within the states. The candidate who wins the popular vote in a state wins all the pledged votes of the state's electors in the 48 winner-take-all states and District of Columbia, which gets three electors. Nebraska and Maine award electors proportionally. Maine has four Electoral votes. Beginning in 1972, the state began to award one Electoral vote for each of its two Congressional districts and two by the statewide vote. Nebraska has five Electoral College votes. Since 1996, three have been given to the Congressional district winners and two by the statewide vote. Overseas territories such as Puerto Rico and Guam, have no say in presidential elections, even though their residents are U.S. citizens.

These days, a candidate must win 270 of the 538 available electoral votes. Back in 1876, it took 185 of the 369 electoral votes. Should none of the candidates win the required number, the 12th Amendment mandates the election be decided by the House of

Representatives. This has happened twice. Both President Thomas Jefferson in 1801 and John Quincy Adams in 1825 were elected by the House. The state electors "pledge" to vote for the candidate of the party that chose them, though nothing in the Constitution requires them to do so. In rare instances, an elector will defect and not vote for their party's candidate. Such "faithless" votes rarely change the outcome of the election, and laws of some states prohibit electors from casting them. However, no state has ever prosecuted someone for not voting the way they were pledged. The 2016 election had seven faithless electors, the most ever. The previous record was six who changed their votes in 1808. The 2020 election didn't have any faithless electors.

It's not until the first Monday after the second Wednesday in December, though, when the members of the Electoral College meet in their respective state capitals to cast their votes, that a President-elect and Vice President-elect are named. The results are then sent to and counted by the Congress, where they are tabulated in the first week of January before a joint meeting of the Senate and the House of Representatives, presided over by the current Vice President, who is also President of the Senate. The reason for all the delays was that during the 1800's, it took that long to count the popular votes, for all the electors to travel to the state capitals, and for the certificates to be sent from the states to Washington.

A full decade after the 1876 election, Congress enacted a law empowering each state to determine the authenticity of its selection of electors. It was not until 1933 that the Constitution directly provided for the nightmarish possibility that the incumbent President's term might expire before the next President or Vice President could be chosen. The Twentieth Amendment, adopted that year, specifies that Congress may in such a case declare "who shall act as President, or the manner in which one who is to act shall be selected, and such a person shall act accordingly until a President or Vice President shall have qualified." (110)

But no amendment or statute has yet solved the central problems which bedeviled the election of 1876. Irregularities in the selection of people for the Electoral College can still occur in the states. A "minority President" who receives the most electoral votes but not popular votes, can still be elected. Also, a "majority President" who receives the most popular votes but not electoral votes can lose an election. The disturbing flaws in the Presidential Election system will, no doubt, arise to haunt us again.

Election Day Tuesday was particularly long and arduous for Governor Rutherford B. Hayes. He knew full well of the complexities of the Presidential Election system and how much could go wrong. He also was aware of the fact that it would take some time to get the complete voting results. He couldn't conceive, though, of just how long it would ultimately take. Rud began the day by writing in his diary:

> "November 7. A cold but dry day. Good enough here for election work. I still think Democratic chances the best. But it is not possible to form a confident opinion. If we lose, the South will be the greatest sufferer. Their misfortune will be far greater than ours. I do not think a revival of business will be greatly postponed by Tilden's election. Business prosperity does not, in my judgment, depend on government so much as men commonly think. But we shall have no improvement in civil service -

deterioration rather, and the South will drift towards chaos again."

Rud travelled to Columbus, Ohio in the afternoon to give this speech to his supporters:

> "I will say something to you which I think it is my duty, under the circumstances, to say. While our present advices look favorable, we must remember that several of the States which have been considered doubtful have a large territory remote from railroad or telegraphic communication, and it will naturally take some time to receive definite returns from them. I therefore take this call as an earnest sign of your loyalty to the Republican party, and your desire for its success. If later advices should change the result from what it is announced at present, I assure you I shall frequently recall this visit during the time I shall live among you with pleasure." (111)

He was surrounded that night by a group of reporters in the spacious living room of his home at Spiegel Grove, located at the corner of Hayes and Buckland Avenues in Fremont, Ohio. Spiegel is the German and Dutch word for "mirror." It signifies the reflective pools of water that would collect on the property after a rainstorm. The small group of family and friends who gathered at Hayes's home on that raw and windy election night found little to cheer about. The candidate was not doing as well as they had hoped in Ohio, and the news that Tilden had carried several doubtful northern states added another layer of gloom to an already somber evening. Lucy kept mostly to the kitchen, busying herself with refreshments, before disappearing upstairs with a headache. When word came that Tilden had carried New York City by fifty thousand votes, Hayes resigned himself to defeat. "From that time, I never supposed there was a chance for Republican success," he confided to his diary. A galaxy of famous Republican speakers, and even Mark Twain, had stumped for Hayes. It was appearing that their efforts would turn out to be in vain. Rud was receiving election news from a procession of messenger boys trooping through his parlor with the latest dispatches. Shortly after midnight, Hayes was ready to go to bed convinced of his defeat after what he called "a very close contest." Results were coming in by way of telegraph. Telephone would have been a more efficient means of communication but it was not yet available. Alexander Graham Bell was awarded the patent for the telephone on March 7, 1876 and would go on to start his Bell Telephone Company the following year.

"Well, boys, I guess that's about it," shrugged Hayes as he dismissed the reporters who had gathered in his home. "Tilden is ahead by 260,000 popular votes and preliminary results show he has 184 electoral votes which is one shy of the majority needed to win the election. I have just 165. I'm calling it a night."

"Does that mean you're conceding?" asked one of the reporters.

"Yes, I suppose that's what it means," shrugged Hayes.

After shaking his hand and wishing him well, the reporters quietly filed out of the house thinking the Democrats had won the White House for the first time in 20 years. After everyone left, Lucy came back downstairs only to put her arm around him and try to console him as they went up to bed shortly after midnight saying, "At least we won't have to uproot the kids and move to Washington."

"That's true," Rutherford said wistfully as he kissed her goodnight, "but I wish it were otherwise." Lucy was always someone he could count on to find the good in a bad situation. As Hayes recounted in his diary, "We soon fell into a refreshing sleep, and the affair seemed over."

Tilden, on the other hand, spent the day walking through the streets to greet eager crowds during the day. He accepted premature congratulations from admirers encouraging him to go to Washington to eliminate the corruption there. That night, Tilden shared a quiet dinner with friends in New York City. Afterwards, he made a quick visit to Democratic headquarters at the Everett House in Union Square. There, he heard the good news that he had carried the swing states of Indiana, New Jersey, and Connecticut. With his own state safely in hand and a blizzard of electoral votes expected momentarily from the South, it now seemed increasingly likely that "Centennial Sam" Tilden, boasting a brand new nickname and an equally sportive red carnation in the buttonhole of his somber black suit, was about to exchange one executive mansion for another. (112)

Hayes had experience with close elections. In his first election, he had been sent to Congress by a slim margin of 2,400 votes, in a wartime election that was tailor-made for Republicans. His first campaign for governor had gone down to the wire as well, with him eventually winning by 0.6% of the vote. His following two terms had been won by slightly larger, but scarcely landslide, margins. The distinction of his never having lost an election, though, seemed to be coming to an abrupt, decisive end. Dan Sickles, the Civil War

General who had been put in charge of federal troops in North and South Carolina during Reconstruction, would turn out to play a critical role in the 1876 election. An ardent Hayes supporter, he had what might be called a "spotty" record. After attending Law School at the University of the City of New York, he was admitted to the bar in 1846 and elected to the New York Assembly. Sickles carried on an indiscreet affair for years with a well-known prostitute by the name of Fanny White. He loved nothing more than to introduce her to guests at formal events to stir up gossip. As a member of the New York assembly in 1847, he earned a censure from the opposition Whig party for bringing White into the assembly chamber. Sickles carried the nickname of "Devil Dan" with pride.

General Dan Sickles (Courtesy Library of Congress)

Sickles married Teresa Bagioli in 1852 when he was 33 years old and she was 15 and pregnant. Needless to say, the Sickles and Bagioli families were not thrilled with the course of events. Upon learning of the marriage, Fanny White was so angry that she followed him to a hotel room, attacking him with a riding whip. Devil Dan arranged for the mortgage on White's brothel using the name of his father-in-law Antonio Bagioli.

In addition to serving as a two-term member of Congress representing two different New York Districts, Sickles was personal secretary for the Ambassador to the Court of St. James in London. He left his pregnant wife behind and chose to bring Fanny White instead. Meeting Queen Victoria at Buckingham palace, Sickles introduced the prostitute as "Miss Bennett", using the surname of one of his enemies - New York Herald Editor James Gordon Bennett, Sr. – who was furious at the use of his name. Sickles was particularly amused when he learned about that.

Devil Dan's wife Teresa confessed to having an adulterous affair with the Washington, D.C. District Attorney Philip Barton Key, son of Francis Scott Key, composer of "The Star-Spangled Banner." On Sunday, February 27, 1859, Sickles confronted Key in Lafayette Square, directly across from the White House. He declared in very theatrical terms, "Key, you scoundrel, you have dishonored my home. You must die." He then shot and killed the unarmed Key. (113)

Sickles then went to the home of Attorney General Jeremiah S. Black to admit his crime and surrender. The next week, a Grand Jury charged him with first degree murder. He retained the services of attorney and future Secretary of War Edwin M. Stanton. By the time the defense had rested, Washington newspapers were praising Sickles for "saving all the ladies of Washington from this rogue named Key." (114) The trial gained nationwide media attention for both its scandalous nature and its proximity to the White House. The courtroom proceedings began on April 4. The prosecution tried to advance the theory that Sickles had also committed adultery and didn't pay much attention to his wife. The judge, however, disallowed this. Instead, the State's approach was to highlight the heinous nature of the murder and not address his reasons for committing it. Sickles' defense countered that he had suffered from a temporary bout of insanity.

Stanton delivered an impassioned closing argument stating that marriage is sacred and a man should have the right to defend it against those who chose to defile the purity of the sacrament, causing the courtroom to erupt in cheers. The jury in the case deliberated for just over an hour before delivering a "Not Guilty" verdict. Outside the courthouse, Sickles and Stanton met a throng of people rejoicing in the victory.

It was the first successful use of the temporary insanity defense to justify a murder. Supporters and detractors alike seemed more upset with Sickles' public reconciliation with his wife than with the original charges. The thirty-nine-year-old disgraced politician rehabilitated his career, raising and leading a Union brigade during the Civil War. On the second day of the battle, Sickles was ordered to protect the Union troops left at the base of a hill called Little Round Top, the smaller companion to the adjacent, taller hill fittingly named Big Round Top. He disobeyed those orders and moved his Third Corps a mile out front, taking a position in a peach orchard. Left alone, the Third was shattered by the Confederate assault.

During the height of the Confederate attack, Sickles was wounded by a cannonball that mangled his right leg while he was propped up on one elbow on a rock and smoking a cigar as he watched the destruction from the sidelines. He was carried by a detail of soldiers to a farmhouse, where a saddle strap was applied as a tourniquet. As Sickles was carried by stretcher to the III Corps hospital on Taneytown Road, he attempted to raise his soldiers' spirits by grinning and puffing on another cigar along the way. His leg was amputated that afternoon.

Sickles continued his service through the end of the war, though he was disappointed that he never received another battlefield command. That may have been due to his life-long feud with General George Meade. Devil Dan fabricated a story that he and not Meade was the "Father of the Union victory." He claimed that Meade was ready to retreat from Gettysburg but it was he who valiantly led the offensive that turned the tide in the Civil War in favor of the North. Sickles is one of only two Union Corps commanders not represented by a statue at Gettysburg. One had been planned for him, but the New York Times reported that he "reappropriated the $27,000 in funds." He was once asked where his monument was. Never one to be accused of being modest, he replied, "The entire battlefield is a memorial to Dan Sickles." (115) He liked referring to himself in the third person.

Devil Dan was brought to Washington, making a grand entrance on July 4, 1863 and bringing some of the first news of the Union victory. The next afternoon, President Lincoln visited General

Sickles as he was recovering. Dan also started a public relations campaign to defend his behavior in the conflict. After 34 years, his lobbying finally paid off as he was **presented with the Medal of Honor**. His citation read, "Displayed most conspicuous gallantry on the field vigorously contesting the advance of the enemy and continuing to encourage his troops after being himself severely wounded." (116)

Sickles preserved the bones from his amputated leg and donated them to the Army Medical Museum in Washington. They were displayed in a small coffin-shaped box, along with a note saying, "With the compliments of Major General D.E.S." He reportedly visited the limb a number of times on the anniversary of the amputation. The museum, now known as the **National Museum of Health and Medicine**, still displays the morbid artifact.

Having begun his political life as a Democrat, Sickles switched sides after the Civil War, becoming one of the leaders in the unsuccessful efforts by Republicans to remove President Andrew Johnson from office. Ignoring Sickles' less-than-stellar reputation, President Ulysses S. Grant appointed him to be the American Foreign Minister to Spain, where it is said he had an affair with no less than the deposed Queen Isabella II, earning him the nickname "the Yankee King of Spain" in a Times Magazine article. (118) On Election night, Devil Dan, wanting to get away from politics for a few hours, went to a Broadway play and followed it with a late dinner. On his way home around midnight, he made a spur-of-the-moment decision to drop by Republican Party Headquarters at the nearby Fifth Avenue Hotel. Sickles entered the headquarters expecting to find it a beehive of activity. Instead, he found it nearly deserted. There was a single clerk left there by the name of M.C. Clancy who told him everyone had gone home and Tilden had won. Clancy was in the process of packing up the records.

Devil Dan asked to see the latest returns. "You will find them on the desk of Mr. Chandler," Clancy said, referring to Republican Committee Chairman Zach Chandler. "He retired an hour ago, saying he didn't want to see anybody." The clerk added that the Chairman had taken a bottle of whiskey upstairs with him and gone to bed. (117)

Sickles sat down at Chandler's desk and rifled through a stack of telegrams from Republican state headquarters across the country. What he saw on paper gave him hope. Quickly scanning the returns, he was disappointed to see that Tilden was winning New York, New Jersey, Connecticut, Indiana, and apparently the entire South, with a plurality of about 250,000 votes and, it seemed, 203 electoral votes with only 185 needed for victory. But then he noticed something else. Something important. "After a careful scrutiny," Sickles recalled, "I reached the conclusions that the contest was really very close and doubtful, but by no means hopeless. According to my figures, based on fair probabilities, Hayes was elected by at least a one vote majority in the Electoral College." (118) Sickles' estimate assumed that Hayes would win the electoral votes of South Carolina, Louisiana, Florida, and Oregon, giving him the exact number of 185 electoral votes needed for victory. As subsequent events would demonstrate, that was a very large assumption to make, but Sickles followed up his intuition by drafting telegrams to leading Republican functionaries in the four questionable states, each containing the same urgent message: "With your state sure for Hayes, he is elected. Hold your state." (119)

Sickles called Clancy to his side, showed him the telegrams, and asked the clerk to sign Chandler's name to the dispatches. Before Clancy could respond, Sickles heard the familiar voice of Chester A. Arthur, the longtime Collector of the Port of New York, outside in the hall. He was an actual government official which was good enough for Sickles, who went to the door and asked Arthur to come into the room. Sickles showed him a copy of the election returns and the various telegrams. "If you advise it," said Sickles, "I have no doubt the chief clerk will feel authorized to send off these telegrams with the signature of the Chairman." Arthur agreed, the telegrams were sent, and Sickles prepared to leave, having functioned for the last hour as a one-man Republican National Committee. (120)

At 3 a.m., Republican Governor Daniel Chamberlain responded, "All right. South Carolina is for Hayes. Need more troops. Communication with interior cut off by mobs." By 6 A.M., he had received an encouraging answer from Oregon. At that point, Sickles again "telegraphed all four states, informing them that the enemy claimed each of them and enjoining vigilance and diligence." (121)

Rud woke and went to his office as usual and wrote to his son Rutherford, who was away at Cornell University, to let him know how the folks at home were taking the defeat. "Scott Russell is rejoiced because now we can remain in Columbus where the cousins and friends live, and will not have to go away off to Washington, which he evidently thinks is a very bad place. Fanny shares in this feeling, but has a suspicion that something desirable has been lost. Birch and Webb don't altogether like it, but are cheerful and philosophical about it." (122)

Democratic newspapers trumpeted a Tilden victory. "GLORY! Tilden Triumphant," the Buffalo Courier headline said. A "Solid South Buries Sectional Hate," blared the Kansas City Times.

"The new era begins," blared the New York World. "Peace on Earth and to men of good will is the glorious message of this glorious day. THE RESULT is Tilden and Hendricks Undoubtedly Elected. Connecticut, New York, New Jersey, and Indiana Join the South. Which Gives Them 123 Votes and Swells the Aggregate to 188." An editorial in the World on November 8 read:

> "With the result before us at this writing we see no escape from the conclusion that Tilden and Hendricks are elected. The Democrats have doubtless carried every Southern state, together with the states of New York, New Jersey, Connecticut, and Indiana, with possibly Wisconsin. No returns have been received from the Pacific coast, but none that may be received can materially alter the present aspect of the case. Tilden is elected."

This article from the Nov. 9, 1876 Richmond Dispatch described the excitement in the city as people waited for Tilden to be officially declared the winner:

> "Business came to a stand-still in Richmond yesterday. Young and old abandoned ordinary pursuits and devoted themselves to the consideration of the election returns. Main Street, at the prominent points, where news was obtainable, was crowded with men, and every phase of the election was

discussed with an eagerness and interest uncommon in this usually unexcitable community. In the forenoon all the telegrams that came from our special correspondent in Washington and from other parties confirmed as to general results our dispatches published yesterday morning.

The glorious intelligence was declared by many to be 'too good to be true,' and consequently not a few worthy Conservatives agitated themselves with forebodings that later news would change the appearance of our victory to defeat. But the telegraphic dispatches, which were prominently displayed at the Dispatch windows as fast as received, kept up the even-tenor of their way till nearly night. There was then given an extract from the New York Tribune's extra. It stated that Tilden had 184 votes, and did not know exactly where to get the other one from. To the faint-hearted this was a heavy blow, but the great public never wavered in the faith in the election of Tilden, and were confirmed in their opinion by this information, coming as it did from an unfriendly source.

The day will be long remembered. The best feeling prevailed and the weather was bright and inspiring. It was without a doubt the gladdest season in Richmond's history for many years, and cancelled much of the trouble that has fallen to our lot. Countenances that are not often illumined yesterday and last night were radiant with unspeakable joy.

> Every man congratulated his neighbor, and there was a universal hand-shaking. In the midst of the general rejoicing there was nothing done to irritate the Republicans, or add a pennyweight to the mountain of misery under which they now labor. Gentlemen from the custom-house were not seen on the streets quite as frequently as usual, but their absence was deemed excusable, and no harsh comments were made thereupon." (123)

During the wee hours of election night, a New York Times Editorial Council in a dirty office littered with proof sheets was calculating the position to be taken in commenting on the election in the morning edition. The editorial they wrote warned:

> "At the time of going to press with our first edition the result of the presidential election is still in doubt. Enough has been learned to show that the vote has been unprecedentedly heavy, that both parties have exhausted their full legitimate strength and that in some of the states where the shotgun and rifle clubs were relied upon to secure a Democratic victory, there is only too much reason to fear that it has been successful." (124)

The most fragmentary information was available from Florida, Louisiana, and South Carolina, the only ones still under Republican control in the South. The Democratic managers in those states had not sent in their reports of the popular vote cast—the usual basis of party claims to the electoral vote. In light of the unexplained Democratic silence, the Republicans might conceivably be able to claim those three slates, although ultimately any claims would have to be verified by the official vote count.

The Times Editors were thinking of one long-shot possibility. In each of the three states in question the official canvassing boards could, if the count was close enough, manipulate a popular majority for Hayes that in turn could be transformed into electoral votes. They realized, as Devil Dan did, that the 20 electoral votes of Louisiana, Florida, and South Carolina, when added to the 165 already awarded to Hayes, would give the Republican candidate 185 electoral votes, enough for the victory, to 184 for Tilden.

The New York Times, citing disputed results in Florida, Louisiana, South Carolina and Oregon, declared in its first edition, "The Results Still Uncertain." Encouraging reports from Oregon, South Carolina, Louisiana, and Florida and a sense of Democratic uncertainty reinforced the hopes of John C. Reid, the paper's rabid Republican Managing Editor. Later that morning, Reid rushed to Republican headquarters to tell Chandler that Associated Press dispatches had given both Florida and Oregon to Hayes. There, Reid found only one member of the National Committee, New Hampshire Senator William E. Chandler, no relation to Zach, who had just arrived. Together, they read the dispatches on Republican National Committee Chairman Zach Chandler's desk and roused him from his whiskey-induced stupor.

"I immediately telegraphed to Florida, Louisiana, South Carolina, Nevada & Oregon," William Chandler later bragged to Hayes, "that all depended on them and that with them we were safe, to look out for Democratic frauds & to telegraph us when sure." Chandler got off his dispatches at 6:30 a.m. Responses began arriving that morning as other Republicans realized the race was far from over. According to Chandler, "It seemed as if the dead had been raised."

Unaware of the frantic activities going on in New York City, Hayes awoke, writing that he felt "contented and cheerful." Hayes rationalized that he and Lucy had escaped the difficulties of high public office but wrote in his diary that he regretted that he "would not be able to establish Civil Service reform and to do good work for the South." He said that he worried "about the Colored people especially." He was convinced that Tilden would be unable to control the baser elements of southern leadership. He warned in a diary entry, "It would prove of untold evil and calamity to the Southerners themselves. Not only would southern Negroes be harmed but the entire South would suffer because northern capital would cease to flow and a tremendous out-migration would occur." Soon after writing that, however, Hayes learned that good luck had not deserted him. During the day, the news indicated that he had carried the Pacific states and, with a few states in the South, he could be victorious.

He then received a dispatch from a trusted friend that "opened it all up again" in his mind. Former Ohio Governor William Dennison, called by Hayes "a prudent and cautious gentleman" wired him, "You are undoubtedly elected next President of the U.S. Desperate attempts are being made to defeat you in Louisiana, South Carolina, and Florida but they will not succeed." Hayes stopped talking about conceding defeat or accepting the inevitable. He began to believe he had a real chance at winning. He claimed, "The whole country was full of excitement and anxiety." Hayes, in effect, then announced to reporters that he had "unconceded."

Rumors were rife, including a false claim on Wednesday evening that New York was for Hayes, which resulted in "a shouting multitude rushing to his home." Hayes tried to calm things down by telling the crowd he didn't believe the rumor:

> "I will say all that is proper to say at this time. In the very close political contest, which is just drawing to a close, it is impossible, at so early a time, to obtain the result, owing to the incomplete telegraph communications... I accept your call as a desire on your part for the success of the Republican Party. If it should not be successful, I will have the pleasure of living for the next year and a half among some of my most ardent and enthusiastic friends as you have demonstrated tonight." (125)

Also on Wednesday evening, Republican National Committee Chairman Zach Chandler claimed victory was "beyond a doubt." Several days would elapse before unofficial tallies were available in South Carolina, Florida, and Louisiana, and they were subject to review by Republican-controlled returning boards, which were empowered to throw out votes where they believed fraud or intimidation had been practiced. With the sudden power to pick the next President, these boards would be pressed by Democrats to count the actual ballots and by Republicans to throw out votes.

Ch. 10 - Chaos, Confusion, & Corruption

It was a pivotal moment for America, amid political tensions over the role of the federal government in the aftermath of the Civil War. Would control go to the Republicans - who had pushed for more federal power and for the rights of Black citizens via the 13th, 14th and 15th Amendments - or the Democrats, who favored an end to federal intervention in the South and limiting the rights of those formerly enslaved? There were some states where the answer was obvious. The strongest states for Hayes were Vermont at 68.30%, Nebraska at 64.70%, and Kansas at 63.10% while Tilden enjoyed significant victory margins in Georgia at 72.03%, Texas at 70.04%, and Mississippi at 68.08%. Other states had results that were far less clear. After receiving an initial report that his vote tallies in the South should have been higher because Blacks had been kept from the polls there, Hayes was uncomfortable with any attempt at retaliation. "We are not to allow our friends to defeat one outrage and fraud by another," he declared. "There must be nothing crooked on our part." Both he and Tilden were upright and honest men, rejecting any notion of bribery or dirty dealing. As for the people around them, that was a different story.

Most of the Republican politicians who observed the count in South Carolina, Florida, and Louisiana were there by invitation from President Grant, who ordered the army to "protect the returning boards in the performance of their duty." The Republican Party, which controlled the boards, quickly challenged the legitimacy of the votes in those three southern states. Many of Tilden's votes began to be disqualified for unspecified "irregularities."

Convinced that "the Democrats were desperate" and that "Republicans had to prepare for any & every possible emergency," Republican Senator William E. Chandler quickly left for South Carolina, Florida, and "Louisiana if necessary." The explanation he gave to Hayes was that he was going "to aid in preventing our being defrauded out of what we have fairly won." What he didn't tell Hayes is that he was carrying a carpetbag filled with $10,000 for members of the Election Commissions.

Tilden was encouraged by his election team to agree to pay $50,000 to secure the South Carolina electoral votes. It was reported that Sam refused, however, saying he was "putting my trust in the American people and the Constitution." (126)

As ballots were still being counted, recounted, and scrutinized, the Saturday Evening Post published an editorial that had an upbeat, positive message about the election. Its intent, obviously, was to lift people's spirits. It read:

> "As the date of this writing, November 10th, when this page must be sent to press, it is known that *somebody* is elected President of the United States, but whether Tilden or Hayes is not fully decided, although appearances favor the former.
>
> The fact that the election has been such a close one we believe is a most happy one for the country. Neither party can afford to conduct the administration loosely or corruptly when its hold on power is so slight; so that in either case we may expect the incumbent to 'put the best foot forward.'

"The closeness of the result will also, or ought to be, a consolation for the defeated, although many will be disposed to consider it an aggravation. Let it be remembered, however, that we are all in the same boat, whoever holds the helm. The party in power cannot afford to peril the interest of the country, for their own interests are thereby placed in jeopardy. Let the defeated comfort themselves with the thought, 'we can stand if you can.' If taxes are increased, the party who increases them must pay their share, and so of other results which partisans are apt to fear.

The country may congratulate itself on the fact that either of the candidates, personally, is not only unobjectionable, but of a character that will well sustain the dignity of the Presidential office and the honor of the nation. So then, now we lift our hats and say: three cheers for -----."(127)

In the weeks that followed the election, battalions of political party officials, called "visiting statesmen" by newspapers, were descending upon the three contested southern states. Their mission was to watch out for their party's interests locally and to gather evidence for presentation to the state canvassing boards and eventually to courts and congressional investigating committees.

In Oregon, Democratic hopes were suddenly uplifted by a totally unexpected development. Although the state had gone for Hayes by a narrow margin of 3.5%, it was discovered that a Republican elector, John W. Watts, was employed as a part-time Deputy

Postmaster at an annual salary of $268. The Democrats argued that was prohibited to Presidential Electors by Article II, Section 1 of the Constitution which states that "No person holding an office of trust or profit under the United States shall be appointed an elector." Watts wound up resigning from his office a week after the election, long before the scheduled meeting of the Electoral College. However, the state's Democratic Governor, La Fayette Grover, with the support of state and national partisans, still substituted a Democratic elector, E.A. Cronin, to take his place.

The fact that Watts was a Deputy Postmaster had attracted no attention during the campaign but assumed vast importance after the election, not only to the people of Oregon but to those of the whole country. After telegrams from the East announced that a contest had arisen over the eligibility of a similar Postmaster-Elector in Vermont, Democratic leaders realized that here was an opportunity to secure the one additional vote which Tilden needed to win his election. The Vermont elector, like Watts, wound up resigning from the post office.

Grover was actually acting without legal authority. The existing State Electors Act provided that the remaining electors, not the Governor, fill any vacancy in the Electoral College. Even though his appointment was questionable, Oregon's Cronin represented the one electoral vote Samuel J. Tilden would need to win the Presidency, even if Hayes was awarded the 20 votes in the South. In that case, the final result would have been the election of Tilden, 185 to 184. The outcome would remain in limbo until the electors met at the state capital on December 6.

The common tasks of the canvassing boards of South Carolina and Florida and of the returning board, as it was known in Louisiana, were to investigate the accumulating allegations of violence, fraud, or other irregularities in local voting to eliminate irregular ballots, and ultimately to certify the official count of the legally cast popular vote. Whichever candidate a board decided had received the greatest number of popular votes in a given state was entitled by law to that state's entire electoral vote. The Louisiana board had a less-than-stellar reputation. The mere fact that it was Republican in make-up did not mean that it would automatically favor the Republicans. The board made it clear, in fact, that its decision was for sale. There is strong evidence that it offered to certify, in consideration of $1,000,000, that the Louisiana popular vote had gone Democratic. The deal, which was offered to the Democratic National Committee, was promptly rejected.

Although John Sherman assured Hayes that J. Madison Wells, chair of that all-Republican Louisiana returning board, was "thoroughly honest and conscientious," Wells was auctioning off the Presidency. Despite, or perhaps because of, Tilden's nephew William T. Pelton's interest, the enterprising Wells reportedly realized a tidy sum by negotiating with his own party. To overcome the substantial Democratic lead in Louisiana, Republican visiting statesmen, led by Sherman, James Garfield, and Charles Farwell, assumed that since Blacks constituted a majority of the state's registered voters, the Democrats had intimidated enough of them to carry the state. They ignored the fact that Republican factionalism had alienated some Black voters. Telling Hayes of the "atrocious means" used to prevent Black Republicans from voting, Sherman assured him that he "would have the vote of Louisiana, according to the letter and spirit of its laws." (127) Farwell's confidence most likely resulted from expenditures he made out of his own pocket. One year later, Rud's friend William Henry Smith told Hayes that Farwell "in all delicate and important matters last year was our right-hand man and his wealth supplied the means when no other could be reached." On November 22, Farwell assured Smith that he was "in constant communication with those who know, and they assure me that all will be well." (128)

In Louisiana, early unofficial tallies indicated that Tilden had carried the state by over 6,000 votes, but the Republican-controlled returning board rejected over 15,000 votes for reasons of suspected fraud and voter intimidation. Of those rejected, 13,000 were for Tilden and 2,000 for Hayes. As a result, Hayes won Louisiana's eight electoral votes, while Republican candidate Stephen B. Packard won the simultaneous election for Governor of Louisiana. In response, the Democratic Party instituted a rival state government under Francis T. Nicholls, and this rival administration, in turn, certified that Tilden had won. (129)

Murat Halstead, Editor of the Cincinnati Commercial newspaper and a leading Republican, confided to Hayes that many in their party were "staggered at the idea of taking the Presidency by throwing out 13,000 votes in Louisiana." Hayes continued to stay above it all maintaining, "I have no doubt that we are justly and legally entitled to the Presidency" and that he was "anxious that in the canvassing of results there should be no taint of dishonesty among Republicans."

Hearing from Sherman, Garfield, and other visiting statesmen that "murder and hellish cruelties at many polls drove the Colored people away, or forced them to vote the Democratic ticket" in Louisiana,

Hayes believed that the board had made a brave as well as a correct decision.

In South Carolina, initial returns suggested that Hayes had won the Presidential election. The Republican-controlled returning board rejected several thousand votes, ensuring the election of Republican governor Daniel Henry Chamberlain and legislature. On November 22, the all-Republican five-member South Carolina board invalidated the votes in both Edgefield and Laurens Counties and ensured that Republicans would carry the state for Hayes as well as win the legislature and the governorship. When the legislature met on November 26 and Republicans in the lower chamber refused to seat Democrats claiming to be elected from those counties, the Democrats withdrew and organized a rival state government under Wade Hampton, which the federal troops in the state did not disturb. Hampton declared Tilden the victor in the Presidential election. Meanwhile, in Florida, the initial count showed Hayes ahead by 43 votes, but after corrections were made, Tilden took the lead by 94 votes. Subsequently, the returning board rejected numerous ballots, delivering the election to Hayes by nearly a thousand votes. The board also declared that the Republican candidate had won the gubernatorial election. However, the Florida Supreme Court overruled them, instead awarding the victory to Democrat George Franklin Drew, who announced that Tilden had carried Florida. On December 6, Florida's returning board, which had a Democratic member, threw out enough votes to declare Hayes the victor by 900 votes and the state Republican ticket victorious by a narrower margin.

Florida was the only one of the three disputed states where the majority of the population was White. This necessitated the most serious juggling on the part of the state canvassing board which consistently used its discretionary powers in favor of the Republicans. It was impossible to determine who would have won a fair. Repeaters, stuffed ballot boxes, and phony ballots had all been used. In addition, returns from remote areas had been delayed, to be altered as needed. William E. Chandler supervised the struggle to save Florida for Hayes and was aided by agents from the Justice, Treasury, and Post Office Departments.

Thomas Nast cartoon from Harper's Weekly of a ballot box being kicked around by politicians. (Courtesy National Archives)

Most visiting statesmen and officials justified their partisans' unlawful acts and zeroed in on those of the opposition. The few who were truly reform-minded were both troubled and ignored. Former Union General Lew Wallace, whose "Ben Hur" would be published in 1880 and go on to become the best-selling novel of the 19th century, visited Florida at Hayes's request. Horrified by what he saw, he wrote to his wife that:

> "It is terrible to see the extent to which all classes go
> in their determination to win. Conscience offers no

restraint. Nothing is so common as the resort to perjury, unless it is violence—in short, I do not know whom to believe. If we win, our methods are subject to impeachment for possible fraud. If the enemy win, it is the same thing exactly—doubt, suspicion, irritation go with the consequence, whatever it may be." (130)

Francis Barlow, another General dispatched by Hayes, declared flatly that he could not back the Republican vote tally in Florida's Alachua County. No one thought that the county, with a large Black electorate, would go for anyone but the Republicans, but it was the size of the victory that was in dispute. The Democrats obtained affidavits from Poll Inspectors Green Moore and Floyd Duke, who said that the actual vote in the county was 180 for Hayes to 136 for Tilden, even though they had falsely certified that the Republicans had received 390 votes. The Republicans countered with affidavits from the same two men in which Duke, a Black man, claimed he had been intimidated by the Democrats into signing the affidavit alleging fraud. The two poll inspectors then claimed that their original certification was correct. Similar challenges and allegations of fraud were lodged in regard to other counties. Charges included the exclusion of the votes of whole precincts by the Republicans and the importation of Georgian Democrats into Florida by train to vote.(131)

In Archer Precinct No. 2 of Florida's Alachua County there was undeniable proof that 219 names had been added to the polling list after the election was over. That exact same number was then added to the Republican majority. The fraudulent vote was allowed to stand.

A former Colonel in the Irish 9th Massachusetts Regiment, immigrant Patrick Robert Guiney eloquently wrote to his daughter Louise, a future poet who was away at school, that he hoped "the monster of corruption will writhe under the lances of honest men" like Tilden. (132) On November 23, he gave this bleak assessment of the status of the election:

> "Our beloved country is in danger, nay in actual peril of its life. The people have just lawfully elected a President of the United States, but the corrupt set of fellows who have the counting of the people's votes in Florida, South Carolina, and Louisiana defy law, justice and truth, and declare that Hayes got the most votes. They know better, but they insist upon the falsehood. Grant seems to back them up, and there is the end of it. He commands the army and the navy and justice has no armed battalion. The country seems about to break up into sections, or go into a state of anarchy and civil war of the worst kind. My heart is nearly broken at the sight, the more so that I am not able to draw my sword again in its defense. Fraud and force are now the factors of our political life. I know not what to say about the future." (133)

There were Democratic newspapers with headlines such as "March to Washington to Install Tilden as President." Republicans cried out, "We're on the verge of another Civil War." Fears of dueling Presidencies lingered as some key Democrats urged Tilden to "take the oath of office anyway." In a dozen states, club-wielding "Tilden Minutemen" had formed threatening to march into Washington to take the White House for their candidate. Plans were made for a counter-inauguration for Tilden in Manhattan, in which he would "seize the federal treasury building and fund a shadow government through customs revenues." All this was to Tilden's chagrin, who sought to calm the rowdiness and didn't want to be responsible for an insurrection. With all the divisive accusations and threats of violence in the weeks that followed the election, the tone of another Saturday Evening Post editorial on December 9, 1876 changed to something very somber and serious:

> "The madman who would recklessly scatter matches in a powder magazine would soon be placed where his freaks would be harmless. There are crazy heads of the press just now more dangerous to the community than the lunatic referred to; writers who for sensational purposes are appealing to partisan spirit already raised to the highest pitch by the exciting political contest through which the country has just passed. Pending the decision for which all are anxiously waiting as to who are the successful candidates, threats of violence, bloodshed, and civil war are covertly or openly uttered apparently with the hope of influencing the results, or at least of keeping up an excitement and profiting by it.
>
> Unfortunately, there is too much powder lying around loosely to permit such firebrands to be scattered harmlessly. Disappointed office-seekers, men wrought up by party feeling, gamblers who have large sums staked upon the issue, desperate speculators mindful of fortunes rapidly acquired

during the recent war and ready again to peril the nation to fill their pockets, and that large class of thoughtless men who are ready to rush into any tumult, are now slow to catch such incendiary utterances.

Such words, whether thoughtlessly or maliciously uttered, should be met with the sternest indignation... The people of the United States are law-abiding. They know that for every wrong there is legal remedy; that retribution can be speedily meted out to offenders even in the highest places, by peaceful but sure methods. No wrong would be so monstrous as the kindling of civil war, and those who even indirectly lead their followers to its contemplation are guilty of a higher crime than the worst of election frauds." (134)

The situations that came before the canvassing boards for investigation and decision followed a distinct pattern. The Republicans, finding themselves widely in control of local voting machines, practiced the time-honored techniques of stuffing the ballot boxes, throwing out Democratic votes, and making things as easy as possible for Republican "repeaters."

As late returns were still being received and tabulated, both the press and Democratic party spokesmen were claiming that Tilden had received a popular majority in all three states. But Tilden's backers feared that the Republican-controlled canvassing boards, applying "discretionary" powers and tossing out Democratic ballots on the flimsiest pretexts, would nibble away at the vote counts. The

Democratic visiting statesmen therefore contended, before the boards themselves and subsequently in the courts, that the function of the boards was limited under law to the "ministerial" or non-discretionary act of counting the popular vote actually cast. But the Democratic spokesmen were consistently and unqualifiedly defeated on this point in all three states. Many a Democrat interpreted the combined defeats as nothing less than the end for the Tilden cause. Republican success appeared to be stemming from the corrupt power of obscure local officials in the contested states, many of whom allowed their personal views to guide policy. (135)

Their chief object of attack by the Democrats in 1876, as it had been since the Civil War, were the predominantly Republican Black voters. The Democrats, organized as rifle clubs and night riders, sometimes employed the most extremes imaginable such as hanging Blacks who attempted to vote. Most of their outrages, however, were more subtle, taking the form of economic and social pressures. Black renters might be threatened with eviction or field hands faced with the prospect of losing their jobs if they dared to try to vote.

The canvassing boards were swamped not only with the facts of actual outrages and irregularities, but with hearsay, gossip, and the fabricated stories of witnesses carefully coached by unscrupulous Democratic and Republican partisans. Given the difficult task of the boards to try to sift the true from the false, and the enormous implications of their decisions, service on them would seem to have been a duty only for well-trained and most competent members of the community. In point of fact, unfortunately, the canvassing boards were by and large composed of the least responsible and qualified people. Investigating a Louisiana election, then Republican Speaker of the House James A. Garfield, declared that the state returning board was a "graceless set of scamps." (138) The big Democratic money never materialized, and the boards in all three disputed states settled down to the business of finding ways to award the vote to Hayes.

The next stage in the drama of 1876 entailed the official issuing of the electoral votes. On the basis of the canvassing board findings, the Republican electors assembled in their respective state capitals on December 6 and cast their votes for Hayes. The Democratic electors, however, gathered independently, voted for Tilden, and also forwarded their results to Washington. Accordingly, two sets of conflicting electoral votes from Florida, Louisiana, and South Carolina would arrive in the Nation's Capital.

It was in the climactic hours of these proceedings that another irregularity was found. The culprit was a man named T. C. Anderson, who carried Louisiana's Republican electoral votes to Washington. Upon examining the certificates accompanying them, President Pro Tempore Thomas W. Ferry noticed that the electors had not properly endorsed them. He allowed Anderson to haul the certificates back to New Orleans to tidy up the defect. Under the deadline specified by law, Anderson had but a day to secure the endorsements which was too short a time to allow two of the electors from remote counties to reach New Orleans. So, Anderson had their signatures forged.

The central issue emerging was simple. Who would choose between the conflicting returns submitted by the rival electoral colleges of South Carolina, Florida, Louisiana, and Oregon? Who would decide the momentous question of who would be the next President of the United States? No one was especially surprised when Rutherford B.

Hayes and most Republicans in Congress began to argue that Article II, Section I of the Constitution provided the answer to those all-important questions in these words: "The President of the Senate shall, in the presence of the Senate and House of Representatives, open all the certificates, and the votes shall then be counted." Hayes and like-minded Republicans read this to mean that the President of the Senate, their fellow party member, Senator Thomas W. Ferry, should determine which of the conflicting electoral votes would be counted.

The Constitution, however, also specifies further that if no candidate secures a majority of the vote, the House of Representatives, then controlled by Democrats, shall select a President. Naturally, the Republicans then began aggressively maneuvering to have the election dispute decided in the Senate. The Democrats championed the House as the final forum claiming the act of "opening the votes" was purely ceremonial and was very different from "deciding which Electoral votes to count."

Tilden personally led the counterattack by compiling a learned and exhaustive History of Presidential Counts, and having a copy distributed to each member of the Congress. He succeeded in establishing that on no occasion had a Senate president exercised any discretionary power in counting the electoral votes.

With party lines firmly drawn, Congress became locked in a standoff. From the massive effort of heated debate, one overriding conclusion became clear - no path forward was clearly provided for in the Constitution and there were no precedents.

While the congressional debate over how to handle the election results churned on inconclusively, developments of a more ominous sort were taking place elsewhere in the country. Their common ingredient was the threat of Civil War. The press was working overtime. "Tilden or Blood!" was the cry of many Democrats. The Albany Argus newspaper saw the grim "prospect of war in every street and on every highway of the land" if Tilden was denied the Presidency.

Thomas Nast Cartoon from Harper's Weekly (Courtesy National Archives)

The Democrats were by no means confining themselves to flaming oratory. They were actively girding for a contest of force. There were Battalion Commanders of state militias who wrote to Tilden, placing their troops at his disposal. A distraught friend reported to Hayes that the Democrats were secretly organizing into military companies and inventorying every gun and bullet they could lay hands on, to be ready to spring to Tilden's rescue.

Henry Watterson, publisher of the Louisville Courier-Journal and a Democratic congressman from Kentucky, on Jan. 8, 1876, called for "the presence of at least 10,000 unarmed Kentuckians" to march on Washington to ensure Tilden was elected.

Not to be outdone, Joseph Pulitzer, best known for the Pulitzer Prize, was working at building up his newspaper empire at the time. But he was also very active in Democratic politics. He called for 100,000 armed Democrats to descend on Washington and demand that they put Samuel Tilden in the White House, in his opinion, "to honor the wishes of the people." (136)

Violent threats were by no means the monopoly of the Democrats. Some Republicans were also threatening war. The Chairman of the Iowa Republicans reported that 100,000 men were ready to back Hayes if the Senate declared Tilden elected. One Texas Republican topped that, pledging to organize "hundreds of thousands" of ex-soldiers to fight for Hayes.

President Grant had the military on stand-by. Troops with light artillery were concentrated near Washington. He ordered General William T. Sherman to alert all federal troops stationed in Louisiana and Florida to prevent any attempted molestations of the boards of canvassers in the performance of their duties. Additional companies were sent to likely trouble spots in both states. South Carolina was already stocked with federal troops. Supporters of Tilden were distressed by the President's military moves. They were worried that Grant's military order had erected an armored facade which would keep Tilden from the Presidency.

Rumblings of a new Civil War continued to roll across America. There was even talk of the country being left without a President at all. There were drills and parades and wartime units started to be brought together. Some discussed the possibility of the State National Guards, under the command of Democratic Governors, marching on Washington to install Tilden by force, if necessary. In that case, the federal Army under Grant stood ready to oppose the Guard. One supporter suggested in a letter to the New York Post, "A little bit of war to inaugurate Mr. Tilden would do us no harm." (137)

Some were fearful that Grant was merely using the crisis as a pretext to prolong his presidency and establish himself as a dictator. A band of Democratic congressmen led by Fernando Wood of New York sought to impeach Grant "for misuse of the army and other offenses." He replied that if the impeachment venture made its way to the House of Representatives, he would clap the Democratic ringleaders into a Fort Monroe prison.

Despite the menacing talk and gestures, there were also forces working for a peaceful settlement of the crisis. "The Democratic businessmen of the country," James A. Garfield wrote to Hayes, "are more anxious for quiet than for Tilden." (138) In the eyes of many Southerners, the end of carpetbag rule and the restoration of local self-government clearly was a higher priority than the inauguration of Tilden.

On the day the Oregon Electoral College was scheduled to meet, E.A. Cronin, the substitute Democratic Elector appointed by the Governor, and the three Republican electors assembled in a room set aside for their use in the state capital. The Secretary of State arrived with the electoral certificates and handed them to Cronin. The Republican electors asked for their certificates, but Cronin refused to surrender them. Retiring to a remote corner of the room, he turned himself into a one-man Electoral College. Cronin's next action was to declare that not one but two vacancies existed and he promptly filled both with Democrats. Just to make things look good, since only one vote was necessary to tilt the scale for Tilden, Cronin arranged for one vote to go to Tilden and the other two to Hayes. For the half-day he put in, Cronin was paid $3,000 by grateful officials of the national Democratic organization. The three Republican electors, holding their ground in their corner of the room, dutifully cast their votes unanimously for Hayes.

Republicans, both at the state and national level, denounced the Democratic procedure as an "outrage" and an attempted "steal." In Oregon itself, the indignation ran so high that Governor Grover was burned in effigy. The Democrats, on the other hand, characterized the matter as a "good joke," and a "shrewd trick." They were now confident that whatever course the Republicans should take, Tilden was sure of the necessary number of electoral votes. It was a fail-safe that they hoped would lead to a Tilden win even if Hayes would wind up victorious in the three Southern states. It could give Tilden the 185-184 Electoral vote win.

The returns of both of Oregon's electoral colleges went on to Washington. The Republican electors challenged the governor's actions and reported that the state was casting all three of its electoral votes for Hayes. They prepared a certificate of election and had Oregon's Secretary of State sign it and send it on to Washington, D.C. Watts, in turn, prepared a certificate that gave two of the state's votes to Hayes and one to Tilden. This certificate was signed by the Governor and likewise sent on to the nation's capital.

Abram S. Hewitt, New York Congressman and Chairman of the Democratic National Committee, clearly perceived the necessity of compromise. On the basis of a frank discussion with President Grant, Hewitt concluded that Tilden could be inaugurated only by force of arms. Hewitt was quoted in the New York Times as saying, "After carefully considering the facts, I became satisfied that we could not wage war with any hope of success." (142) So, it was not a case of doing what's best for the country. It was that Hewitt felt the second Civil War wasn't winnable. Hewitt hoped that the Oregon maneuver would force the Republicans to reject the state's official certified electoral vote. If such a move could work there, Hewitt reasoned that it might enable the Democrats to do the same thing with the certificates from the Governors of South Carolina, Florida, and Louisiana. It was a last-ditch desperate move. Hewitt thought it was worth an attempt.

Rud believed that by "improper interference with the rights of the Colored people," the Democrats were trying to deprive him of the presidency. "A fair election in the South," he insisted, "would undoubtedly have given me a majority of the electoral vote and a decided preponderance of the popular vote."

On the evening of December 6, surrounded by family and friends, Hayes and Lucy awaited dispatches confirming the electoral vote. They had what they described as "a lively, happy little gathering," believing that the decisions of the returning boards would be made official and everything finalized.

Hayes was concerned that the one disputed electoral vote from Oregon would "be treated as the true one" and give the election to Tilden. Not anticipating the continuation of the dispute over the votes of Louisiana, Florida, and South Carolina, Hayes initially felt the Oregon dispute was a potential crisis calling it, "perhaps fatal to free government" and indicating, "I would gladly give up all claim to the place if this would avert the evil." But he soon concluded that "the Oregon fraud was so obvious and disgraceful that, at worst, it would only complicate matters and at best be thrown aside without dissent." The gathering at Spiegel Grove quickly and quietly dispersed when it was announced that the election results were stalemated in the four states. Embarrassed, Rud explained that he still believed he was "fairly, honestly and lawfully elected," and expected "a general acquiescence in the result among judicious men of all parties." Unfortunately, he had no idea how or when that would happen. As it became more and more evident that the results were not going to be easily settled, Hayes began to support efforts to secure his election and to assure there could be both reconciliation and protection of the rights and obligations conferred by the Civil War amendments. He recorded in his diary on December 12, 1876, that he had received assurances from southern Democratic leaders, including Lamar of Mississippi, Hampton of South Carolina, and "probably" Gordon of Georgia that they would not oppose his Presidency, that they would support abolition of the color line, and that they would support "measures to secure the Colored people of all of their rights."

South Carolina, Florida, and Louisiana all had self-appointed rival State governments of the other party. In each case, one group of electors was committed to Hayes and the other to Tilden, reflecting the rival parties vying for control of the State governments. With time running out and no President-elect yet named, Congress would be forced to grapple with the extra-Constitutional issue of which slate of electors to count and how to validate their votes.

Tilden had won the popular vote by just over a quarter of a million votes, but he did not have a clear Electoral College majority. He received 184 uncontested electoral votes, while Hayes received 165, and both sides claimed the remaining twenty which consisted of four from Florida, eight from Louisiana, seven from South Carolina, and one from Oregon. As 185 votes constituted an Electoral College majority, Tilden needed only one of the disputed votes. Hayes needed all twenty. Thus began the longest stalemate of a Presidential election in U.S. history. Backers of both Hayes and Tilden charged the election was being stolen. They engaged in the time-honored tradition of "what-about-isms." When confronted by an accusation, they would respond with "what about" something that the other party did. It was a circular argument that would never reach a conclusion.

The events of the Centennial Election likely sound familiar to Americans today. Voter intimidation. The threat of violence in state capitals. Name-calling. A nasty Presidential campaign that was called unprecedented. Hate groups threatening to organize a march to take over the Capitol. Talk of a Supreme Court poised to rule in favor of the candidate that shared a party with their majority. Bickering, name-calling, and finger-pointing. Votes in Congress going strictly by party lines. In effect, both sides in 1876 were right. There was `clear evidence of widespread corruption by the two political parties. No one knew how to break the impasse.

Ch. 11 - The Election Commission

The size and scope of the country has changed dramatically since 1876. Back then, a total of 8,418,659 people voted. In the 2020 election, it was 155,120,887. That's an increase of 146,702,228 voters or 1,743%. Seemingly though, the only difference between the political threats, partisanship, and tensions that followed that Presential election versus the 2020 election is that in 1876 nobody used social media.

The Electoral College ballots from all of the then-37 states arrived in Washington, D.C. for the ceremonial count by the President of the Senate. However, there were eight sets of returns that arrived from four of those states. There were two separate sets, one from the Democrats and one from the Republicans, from South Carolina, Louisiana, Florida, and Oregon. Whose votes were valid? Was either set really representative of the will of the people? Who would sort out all the widespread voter fraud? How would they decide? Who was trustworthy, if anyone, in the disputed states? No one had the answers. In total, twenty electoral votes remained in limbo. To win, Hayes still needed all of them while Tilden needed only one.

The 1876 election showed us that our laws and democratic institutions were not up to the task of resolving an election crisis. The Constitution didn't provide a roadmap for how to decide an election when there were disputed electoral votes. Both Hayes and Tilden stayed above the fray, leaving it to their representatives to do the negotiating, name-calling, and finger-pointing. They were informed of important developments as they unfolded.

One Washington newspaper reported on plans in 1876 "to send a threatening and bellicose mob to the National Capitol to see that the count is made according to their wishes." That never happened. But, of course, it did on January 6, 2021. President Donald Trump claimed that Vice-President Mike Pence could summarily reject the electoral votes from states that did not vote Republican. Pence responded by stating the obvious - the Constitution doesn't authorize him to do that. The counting of the Electoral Votes is purely a ceremonial function.

Trump indicated his displeasure with Pence and called for the storming of the Capitol Building by supporters. Many came looking for Pence chanting, "Hang Mike Pence!" It's not sure what would have happened if they had found him or any of the other members of Congress. Gallows had been erected by rioters outside the building and at least one carried plastic ties inside evidently in preparation for kidnapping or subduing government officials. Significantly, one of the rioters carried the Confederate flag into the Capitol Building. This had never happened before, even during Civil War times. The Insurrection led to the ignominious second impeachment of Trump. He was acquitted in a Senate trial.

W.E.B. Dubois' explanation as to why violent White supremacist mobs seem to be an endemic part of America seems as fitting today as he did when he spoke these words in 1876:

> "How is it that men who want certain things done by brutal force can so often depend upon the mob? Total depravity and human hate do not explain fully the mob spirit in America. Before the wide eyes of the mob is ever the Shape of Fear. Back of the writhing,

yelling, cruel-eyed demons who break, destroy, maim and lynch and burn at the stake, is a knot, large or small, of normal human beings, and these human beings at heart are desperately afraid of something. Of what? Of many things, but usually of losing their jobs, being declassed, degraded, or actually disgraced; of losing their hopes, their savings, their plans for their children; of the actual pangs of hunger, of dirt, of crime." (139)

The person who played the "caught-in-the-middle" Mike Pence role in the 1876 election turned out to be Democrat Samuel Randall, Speaker of the House. He was able to avoid a situation where Hayes and Tilden might each be regarded as the lawfully elected President by their respective parties. Decisions that Randall made likely forestalled any violent conflict, both inside and outside of the congressional chamber.

Hayes was aware of what he called New York Senator Roscoe Conkling's "lack of hearty support" and of his view that Congress, rather than President of the Senate Thomas W. Ferry should decide which votes to count. From an emissary, Hayes learned that Conkling would be willing to support him on how the count should proceed if he would repudiate the Republican reformer wing. Hayes also found out that the more conservative southern senators would remain loyal if he would continue to back them. Despite these backroom feelers, Hayes made no commitments. He repeated his pledge to "deal fairly and justly by all elements of the party" and reiterated the views he had expressed in his acceptance letter that "to achieve peace and prosperity, the Southern people must obey the new amendments, and give the colored men all of their rights." To encourage Ferry and to lead congressional Republicans before the count began, Hayes thought of resigning his governorship and boldly claiming the role of president-elect. He consulted Senator John Sherman who convinced him to continue silently waiting. Inauguration Day of March 4 was looming on the horizon, and there seemed no clear way to name a President-elect.

Just as in the 2020 election, people were using terms such as "Constitutional Crisis" and "End of Democracy." After the 1876 election, former Secretary of State and Pennsylvania Democrat Jeremiah S. Black offered this warning to future Americans:

> "We can never expect such a thing as an honest election again. If you want to know who will be President by a future election, do not inquire how the people of the states are going to vote. You need only to know what kind of scoundrels constitute the returning boards, and how much it will take to buy them." (140)

Some Republicans were also fearful that a plot to seat Tilden had been organized. A group of approximately 30 well-known Republicans appointed four people to keep guard night and day at Tilden's country home to prevent him from sneaking off to Washington and declaring himself President of the United States. According to White House guard William Crook, some of Tilden's supporters were so violent, "it was common to hear threats made on the streets that they were determined to seat him in the White House if they had to bring an armed force to Washington for that purpose." (141)

Yet another complication was that Grant's Vice President, Henry Wilson, had died on November 22, 1875 after suffering a stroke while in the United States Capitol Building. Michigan Republican Senator Thomas W. Ferry took his place as President of the Senate. However, he was not officially the Vice President. Ferry chose not to take the title, citing lack of direction from the Constitution. There was much speculation as to whether Ferry would have been forced to temporarily become the acting President of the United States if the Electoral College vote was not certified by March 4, 1877. Could someone who did not have the title of Vice-President be second in line to become the President? If President Ulysses S. Grant continued in office, which from duty or ambition he might feel driven to do, he could be labeled an outright usurper. Those were among the many dizzying options discussed.

Arguing that Ferry should decide which votes to count, Hayes stated, "My judgment is that neither House of Congress, nor both combined, have any right to interfere in the count. It is for the V.P. to do it all. His action is final. There should be no compromise of our constitutional rights."

Republicans, especially in Rud's circle of Ohio friends, argued intensely that Ferry had the sole constitutional authority to certify the presidential election. Other Republicans and virtually all Democrats objected to such a narrow congressional role. They didn't believe the election should rest on the shoulders of one person. Ferry himself felt that if he simply awarded the Presidency to Hayes, it would undermine his legitimacy.

Things became more and more contentious between the Republicans and Democrats. Some Senators and Representatives on both sides began to jockey for power saying they'd be willing to sacrifice a national victory for regional, local, or factional advantages. In the meantime, President Grant admitted to his cabinet, and even to Democratic National Committee Chairman Hewitt, that he was particularly uncertain who had carried Louisiana. A number of Republicans began to talk of conducting a completely new election in that state. Recognizing that he would likely not become President if Grant were opposed to him or even neutral, Hayes wrote a friendly letter to him just before Christmas. Although Hayes declined Grant's invitation to meet with him directly, he did send Ohio State Journal Editor Comly to Washington. Grant reportedly "drew the friendly cigars from his pocket," and they engaged in a productive talk. Hayes was still reluctant to enter into negotiations with anyone directly saying, "I do not wish to be committed to details."

The decisions of the returning boards and Tilden's caution made many members of his party anticipate defeat. Having lost elections for sixteen years, many of them felt like habitual losers. Although the Democrats preferred a Tilden victory, some Southerners began to explore what they might gain from capitulation. These Southerners wondered whether Hayes would concede the South to the control of the Democrats if they acquiesced to his election. They began to debate just what "home rule" would look like along with how much and what kind of autonomy they'd want. In an effort to reach an understanding, Col. William H. Roberts of the New Orleans Times reportedly had a discussion with Hayes about this possibility on December 1.

Other Southern Democratic newspapermen and politicians met with counterparts close to Hayes. The Editor of the Memphis Avalanche, Col. Andrew J. Kellar, conferred with both William Henry Smith and Richard Smith of the Cincinnati Gazette. According to the Avalanche, Kellar wished to involve "the better class of White southerners" in building a conservative Republican party in the South that would "destroy the color line & save the poor Colored people." After meeting with the Gazette Smiths, Kellar left for Washington on December 14 to "enter zealously on the great work." Informed of Kellar's activities by William Henry Smith, Hayes was "hopeful that much good will come from friendly relations with good men" in the South. But he did not move beyond his promise in his letter of acceptance that, if the rights of all were recognized by all, the federal government would promote southern efforts to obtain "honest and capable local government." Confident that Ferry would count him into the presidency, Hayes felt he remained "perfectly free from committals as to persons and policies."

Hayes refused to go to Washington to confer on important points and did not designate a Washington spokesman. "There are too many cooks in Washington," he said and reiterated, "The true thing is a firm adherence to the Constitution. The V.P. ought to be able to finish the work at one sitting." Hayes continued to rely on Ohio Republicans in Washington to unofficially represent him.

Hayes told Senator John Sherman, "I wish you to feel authorized to speak in pretty decided terms for me whenever it seems advisable to do this, not by reason of specific authority but from your knowledge of my general methods of action." (142) Hayes avoided firm pledges but left his lieutenants free to give assurances. He feared that an authorized friend might become the focal point of negotiations and "fuel charges of intrigue - bargain and sale. At any rate, I see the true position to be hands off."

He told the Cincinnati Gazette's William Henry Smith that he desired in general terms "to restore peace and prosperity to the South" and "would be exceptionally liberal about education and internal improvements of a national character." That's as specific as Rud wanted to be during the post-election period. Hayes' thoughts were more on Republican solidarity than on the dissatisfaction among southern Democrats. "We are in some danger from treachery" he wrote on December 31, "but most of all from lack of backbone." Of course, Hayes detractors could say that he showed "lack of backbone" by his insistence that he stay in Ohio and speak only in general terms. "My position was described in my letter when I accepted the nomination" continued to be Hayes' standard answer when asked virtually any question about his intentions.

Days turned into weeks. Thanksgiving had come and gone. Lincoln had established its celebration as a national holiday in 1863, during the height of the Civil War, as a day of national unity. It was anything but that in 1876, as the country seemed hopelessly divided once again. Then, Christmas came and New Year's Day welcomed in 1877. There were continued meetings, caucuses, back-room discussions, and political maneuverings.

The candidates took very different approaches to the election crisis. Tilden hid out in his Manhattan mansion, forbade his supporters from holding rallies, and assembled the exhaustive analysis concluding that the election should be decided by the Democratic House of Representatives. It was an earnest, intellectual response, entirely out of touch with what was going on around him. Hayes denounced fraud publicly, even as his operatives worked to disqualify Democratic votes. He also held friendly meetings with officials on both sides, listened to their concerns, and allowed the opposition to propose possible solutions.

Suddenly, there was a proposal, called by Edward S. Corwin, the President of the American Political Science Association, "The most extraordinary measure in American legislative history." (143)

Iowa Republican Congressman George W. McCrary introduced a resolution calling for a special bipartisan Election Commission to make recommendations to Congress as to how to deal with the situation. Set up as an open trial with members of the House and Senate allowed to observe the proceedings, the commission would be composed of five U.S. Representatives (three Democrats and two Republicans), five U.S. Senators (three Republicans and two Democrats), and five Justices of the U.S. Supreme Court (two appointed by Republican presidents, two by Democratic presidents, and one independent who would be expected to be the tie-breaker if things became too partisan. Under the proposal, a decision by the commission would be final unless it was overridden by both houses of Congress. That would be unlikely since each party controlled just one of the houses. On January 25, 1877, the Senate passed the bill, 47–17. The House did the same the next day, 191–86. The law officially creating The Electoral Commission was signed by President Grant on January 29 to try to solve the crisis.

The new law formalized the process that would be followed for future elections. The President of the Senate opens the electoral certificates in the presence of both chambers, and hands them to the tellers, two from each chamber, who will read them aloud and record the votes. In the event of a state sending multiple returns to Congress, whichever return has been certified by the executive of the state will be counted, unless BOTH houses of Congress decide otherwise. If that last provision had not been part of the procedure, the election of 1876 might still, to this day, be unresolved.

Just like everything else with this election, putting together the Electoral Commission proved to be more complicated than anyone could have imagined. The justices initially selected David Davis to be the fifth Supreme Court member on the Commission. Justice Davis was largely viewed as a political independent. Since there were 7 Republicans and 7 Democrats in the Commission, the crucial spot to be filled by Davis could decide the outcome of the entire election. At least, that was the plan.

Before the Electoral Commission could convene, the Illinois state Legislature's Democratic-Greenback coalition majority voted 101-99 to make Davis the state's new U.S. senator. Prior to the passage of the 17th Amendment, State Legislators appointed their Senators. So, when Illinois Democrats, inspired by Tilden's nephew William T. Pelton, chose Supreme Court Justice David Davis, it was clearly a political move. It wasn't based on any election. Since Davis' political leanings were unknown, the Democrats who controlled the Illinois legislature thought this would be a way to stroke his ego and ensure his loyalty to their party. This proved to be a miscalculation.

Upon being notified of his election to the Senate, Davis shocked everyone by resigning from the Court and from the Electoral Commission to actually accept the appointment to the Senate. The legislation that created the commission required that the vacancy be filled by a member of the Supreme Court. The four remaining members of the Court were all Republicans. Justice Joseph P. Bradley, an appointee of President Grant, was the one selected. He was considered the most impartial of the choices. If the commission's vote split along party lines, he would be the one to break the tie. In a letter to Senate and House leaders asking for leave to sit on the commission, the five House members and five Senators vowed their efforts would be totally nonpartisan and uncorruptible. It was assumed, of course, the same would be true for the Supreme Court Justices.

The idea of an electoral commission met with a mixed response. Tilden accepted it and most Democrats, except those in the South, thought it was their best shot at victory. Some Republicans were against it but, most importantly, President Grant lobbied for the idea. Rud privately called it "a surrender, at least in part, of our case" and still insisted that Ferry should decide which votes to count. Recognizing that the bill was going to pass and that his opposition might hurt his cause, Hayes never spoke publicly against it, though. Some called the bill an unconstitutional "surrender of a certainty for an uncertainty." Cincinnati Gazette Editor William Henry Smith grumbled, "The truth is we have had blunder upon blunder at Washington."

President of the Senate Thomas W. Ferry continued insistence that he did not want to, in effect, decide the Presidency himself, thus disenfranchising the voters, helped Hayes accept the proposed commission. When the bill forming the commission finally passed, Rud admitted, "It is a great relief to me." Although he was confident that "the measure will turn out well," he rationalized that, in the worst case, "defeat in this way after a full and public hearing before this commission is not mortifying in any degree, and success will be in all respects more satisfactory."

On January 3, Rud told Smith that he was "hoping to "divide the Whites and help obliterate the color line." Hayes's also reiterated, "I look for nothing of value growing out of southern conservative tendencies in this Congress." Reiterating his staunch belief in the Republicans, Rud added, "Whatever the caucus decides to do will be done." Ardent Hayes supporters were outraged when Democratic Speaker Samuel J. Randall appointed moderate Republicans to the House committee and were dismayed when Ferry named Senator Conkling to the committee. Having heard that Conkling believed that the Louisiana returning board had "greatly abused" its power, Hayes feared that Conkling would inspire a compromise measure that would change the result of the election.

Hayes' luck held out when Conkling, who thought the commission's duties would be "inconvenient if not distasteful," turned down a chance to serve on it. Then, Morton and Garfield, two of Hayes's staunchest allies, were selected for it.

This was the final composition of the commission from the Democratic side:

- Josiah Gardner Abbott, Massachusetts, House
- Henry B. Payne, Ohio, House
- Eppa Hunton, Virginia, House
- Allen G. Thurman, Ohio, Senate
- Thomas F. Bayard, Delaware, Senate
- Nathan Clifford, Maine, Supreme Court
- Stephen J. Field, California, Supreme Court

These were the Republicans chosen:

- James A. Garfield, Ohio, House
- George F. Hoar, Massachusetts, House
- George F. Edmunds, Vermont, Senate
- Frederick T. Frelinghuysen, New Jersey, Senate
- Oliver H.P. Morton, Indiana, Senate
- Joseph P. Bradley, New Jersey, Supreme Court
- Samuel Freeman Miller, Iowa, Supreme Court
- William Strong, Pennsylvania, Supreme Court

After learning who would participate, Hayes commented, "The commission seems to be a good one." While he was calm, much of the nation was not and threats of violence continued to be widespread. Newspapers published reports of militias consisting of former Union and Confederate soldiers preparing for battle. One night, shots were fired through the window of Rutherford B. Hayes' house, though the incident was kept quiet. No one was hurt and most took it as a warning rather than an attempt at murder. The person doing the shooting was never identified and no group took credit for it.

Following the disputed election, John S. Mosby, a former Confederate Army Commander who became a friend of Grant's and worked in the Justice Department, warned the outgoing President "to be careful of his own person" and predicted "an effort would be made to assassinate him." Mosby said the language of the Democrats "was now more desperate and more threatening and violent than that of the Southern men on the election of Lincoln in 1860." Mosby feared there would be bloodshed if the Electoral College voted Hayes into office. (144) On February 1, 1887, at 1 p.m., a Joint Session of Congress met in the House Chamber to begin the electoral vote count. The galleries were full and privileged visitors crowded the floor. After tellers representing each house were appointed, the President of the Senate turned to a wooden box, a little more than a foot long on each side, selected the return of Alabama, and the count began. All went well until Florida was reached and the two conflicting returns read. Each side made its objections and all the papers involved were turned over to the Electoral Commission. The Joint Session then put the commission to work, submitting the Florida returns for investigation.

According to the New York Times, "There was a great desire to witness a fair count and curiosity was increased by the expectation that the new law would afford some new diversion to the formality of the counting." Congress would meet in Joint Session 15 times in the next month, until, acting on the decision of the commission, it would go on to finally award the disputed votes.

Election Commission meeting drawing from Frank Leslie Illustrated Newspaper (Courtesy of Library of Congress.)

Two batteries of able lawyers, personally selected by Hayes and Tilden, presented their opposing arguments to the commission's first meeting. The Republicans contended that the language of the Constitution limited Congress to the ministerial act of counting the electoral votes presented by the officially established state authorities. The Republican lead counsel, New York Senator William Evarts, argued for only allowing evidence that previously had been submitted to Congress. His position, largely a practical one, was that trying to investigate the Florida vote at the county and local level would drag on and not wrap up in time for inaugurating a new President in March.

His opponent in this case, Democratic counsel Charles O'Conor, former U.S. Attorney for the Southern District of New York, argued for admitting additional evidence to attempt to make the case that Tilden had carried Florida. The Democrats pleaded that Congress, or its agent, the commission, had the duty to inquire into the circumstances surrounding the choice of electors in all the disputed states. Such an inquiry, the Democrats contended, would uncover gross irregularities that would compel the award of the electoral vote to Tilden. After hearing argument, the commission spent a full day trying to decide the disposition of the Florida case. The country was holding its collective breath. Justice Bradley's vote was expected to hold the balance.

On the night before the decision was due, Democratic National Committee Chairman Abram Hewitt dispatched his good friend Pennsylvania Representative Thaddeus Stevens to Bradley's house. The Justice graciously read the opinion he intended to hand down the next day. To Stevens' great joy, which he struggled to keep within discreet bounds, the opinion upheld the Democratic position and thus, by adding Florida's three electoral votes to his uncontested total of 184, ensured Tilden's election with two votes to spare.

Stevens returned to Hewitt with the great news at about midnight. Next morning, however, the two were dumbfounded when Bradley did a complete about-face and presented a decision in favor of the Republicans.

Sometime between midnight and sunrise, Bradley had changed his mind, reportedly under the influence of the Republican senator Frederick T. Frelinghuysen of New Jersey and Secretary of the Navy George M. Robeson, who had arrived after Stevens had departed. There was also information leaked that they were strongly aided by Justice Bradley's wife Mary who evidently had strong opinions on the matter. The tenor of the trio's argument was that whatever the strict legal equities of the situation, it would be a national disaster if the government fell into Democratic hands.

In a party-line vote of 8-7 on February 9, Bradley tipped the scale to block additional evidence the following day giving Florida's four electoral votes to Hayes. When the Florida vote went to Congress, the Republican-controlled Senate voted to affirm Florida for Hayes and the Democratic-controlled House voted to reject the Electoral Commission's findings. Remember, though, it would take a rejection by both chambers to nullify the commission's decisions. So, the decision became official.

Next on the docket would be Louisiana. Angry and stubborn, the Democrats fought on hoping they could win the decision. If not, they started talking about continuing to delay the count to extract concessions from Republicans. Above all, southern Democrats were insistent on home rule, which would mean returning to White-controlled state governments. If Tilden, who would certainly accede to their wishes, were not elected, they wanted a commitment from Hayes.

The Louisiana Returning Board was seen as disreputable. Because it lacked any Democratic members and Republican frauds were well-documented in the state, it presented the Democrats' strongest case for the commission going behind the returns and hearing evidence. Confident that Bradley and the other Republicans would refuse to probe further into the returns, Representative Samuel Shellabarger of Ohio thought "it is safe for Mrs. Hayes to begin to get the children ready although Lucy's faith in these mixed commissions was weaker than a grain of mustard seed." (145) Shellabarger had once again predicted accurately. On February 16, Louisiana was given to Hayes by an eight-to-seven vote. Democrats thought they had a good shot in Louisiana. Unofficial returns there gave Democrats a big win, which warranted hearing more evidence. From a purely legal standpoint, however, the Democratic case in Louisiana was identical to the one in Florida. It was as impractical to do a county-by-county canvassing in Louisiana as it would have been in Florida if a President were to be named by Inauguration Day.

Congressman Henry Watterson of Kentucky then read into the Congressional Record President Grant's support of the claim of Democratic candidate Francis T. Nicholls to the Louisiana Governorship over Republican candidate Stephen B. Packard. Grant did so as a favor to Hayes, hoping it would give him a boost with Democrats.

The Oregon and South Carolina rulings by this time were looking like just formalities. Hayes began working on his inaugural address.

The only hope Democrats seemed to have was to delay the inevitable decision and threaten more chaos after March 4, with no President in office.

Frustrated Democrats recessed again to delay the count but in their caucus on February 17, they again decided not to obstruct the process, with only one southerner voting for a filibuster. After the caucus vote, Hayes remarked that the "affair now looks extremely well" and remained noncommittal as ever. "I prefer to make no new declarations beyond my acceptance letter," he once again told John Sherman. "But you may say, if you deem it advisable, that you know that I will stand by the friendly and encouraging words of that letter, and by all that they imply. You cannot express that too strongly." (146)

For leadership, southern Republicans looked to Conkling, who appeared willing to see Hayes defeated if it would enhance his own power. The Democrats' last hope was that Conkling and his southern allies would object to the Commission's decision on Louisiana, but on February 19, he was conspicuously absent. Southern Republican senators were then whipped into line.

With defeat certain, delay and the threat of chaos were the Democrats' only bargaining chips. But they were dangerous chips to play. House Speaker Samuel J. Randall accused southern Democrats of bargaining with Hayes. He predicted that Hayes would continue bayonet rule and ruin them. Randall proposed to stop the count and force the Senate to accept a bill naming Secretary of State Hamilton Fish acting President until an entirely new election could be held. When the caucus did not accept this extreme scheme, the delaying tactic remained as an option.

The Commission took up the Oregon count and, once again, voted 8-7 to award the state's three votes to Hayes on February 23. As expected, the Republican Senate approved the finding while the Democratic House rejected it. In the midst of the proceedings, the House adopted a meaningless resolution declaring that Tilden was the duly elected president. They then proposed a last-ditch measure to delay the completion of the electoral count. If no President were declared elected by March 4, no one knows what would have occurred. Neither the Constitution, precedent, nor statute made any provision for such a contingency. Ohio Representative Samuel Shellabarger told Hayes of his fear that "they mean to kill us by filibustering." On February 24, the Democrats forced yet another adjournment. Did Rutherford B. Hayes' positions on issues change as the months dragged on? The answer is an emphatic, "No!" This is a diary entry he made on February 25, 1877:

> "My letter of acceptance in July last expressed what I thought were just sentiments on the leading questions which then interested the country. I thought its doctrines were sound before the election. I think they are sound now that the election is over, and if the issue pending in congress shall be decided in our favor those principles will be the standard by which my official conduct shall be guided. If I were to write that letter now I would give that part on the Southern question greater emphasis.
>
> The great body of the people of this country earnestly desire a wise and just settlement of that question.

They want peace – they long for repose. What is required is:

- That for the protection and welfare of the colored people the 13th, 14th and 15th amendment should be sacredly observed and faithfully enforced according to their true intent and meaning.

- We all see that the tremendous revolution which has passed over the Southern people has left them impoverished and prostrate and we all are deeply solicitous to do what may constitutionally be done to make them again prosperous and happy. They need economy, honesty, and intelligence in their local governments. They need to have such a policy adopted as will cause sectionalism to disappear and that will tend to wipe out the color line.

  They need to have encouraged, Immigration, education and every description of legitimate business and industry. We do not want a united North nor a united South. We want a united country. And if the great trust shall be devolved upon me, I fervently pray that the Divine Being who holds the destinies of the Nations in his hands, will give me wisdom to perform its duties so as to promote the truest and best interests of the whole country."

An unwritten agreement, informally arranged off-site by members of Congress, then helped resolve the stand-off between the Republicans and the Democrats. It stands as one of the most consequential political deals ever made. The agreement would change the trajectory of American history, but not for the better.

Ch. 12 - The Compromise of 1877

On February 26, 1877, a Monday night, eight politicians joined together in an unlikely alliance to see if a deal could be reached to prevent Democrats from continuing to block the Presidential Election vote with delaying tactics. The Republicans side consisted of four Ohio members of Congress close to Hayes - Representatives James Garfield and Charles Foster along with Senators Stanley Matthews and John Sherman. Representatives John Y. Brown and Henry Watterson of Kentucky joined with Representative William M. Levy of Louisiana, and Senator John B. Gordon of Georgia to represent the Democrats.

With the Inauguration just days away, the closed-door discussions were held at the Wormley House in Washington, D.C., a luxurious hotel, owned by James Wormley, probably the most well-to-do Black man in the city of Washington. The secret agreement was struck in the room of W.M. Evarts, who served as counsel to the Electoral Commission and later became Secretary of State in the Hayes Administration.

Some claim that the agreement was captured in writing in a letter from Republican Charles Foster, a member of the U.S. House of Representatives from Ohio's 10th district who would go on to serve as Ohio's Governor in 1880, to Democrat John Y. Brown, a member of the U.S. House from Kentucky's 2nd district and eventually named Kentucky's Governor in 1891. That letter, however, has never been found and both denied its existence. To this day, there are no details as to exactly how the agreement was reached. Nothing was ever leaked to the press or anyone else. It remains shrouded in mystery and denials. Even congressional investigators who later looked into the matter could only get the participants to say, "I don't know anything about it. I wasn't involved."

The essence of the "deal with the devil" was that the Democrats agreed not to filibuster or otherwise disrupt the proceedings of Hayes being named President-elect if the Republicans removed federal troops from of the South so they could run their states the way they wanted. It would be hard to imagine that the Republicans didn't ask obvious questions such as, "What exactly is the way you want?" These Republicans were astute and experienced politicians. They certainly wouldn't have let the Democrats get away with responding with something like, "You'll see soon enough." They also would not have blindly accepted the obvious lie of, "We'll immediately change our ways and behave exactly the way you want."

The truthful answer from the southerners would have been, "We've got a new form of slavery in mind. We're going to call it 'Segregation.' We also have lots of ways that we can disenfranchise Blacks and take away their basic freedoms. We're still pretty angry that you freed our slaves and we're going to make up for it. You can't imagine what extreme measures we're going to take. Just make sure you stay out of our way."

The 1877 compromise essentially stated that the Democrats would acknowledge Hayes as President, but only on the understanding that Republicans would meet certain demands. The following six elements were the points of the compromise:

- All remaining U.S. military forces will be removed from the former Confederate states.

- The southern states will have the right to "control their own affairs." This vague point was interpreted as granting them the right to deal with Blacks without federal interference.

- At least one southern Democrat will be appointed to Hayes' cabinet.

- Another transcontinental railroad will be built using the Texas and in the South.

- Legislation will be passed to help industrialize the South and restore its economy following the Civil War and Reconstruction.

- Democrats will not employ the filibuster during the joint session of Congress and will acquiesce to the election of Rutherford Hayes. (147)

Although the naming of Democratic Senator David Key of Tennessee to the position of Postmaster General seems on the surface like a minor appointment, it was actually the cabinet position with the largest number of patronage jobs. It's important to note that the Wormley agreement occurred after Congress had already awarded the disputed votes of Florida, Louisiana, and Oregon to Hayes. Only South Carolina remained to be resolved. It was likely, although not certain, that it would be just a matter of time before the Democratic filibuster would wind down and Hayes would officially receive their votes, too. The compromise, in effect then, gave both sides greater assurance about an outcome that was probably inevitable. After he learned of the agreement, Hayes confidently wrote in his diary, "The inaugural and cabinet-making are now in order." The possibility of further obstructionism was far from dead, however. A good number of Democrats were fully resolved to carry it on, despite the Wormley Agreement. Democratic National Committee Chairman Abram Hewitt and Speaker of the House Samuel J. Randall, mindful of the dangerous implications, begged Tilden to put an end to the delaying tactics with a decisive statement. Tilden hesitated at first. Only after some long hours of introspection did he conclude that the compromise was the only path forward. Accordingly, he wired Speaker Randall that the recommendation should be accepted. Neither Hayes nor Tilden are the evil culprits that some have depicted. Those who participated in the negotiations brought an end to four months of agonizing partisan bickering. They really couldn't speak for anyone but themselves so it would be unfair to say they reneged on any firm agreements or understandings.

During the election, Republicans "waved the bloody shirt" by emphasizing the Democrats involvement with secession and anti-Black violence. But, with every year that passed since the Civil War, it increasingly became just more political rhetoric. Many Republicans echoed Hayes in his speeches. In an attempt to "heal the nation" and "bring people together," they would talk in general terms about it being a fair and just policy for the South to return to self-government. Democrats lobbied hard for the withdrawal of the occupying federal troops and their efforts were working. The number of troops had already dwindled from 15,000 in 1867 to 6,600 in 1870 and then to just 3,000 by 1876.

Hayes had showed support for Blacks throughout his life. Remember that, long before he ran for President, he was a Cincinnati lawyer fighting in court to win freedom from slavery for those such as Rosetta Armstead. Within the first few weeks of his new administration, Hayes would appoint Frederick Douglass to be the U.S. Marshal of Washington, D.C. This was the first-ever Senate confirmation of a Black Presidential appointment. In his later years, Hayes spent much energy and resources on the issue of Black education.

Thomas Nast cartoon in Harper's Weekly suggesting compromising with the South is betraying the Union dead. (Courtesy Library of Congress.)

With the Compromise, though, the Republican Party and Hayes, in effect, abandoned its active efforts to ensure equal rights for Blacks in the South. Black leaders and activists were incensed. Frederick Douglass quickly concluded that the compromise was "tantamount to being turned over to the rage of our infuriated former masters." Henry Adams, a Black Louisiana activist who was born a slave, lamented, "The whole South - every state in the South - had got into the hands of the very men that held us as slaves." He held Hayes responsible calling him "a third-rate nonentity." (148)

You have to wonder if the "home rule" point of the Compromise, by far the most important one, was made with a wink and a nod. Did the southerners immediately break a promise to protect the rights of Black citizens or did the Republicans know they were going to do the exact opposite? With four Republicans from Ohio involved in forging the agreement, it would be unreasonable to think that Hayes was never briefed on the details. You can blame the Republican negotiators, blame Hayes, blame Democrats, or blame America. All the blame doesn't change history, though.

The Wormley Agreement was not a specific, detailed, step-by-step plan agreed to by both sides. It was more of a general understanding. It was certainly not a few corrupt politicians who conspired against the popular will. It was something simpler. The White majority in America, including most Democrats and many Republicans, was willing to give up on Reconstruction efforts by 1877.

Another interesting question is how it was explained to Tilden. It's doubtful he would have liked the "new form of slavery" that was going to be introduced in the South. He also wouldn't have liked Hayes being named President. It doesn't seem that he was offered any incentive to go along with the deal. Perhaps Tilden was just too timid to fight and challenge the Compromise. Maybe he was taken advantage of. A positive way to look at it, of course, was that he valued the country's well-being over his personal ambition. It may well be that all these things were true.

On February 27, the morning after the Wormley Hotel meeting, it was hoped that the count would proceed smoothly. Yet again, though, there were snags. Unable to overturn the commission's decisions, many Democrats instead tried to obstruct them. Congressman Abram Hewitt, the Chairman of the Democratic National Committee, made a spurious challenge to the electoral votes from Vermont, even though Hayes had clearly carried the state. The two houses then separated to consider the objection. The Senate quickly voted to overrule the objection, but the Democrats began another filibuster in the House of Representatives.

Speaker of the House Charles Randall refused to allow members of his Democratic party to delay the vote count by suddenly producing the competing slate of electors of dubious origins from Vermont. When Randall rejected these efforts, one of his fellow Democrats tried to physically attack him, and others began reaching for their guns. He had to call the Sergeant-at-Arms to restore order.

Randall halted the delaying tactics that would have increased the likelihood of dueling inaugurations and subsequent violence. His actions finally brought the count to an end on March 2, just two days before the inauguration. Upon becoming Speaker, Randall had pledged fairness to both sides in exercising his parliamentary powers. He kept that promise, even when doing so required decisions not in his party's interest.

On February 28, the Democrats filibustered with what James Garfield called "all their might" and forced the House to adjourn until March 1. That would turn out to be one of the longest and stormiest sessions in history. Filibusterers made motions to recess, to reconsider, and to call the roll, but Speaker of the House Randall, in what Hayes referred to as his finest hour, refused to entertain their motions, adding to the pandemonium.

There were two disputed governorships that might have been used as bargaining chips by the Republicans. The New York Herald's Charles Nordhoff warned that continued support of Republican Governor Stephen B. Packard's contested election victory in Louisiana would cause a violent outbreak that would require an army to suppress. Hayes was also reluctant to abandon Republican Governor Daniel H. Chamberlain who was also involved in another controversial election in South Carolina with Democratic candidate Wade Hampton III. Their claims to office and Rud's claim to the Presidency were all based on the actions of the returning boards. The Cincinnati Gazette's William Henry Smith, however, maintained, "You cannot dismiss those gentlemen with a waive of the hand for mere party expediency."

Because winning the presidency was so important, though, supporters of radical Reconstruction did not object to abandoning the two Republican regimes in Louisiana and South Carolina, allowing Democrats to assume the governorships and save face.

Congress began its next session at 10 a.m. on March 1 and it continued through the night. Democrats kept up efforts to further slow the proceedings with various parliamentary motions to reconsider, call the roll, recess, or do anything else to delay things for a few more days and hope the Republicans would back down. The commission awarded South Carolina's seven electoral votes to Hayes in another 8-7 party line vote. The Senate affirmed it and, as expected, the House rejected it one day later.

A few die-hard Democrats reacted with a final but vain outburst when the alphabetical order count of Wisconsin, the last state, was reached in the early morning of Friday, March 2. The high point of the absurdity was a statement by Democratic Congressman Joseph C. S. Blackburn of Kentucky that Friday was the day of Jesus Christ's death and "fittingly the day on which the crucifixion of constitutional government, justice, honesty, fair-dealings was transpiring among a number of thieves." In a last-ditch effort to obstruct, bitter Democratic filibusterers prolonged the struggle until 3:38 a.m. The matter was finally settled at 4:10 a.m. when the Republican President of the Senate, Thomas W. Ferry announced the following:

> "The Chair trusts that all present, whether on the floor or in the galleries, will refrain from all demonstrations whatever; that nothing shall occur on this occasion to mar the dignity and moderation which have characterized these proceedings, in the main so reputable to the American people and worthy of the respect of the world.
>
> Wherefore, I do declare that Rutherford B. Hayes of Ohio, having received a majority of the whole number of votes is duly elected President of the United States for four years commencing on March, 4 1877." (149)

The disputed election was at last decided. March 2, 1877 would go down in history as the day the joint session of Congress declared that Hayes would be the 19th President with the bare minimum of 185 electoral votes to the Democratic ticket's 184. Though some

Democrats were furious, all Tilden did publicly was shrug, "It is about what I expected." Others in the Tilden camp cried foul calling it the "Election Farce of 1876." In bold type, the Cincinnati Enquirer intoned "The monster fraud of the century is consummated." The Democratic New York Sun complained bitterly:

> "These are days of humiliation, shame and mourning for every patriotic American. A man whom the people rejected at the polls has been declared President of the United States through processes of fraud. A cheat is to sit in the seat of George Washington. Every upright citizen must gird himself up for the work of redressing this monstrous crime. No truce with the guilty conspirators. No rest for them and no mercy till their political punishment and destruction are complete." (150)

The country was faced with a "Lose-lose" proposition in 1877. You could say that Hayes was a conservative Liberal and Tilden was a liberal Conservative. They were both moderates wanting to unite the country and neither wanted to risk alienating the South. The final vote tally was Hayes winning the electoral vote 185-184 and Tilden taking the popular vote 4,300,590 to 4,036,298.

Ch. 13 - The Inauguration

In the midst of the turmoil in Congress and with the outcome of the election still undecided, Rud and Lucy had boarded a 1 p.m. train in Columbus, Ohio for the 21-hour, 400-mile trip to Washington, DC on Friday, March 1. Inauguration Day was set for Monday, March 4. Tilden, on the other hand, chose to stay in New York City and await word on the election. He would have had a much easier time if he got good news and needed to suddenly travel to the nation's capital.

1877 Passenger Train (Courtesy American-Rails.com)

Given a private railroad car for security purposes, Rud stared out the window, gazing at the landscape. "What a big, beautiful country this is," he thought to himself. "Someone is going to be President of it all." The problem was that he still didn't know who that someone was going to be. Election Day, November 6, seemed like a lifetime ago. Here it was four months later and there was still no final decision from Congress. He had plenty of gazing time during the long trip. Fortunately, he had his favorite person in the world, Lucy, at his side. As usual, she had her nose in a book.

Rud mentally rehearsed the unifying remarks he would make if he was declared the winner. On the other hand, he had a gracious concession speech in mind if he got disappointing news. Thinking worst case scenario, he wondered if the seemingly-hopeless deadlock was really hopeless. What if there was, in fact, another Civil War as many people were predicting? His mind continuing to race, Hayes pondered how Grant had continued to be President as a lame duck over the four months thinking maybe he could do it for the full four years. No, he concluded that a four-year lame duck doesn't make sense. He wondered to himself, "What does make sense, then? How will this all play out? I've just got to be patient. One way or the other, I wish this was all over."

Lucy looked up at him with a knowing smile. She had a pretty good idea what thoughts were racing through his head.

It would be a futile trip for the Hayes couple if Tilden did turn out to be the winner. They'd have to turn around and head back to Ohio, but it would be a very worthwhile trip if they got the news they were hoping to hear. As the train whistle blew indicating they were approaching Baltimore, a conductor came by with a telegram. Rud looked at Lucy who nodded as if to say, "Okay, go ahead. Open it." He did, quickly read the message, and then turned to Lucy whispering, "It's decided. I won." The two hugged and kissed.

Rud walked to the adjacent train car which carried the members of the Ohio legislature who were accompanying them. He spread the good news, they shook his hand, and he began hearing the long-anticipated "Congratulations, Mr. President-elect."

The train arrived at the designated time of 10 a.m. amidst a driving rainstorm. Still, there was a gathering of people cheering Hayes as they arrived at the station. Included were the two Shermans, Senator John and General William, who escorted the Hayes family to John's K Street residence where they'd be staying. They all enjoyed a big breakfast that morning. For the first time in four months, Rud felt relaxed. He could enjoy himself without being inundated with "What if…" questions.

Hayes then wrote a letter resigning as Governor and it was telegraphed to Ohio. Thomas L. Young, Lieutenant Governor, was sworn in and took the next train for Washington to attend the Inauguration. Rud spent the day meeting with Grant and other officials at the White House and then the Capitol Building. He had a private meeting with William Wheeler, his new Vice President. Many Senators and House members, including Democrats, came to congratulate him and wish him well. He met with the press and, when asked by a New York Times reporter, said he had not completed his Inaugural Address but he "expected it to be shorter than the usual." It was not.

Showing uncharacteristic aplomb, Hayes also announced that his cabinet would contain no one from Grant's administration or who was a former Presidential candidate. He also emphatically said he would "make no appointment to 'take care' of anybody."

Tilden was understandably angry and bitter when he received word of the final results. He would always be convinced he was unjustly deprived of the Presidency, but didn't press matters. That just wasn't in his nature. The nation was still badly divided and Tilden rationalized that he would cause more harm by being openly defiant. In private, though, he continued to maintain, "The country knows that I was legally elected President." As far as for public pronouncements, the New York Tribune accurately predicted, "Tilden won't do anything. He's as cold as a damn clam."

Christie Weininger, the Hayes Presidential Center Director, has speculated that "If either Presidential candidate had more of an aggressive or intense personality, and wanted this presidency for very selfish reasons, the outcome might have been different." (152)

Many of Tilden's supporters, though, believed that he had been cheated of victory, and Hayes was variously dubbed "Rutherfraud," "His Fraudulency," "His Accidency" and "The Great Usurper." On March 3, the Democratic House of Representatives went so far as to pass a resolution for the record declaring its opinion that Tilden had been "duly elected President of the United States." Nevertheless, Hayes would be peacefully sworn in as President.

Ulysses Grant had taken it upon himself to make the arrangements for Saturday evening, March 3. In accordance with a formal invitation that was sent on February 20, the President-elect attended a state dinner at the White House. Among the guests present was Supreme Court Chief Justice Morrison B. Waite. In the course of the evening, General Grant sent his son Ulysses S. Grant, Jr., nicknamed "Buck," for a Bible. The two Grants, Waite, and Hayes then adjourned to the Red Room. It was there that the Chief Justice administered the Oath of Office to Hayes at 7 p.m., the first time that ever took place inside the White House. This was done just in case there would be any last-minute trouble at the Inauguration. Grant gave an after-dinner farewell address to those in attendance, including his Cabinet, saying he was finishing packing the family belongings. Preparations were being made for Monday's events. A large stage was built on the east side of the Capitol building to accommodate the dignitaries who would be present. Rud and Lucy attended Episcopal services at the Church of the Epiphany on Sunday morning and spent a quiet day with the Sherman family.

Shortly before the Inauguration, President Grant ordered the prosecution of Donn Piatt, who used "seditious language" in an article he wrote for a newspaper called "The Capital." Piatt stated that "somebody ought to assassinate President Hayes on his ride to the Inauguration." Piatt was jailed. Grant was determined to stand fast and warned Tilden's supporters not to make any ill-conceived move in support of their candidate. He declared he would not "shirk in his duty" to make sure Hayes was inaugurated. (150)

Monday brought a chill in the air. It was overcast and calm. A few snowflakes fell during the day. Parade Marshalls cleared the streets for the procession from the White House to the Capitol. Hayes arrived at the White House around 11 a.m. in an unmarked horse-drawn carriage with Representative James A. Garfield and two D.C. Constables. Vice President Wheeler and Senator McCreary reached there five minutes after Hayes entered the White House. They wasted no time as President Grant and Hayes stepped into a carriage with Chairman of the Senate Committee on Arrangements, Vermont Senator Justin Smith Morrill. Their procession slowed at that point as a huge throng met to cheer for them. They arrived at the Capitol to the sounds of a 100-gun salute.

The Senate chamber had been opened for invited guests to enter for the Vice-Presidential Inauguration. Lucy Hayes sat with the Ohio delegation next to John Sherman's wife. The Senators sat to the left of the incoming V.P. while the members of the House were seated in the rear of the room. The Supreme Court Justices all wearing their judicial robes, were to the right of Wheeler. Hayes, Grant, and Morrill arrived at 12 noon to a standing ovation. The chaplain opened the proceedings with a prayer, the group of new Senators were sworn in, Wheeler took the oath of office, and followed it with a short speech.

There were 30,000 people outside the East Portico of the Capitol building. Lucy led the procession followed by the Supreme Court Justices and the diplomatic corps. The clerk of the Supreme Court carried the Bible that would be used to administer the oath of office. The crowd cheered as Hayes appeared. The Bible used was opened to Psalm 118:11-13. Not the most uplifting passage, it was likely meant to refer to Hayes' days on the Civil War battlefield. Despite being surrounded by disease, death, and destruction, Hayes often referred to the civil war representing his "golden years" as a time when he came into his own as a man and a leader.

> "They surrounded me on every side, but in the name of the Lord I cut them down. They swarmed around me like bees, but they were consumed as quickly as burning thorns; in the name of the Lord I cut them down. I was pushed back and about to fall, but the Lord helped me."(151)

Rud recited the Oath of Office as required by the Constitution. Few people in the country knew these 39 words had already been spoken for real over the weekend and were being repeated just for show:

"I do solemnly swear that I will faithfully execute the Office of President of the United States, and will to the best of my ability, preserve, protect, and defend the Constitution of the United States, so help me God."

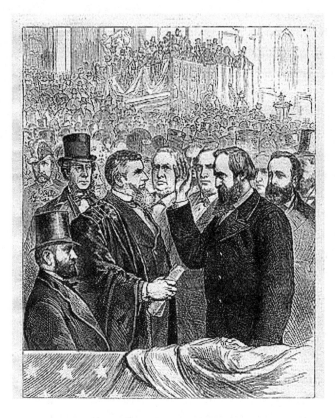

Hayes takes the Oath of Office (Courtesy Library of Congress)

Rud almost didn't make it through the day. A would-be assassin stalked him, planning to shoot him during the Inauguration ceremonies. Days before the Inauguration, an unnamed man had visited Reverend Father D. Reville, a priest at St Dominic's Church in Washington. He told the priest that one of his acquaintances, William Meyers, described as a "well-to-do man from Northern Illinois," had arrived in the city with the intention of assassinating President-elect Hayes. The visitor said he believed Meyers was "insane" and "determined to carry out his act." Father Reville took the man to see Washington detective James McDevitt. He, in turn, advised Major Almarin C. Richards, the Washington Chief of Police and someone who had happened to be present at Ford's Theatre the night Lincoln was shot. Richards assigned McDevitt to investigate the matter. He eventually tracked the would-be assassin to the Imperial Hotel in Washington. On his way there, McDevitt encountered two Secret Service agents, C. E. Anchist and E. W. Maxwell, and enlisted their assistance. The three men agreed not to reveal their identities and simply questioned Meyers about his plans. During their conversation, Meyers asked the men to join him in his plot to kill Hayes and gave Anchist a twenty-dollar gold coin to purchase a pistol after the agent promised to aid him in the conspiracy. (152)

McDevitt immediately arrested Meyers and, after a search of his room, it was discovered the would-be assassin had gathered "an arsenal of weapons." During questioning at police headquarters, he admitted to his assassination plans. According to the Washington Evening Critic, "Myers said he intended to shoot President-Elect Hayes then proclaim himself President and to be sworn in amid the ringing of bells and the firing of cannon." According to the Washington Evening Critic, the authorities were convinced he was mentally ill and sent Meyers to an insane asylum where he was incarcerated for a period of six months then released to the supervision of his sons.

According to the Carroll City Herald, an Iowa newspaper, President Hayes was informed of the assassination plot. He thanked the officers for their diligence and requested that the matter be kept from the public since he believed it might lead to further attempts on his life.

Hayes arranged for Maxwell to be awarded an appointment as a Second Lieutenant of the Twentieth Infantry shortly after the inauguration. Unfortunately, Maxwell soon got into trouble. He signed his pay accounts more than once, doubling his pay, and he also received loans with his pay as security when he had already fraudulently overdrawn his account. Maxwell was sentenced to two years at the Texas State Prison in San Antonio but Hayes pardoned him and he was released early from prison.

In his Inaugural Address, the full text of which is in the Appendix, Hayes attempted to soothe the discord of the past months, saying that "he serves his party best who serves his country best." He pledged to support "wise, honest, and peaceful local self-government" in the South as well as reform civil service and a return to the gold standard. On the other hand, he did not shy away from defending the Reconstruction Amendments. He believed that safeguarding those amendments was needed for a harmonious nation that had gone through a brutal four-year Civil War. He also stressed the need for the country to come together:

> "Let me assure my countrymen of the southern states that it is my earnest desire to regard and promote their truest interest - the interests of the White and of the Colored people both and equally and to put forth

my best efforts in behalf of a civil policy which will forever wipe out in our political affairs the color line and the distinction between North and South, to the end that we may have not merely a united North or a united South, but a united country."

After the address, Hayes and his party were taken by carriage back to the White House as crowds cheered. For a little over a day, the country actually had two Presidents. Both Grant and Hayes had taken the oath of office. It now had only one. So, the public thought a President was added on Inauguration Day. In truth, one was eliminated. Grant's term in office was officially over. Rud finally became the sole President of the United States.

Future President James Garfield reflected the tension felt by those who attended the ceremony when he wrote in his diary that day, "There were many indications of relief and joy that no accident had occurred for there were apprehensions of assassination." (153)

That night, houses along Pennsylvania Avenue were lit with Chinese lanterns as bands played, bells rang, and cannons were fired throughout Washington. There was no Inaugural Ball that year due to the unrest in the country. Instead, the Hayes and Sherman families joined members of the Cabinet in a reception in the Blue Room before heading off to an official State dinner. After the meal, the Grants stayed at the residence of Secretary of State Hamilton Fish, leaving the White House to the Hayes family for the next four years.

Grant and his wife Julia then travelled the world. He enjoyed being hailed world-wide as the Civil War hero and savior of the Union. In

1880, Grant would be urged by Republican Stalwarts to run for a third term but he was defeated at the convention.

In 1881, Grant retired from politics, moved to a New York investment business and later began to write his memoirs, focusing on his military career. He wrote feverishly, often completing 25 to 50 pages a day, despite worsening throat pain and coughing. He grew progressively weaker and had trouble walking. Soon, the president could no lie down without choking. Then he could not swallow food or even breathe without distress. Grant's cigar habit had led to his contracting throat cancer. According to the Philadelphia Enquirer, he suffered terribly, once writing, "I have such difficulty in speaking that I am no company."

Grant had to be propped up in a chair, supported by pillows, as he wrote the story of his life from his cottage porch. He began by dictating to a scribe, but when speaking grew impossible, he scratched out the words on a legal pad in pencil. Grant's physician prescribed cocaine, what was then a legal substance, as a throat spray, in a "French wine tonic" called Vin Mariani. The 6 milligram dose of cocaine numbed the pain, allowing Grant to keep up his writing with the help of multiple bottles of tonic each day.

The Enquirer reported that one time his breathing grew so labored, Grant passed out. A minister performed last rites, but a doctor revived the former president. The minister exclaimed, "It is Providence. It is Providence." The doctor responded, "No, it was the brandy." Grant finished his manuscript on July 18, 1885, and died five days later, the only U.S. President to succumb to cancer. The memoirs were published by Mark Twain and became an instant bestseller, hailed by the critics.

Ch. 14 - The Hayes Presidency

1877 White House illustration from Ernst von Hesse-Wartegg's "Nord Amerika," Swedish Edition (Courtesy Getty Images)

Some American Presidents get memorialized in movies, some are pictured on currency, and some have statues erected in their honor. A few have even had their faces carved on Mt. Rushmore. Then, there are others whose names are all-but-forgotten. Rutherford B. Hayes belongs in the latter category.

If the corrupt election of 1876 had resulted in Hayes being able to achieve great things for America, that would be one thing. But his four years, unfortunately, didn't produce much in the way of accomplishments. Instead, he felt that radical reforms and policies could further divide the nation and so opted to work for the most part at maintaining the status quo. Rud wrote in his diary about the acceptance of the terms of the Wormley Compromise. He defended it because he felt it was, in a way, finally ending the Civil War after 12 years of military occupation in the South. He said:

> "My judgment was that the time had come to put an end to bayonet rule. I saw things done in the South which could only be accounted for on the theory that the war was not yet ended. Many Southern people evidently felt that they were justified in acts which could only be justified in time of war towards the common enemy.
>
> The Republicans, the North, the Colored people, if active in politics, were regarded and treated as the public enemy. My task was to wipe out the color line, to abolish sectionalism, to end the war and bring peace. To do this, I was ready to resort to unusual measures, and to risk my own standing and reputation with my party and the country. My object was to end the war; to restore confidence in the South in the justice and good will of a Republican Administration. The army was withdrawn because I believed it a constitutional duty and a wise thing to do."

All remaining U.S. military forces were, in fact, removed from the South per the terms of the Wormley Agreement which was given the ability to "control its own affairs." This effectively marked the end of the protection of the civil rights of Blacks and ushered in the era of Jim Crow laws, institutional racism, and over 100 years of solid Democratic control of the South. The following is an excerpt from Governor Daniel Chamberlain's bitter address to the Republicans of

South Carolina after President Hayes removed the federal troops and allowed Democrats to take control of the state government:

> "Today - April 10, 1877 - by order of the President whom your votes alone rescued from overwhelming defeat, the government of United States abandons you, and by the withdrawal of troops now protecting the state from domestic violence abandons the lawful government of the state to a struggle with insurrectionary forces too powerful to be resisted."
> (154)

Hayes remained optimistic that the southerners would respond responsibly in their treatment of former slaves, writing in his diary on April 22:

> "We have got through with the South Carolina and Louisiana problems. At any rate, the troops are ordered away, and I now hope for peace, and what is equally important, security and prosperity for the Colored people. The result of my plans to get from those states and by their governors, legislatures, press, and people pledges that the 13th, 14th, and 15th amendments shall be faithfully observed; that the Colored people shall have equal rights to labor, education, and the privileges of citizenship. I am confident this is a good work. Time will tell."

The Redeemer Democrats, who already dominated other state governments in the South, came to dominate what became known as the "Solid South." When Reconstruction died, so did all hope for national enforcement of adherence to the constitutional amendments that the U.S. Congress had passed in the wake of the Civil War. As the last Federal troops left the ex-Confederacy, two old foes of American politics reappeared at the heart of the Southern polity – the twin, inflammatory issues of state's rights and race. It was precisely on the ground of these two issues that the Civil War had broken out, and in 1877, sixteen years after the secession crisis, the South reaffirmed its control over them.

The appointment of a Southern Democrat to Hayes' cabinet was accomplished when David M. Key of Tennessee was named Postmaster General. It was not unusual, nor unexpected, for a President, especially one so narrowly elected, to select a cabinet member favored by the other party.

Points 4 and 5 of the Wormley Agreement were never enacted. They involved construction of another transcontinental railroad using the Texas and Pacific in the South and legislation to help industrialize the South and restore its economy. This had been part of the so-called Scott Plan, proposed by Thomas A. Scott of the Pennsylvania Railroad.

The final point of the compromise was a split decision. Democrats did, as promised, finally accept Hayes as President. They did not, however, keep their word to not employ the filibuster during the remainder of the joint session of Congress needed to finalize the election. As has been described, they did all they could to stop progress in Congress.

After it became clear the Democrats didn't have the ability or willingness to treat their Black citizens as people, Hayes was in a bind. He could have said, "You didn't keep your word. I'm sending federal troops back in." Historians have debated whether more troops would have helped the Reconstruction or caused a larger blood bath. Did Hayes really have any political options? Could he have withheld federal funds from the states? He didn't have the support of the American people or even the support of his own political party for that action. Should he have done it anyway? If Congress wouldn't have gone along with it, maybe he could have withheld funds by executive order. Even if it would mean risking impeachment, at least history would have treated him kinder. What about reviving the "40 acres and a mule" concept? Could he have bypassed the states and directly instituted massive federal assistance and reparations programs?

Well before the end of his four-year term, it was clear to Hayes that the Compromise of 1877 had failed. He rationalized it by noting the loss of northern will to continue the fight to permanently secure Black civil rights as opposed to the racism of southerners.

He asserted in an address to a grand reunion of Ohio soldiers in August of 1880 that the Union had been saved, and slavery abolished, by war. But, he said, securing peace, prosperity, and the protection of human rights required education claiming, "As long as any considerable numbers of our countrymen are uneducated, the citizenship of every American in every state is impaired." He reminded everyone that the South had been devastated by the war and needed education that those states lacked the funds to provide. Hayes insisted that:

> "Where millions of citizens are growing up in the grossest ignorance, it is obvious that neither individual charity nor the resources of impoverished

States will be sufficient to meet the emergency. Nothing short of the wealth and power of the federal government will suffice to overcome the evil."

Hayes admitted, "There is still in our country a dangerous practical denial of the equal rights with respect to voting secured to Colored citizens by the Fifteenth Amendment to the Constitution." He most likely he convinced himself that his policy of restoring the autonomy of the state governments in the South would be worth a try. Hayes believed all along that once the states had been granted their rightful power under the Constitution, the federal government should not intervene in local affairs. We think of racial discrimination now as a national issue. Back then, it was seen as a state's issue. You can still hear the echoes of White supremacists shouting, "We live by our state and local laws. We don't need outsiders coming in and telling us what to do. If you don't like the way we do things here, then get out." In some places today, they're more than just echoes.

As Hayes assumed office, he continued to maintain the position that the protection afforded Blacks by the Reconstruction Amendments must be upheld. At the same time, he was convinced that if the rule of law was ever to return to the South, each state must decide local matters for themselves. He claimed:

> "The real thing to be achieved is safety and prosperity for the Colored people. Both houses of Congress and the public opinion of the country are plainly against the use of the army. The wish is to restore harmony and good feelings between sections and races. This can only be done by peaceful methods. The federal government must adopt the

non-intervention policy, except so far as may be necessary to keep the peace."

Hayes sounded very much like a modern-day progressive when he explained, "Free government cannot long endure if property is largely in a few hands, and large masses of people are unable to earn homes, education, and a support in old age." He also realized the effect of economic injustice. As he said, "Crimes increase as education, opportunity, and property decrease. Whatever spreads ignorance, poverty and, discontent causes crime. Criminals have their own responsibility, their own share of guilt, but they are merely the hand. Whoever interferes with equal rights and equal opportunities is in some real degree, responsible for the crimes committed in the community."

Once again, though, you might have asked him, "So, what bold action are you going to take?" or "How will you lead the country in solving this problem?" He likely wouldn't have had an answer. Acknowledging a problem is nowhere near as valuable as fixing it.

President Hayes promoted financial conservatism. He was content with securing incremental economic gains that brought needed relief to the nation. He agreed to offer the South subsidies to help them rebuild their economy. His conciliatory messages and financial conservative policies were well received by the American public as the economy gradually improved.

Rud wasn't the perpetrator of injustice because he lusted after power of the Presidency. He also wasn't simply an innocent who was duped by others. He was a savvy politician who knew the value of compromising. There's a time and a place for compromising. The

1870's wasn't the time and America wasn't the place, though. Leaders beginning with George Washington could have and should have done more to abolish slavery. Unfortunately, the outrageous behavior of the White supremacists in the South called for stronger action than Hayes, his contemporaries, and his predecessors were willing to take.

Could Hayes, or anyone else of his generation, rationally explain why Black citizens would begin to be beaten for daring to drink water from a "White Only" fountain, sitting at a "White Only" lunch counter, or trying to attend a "White Only" school? Could he justify what was going to happen to someone like Dr. Martin Luther King, Jr. who would say decades later, "To ignore evil is to become accomplice to it"? (156)

In fairness, there were many Republicans who erroneously believed they could build a Southern GOP based on support from reasonable White southerners. They may have underestimated how unwilling the "reasonable" ones would be to face up to the "unreasonable" ones. Hayes offered these conciliatory words:

> "The sacred obligation to the Union soldiers must not and will not be forgotten nor neglected. But those who fought against the Nation cannot and do not look to it for relief. Confederate soldiers and their descendants are to share with us and our descendants the destiny of America. Whatever, therefore, we their fellow citizens can do to remove burdens from their shoulders and to brighten their lives is surely in the pathway of humanity and patriotism."

Rutherford B. Hayes had stated unequivocally from the beginning that, if elected, he would not seek a second term. He didn't have the desire or intention to even consider the possibility of eight years of service. In fact, he advocated for a Constitutional Amendment that would set a term limit of 6 years for the office of US President. There was not support in Congress, though, for the amendment to go anywhere. You can almost hear his sighing in relief as he wrote in his diary on June 6, 1879, in the middle of his term in office:

> "I am heartily tired of this life of bondage, responsibility, and toil. I wish it was at an end. We are both physically very healthy. Our tempers are cheerful. We are social and popular. But it is one of our greatest comforts that the pledge not to take a second term relieves us from considering it. That was a lucky thing. It is a reform - or rather a precedent for a reform, which will be valuable."

Shortly before his death in 2020, Congressman John Lewis repeated his famous saying, "Get in good trouble, necessary trouble, and redeem the soul of America." (159) It was part of a statement he made as he was standing on the Edmund Pettus Bridge in Selma, Alabama to commemorate Bloody Sunday - March 7, 1965. That's the day peaceful protesters were beaten by police for crossing the bridge. Lewis suffered a fractured skull that day and nearly lost his life. In all, he was arrested more than 40 times for daring to take a stand against injustice. Like Lewis, Hayes and other politicians could have gotten in a little more "good trouble" to help "redeem the soul of America."

Instead, this was the weak, disappointing excuse Hayes wrote in his diary:

> "I am loaded down with educational, benevolent, and other miscellaneous public work. I must not attempt to do more. I cannot while attempting to conduct imperative duties."

One can't help but wonder what Lucy would have done if she were President instead of Rud. She was not afraid to take controversial stands for what she thought was right.

A positive outcome of Hayes' Presidency came in February of 1879, when he signed the Belva Bill allowing women to argue cases in all federal courts. As a result, Belva Lockwood became the first woman in America's history to present a case before the Supreme Court. She would later run for President as a candidate from the National Equal Rights Party in 1884. She received 4,100 votes which was unexpected because women could not yet vote. The media did not treat her kindly. The Atlanta Constitution referred to her as "Old Lady Lockwood" and warned of the dangers of "Petticoat Rule."

Another example of a worthwhile initiative was the support Hayes gave to Native Americans. He worked hard to see to it that they received full citizenship status. During his term of office, the number of forced removals of Native Americans from their lands diminished significantly.

Lincoln's death, Andrew Jackson's impeachment trial, and Ulysses S. Grant's corrupt administration had shaken the trust Americans had in politicians in Washington. President Hayes worked to restore the faith Americans had in the White House. He was against the partisan-based appointment of civil servants. He maintained that they should be appointed based on properly defined and objective criteria. This and many more works of his brought him into conflict with Roscoe Conkling of New York, the leader of the Stalwart Faction of the Republican Party. However, none of his political opponents could dissuade him from trying to keep the civil service and his federal appointments politically neutral and nepotism-free. After becoming President, Hayes, in fact, changed the system that employed people in government jobs that party leaders usually had great power to fill. They used the jobs to reward loyal party workers and to increase their own political strength. Rud demanded that federal jobs be given to people because of their abilities, not because they supported a politician. He reformed the civil service by substituting nonpartisan examinations for political patronage. At that time, there were lucrative jobs such as those with the customs service of the Treasury Department. The people who collected customs taxes on imports could keep part of the money for themselves. Hayes instituted reforms and demanded the resignation of top officials in the New York customhouse, including future President Chester Arthur, provoking a bitter struggle with his old rival, New York senator Roscoe Conkling. Hayes also banned all federal workers from taking part in political organizations, conventions, and campaigns. And he prohibited politicians from demanding campaign money from federal workers.

During Rud's first summer as President, the nation became mired in labor strife with The Great Strike of 1877, in which the political power of railroads became evident. An estimated 100,000 workers participated in the strike and around 100 people died in clashes between strikers and troops called to the aid of employers.

Hayes showed political strength during the strike. The nation was still suffering from a serious economic depression with three million people out of work. Factories and businesses reduced the pay of those who still had jobs. Workers with the Baltimore and Ohio railroad protested. They took control of many areas along the railroad, refusing to let the trains move. The strike spread to other railroads. In some places, the strikes turned into riots, and the riots became violent. Some governors ordered their state armed forces to intervene but they weren't able to maintain order, so the governors asked President Hayes for help. He immediately sent federal troops to troubled cities. The troops stopped the riots and ended the strikes.

The United States was experiencing an influx of Asian immigrants, particularly from China. Many workers had come from that country to help build the Central Pacific Railroad. After the railroad was built, many of them remained in California and others came from China to join them. This caused quite a lot of anger among Americans that had to compete with the immigrants for jobs. Whites protested because the Chinese agreed to work for less money which, it was claimed, held wages down for all workers. Congress introduced a number of bills to completely ban immigration from Asia, however, Hayes vetoed them in 1879. He opted for non-discriminatory immigration policies. Unfortunately, his policy would be struck down two years after he left the White House.

During the administrations of Andrew Johnson and Ulysses Grant, Congress had weakened many powers of the president. The Legislature had become the strongest of the three branches of the American government. Throughout his administration, Rutherford Hayes tried to strengthen presidential powers.

The United States Constitution gives the President power to veto bills passed by Congress. In the 1800's, they tried to prevent those vetoes, although Andrew Johnson made regular use of them. Instead, they used the time-honored method of attaching "riders" to legislative proposals that the President would believe necessary. To get the wanted bill, the President would have to accept the "rider," too. President Hayes refused to sign any bills with riders, so the Congress during his administration stopped using the method. A Presidential line-item veto, sometimes referred to as a partial veto, has never been able to find the necessary support from Congress. Forty-four of the fifty U.S. states, though, have given their Governors some form of line-item veto power. Indiana New Hampshire, Rhode Island, Vermont, North Carolina, Nevada, and Indiana are the exceptions.

From the beginning, Hayes set out in clear lines his Southern policy. He wanted to eliminate political acts of violence committed against Blacks. He insisted, and believed, that White southerners would adhere to the tenets of the Civil War constitutional amendments and that honest government would be restored to the South. Hayes refused to accept riders to military funding bills that would have repealed laws protecting Black voting rights. In 1878 and 1879 he vetoed seven consecutive Army Appropriation Bills for that reason. Rud's administration was under continual pressure from the South and West to resume silver coinage, outlawed in 1873. Many considered this proposal inflationary, and Hayes sided with the Eastern, hard-money gold interests. Congress, however, overrode his veto of the Bland-Allison Act in 1878, which provided for government purchase of silver bullion and restoration of the silver dollar as legal tender.

Hayes was right in saying that the United States was strong and prosperous. The late 1800's were a time of growth for the nation. They also were a time of expansion into new territory. In 1880, he became the first President to visit the West Coast, writing in his diary after the 71-day trip that took him past the Rocky Mountains, "A most gratifying reception greeted us everywhere from the people and from noted and interesting individuals." While out West, he and Lucy descended into a silver mine, toured orange groves, visited the new University of Southern California in Los Angeles, attended a Santa Fe fiesta, witnessed whales playing in the Pacific Ocean, and walked through Yosemite Park.

It wasn't a luxurious, relaxing trip. The rail line through New Mexico was incomplete, forcing the Hayes couple to ride in horse-drawn wagons for three days until they reached another rail head. There was another 60-mile stretch when they had to be accompanied by a military guard as they traversed a dangerous territory controlled by Apache and outlaw cowboys. (160) According to an article in The San Jose Times:

> "Nothing so strongly illustrates the true freedom and happy security in the land of liberty than the comparison naturally suggested by the untrammeled movements of our worthy President on his present long journey, when compared with the nervous precautions necessitated in monarchical countries when the crowned head passes through its districts. When the Russian Emperor traveled on a recent train ride, 40,000 troops and 10,000 peasants lined the

route. Happily, America has no such terrors for the head of government."

In truth, there were a number of reports that Hayes had been the victim of assassination attempts during his travels around the country. The Sedalia, Missouri Weekly Baxoo reported, for example, that a man named "Freebolter" had attempted to assassinate him at Muscotah, Kansas, a small railway station on the Union Pacific Railroad near Atchison City. Hayes passed through the area on his way back to the White House from the West Coast. Freebolter was arrested and taken to Atchison County Jail.

The Secret Service would not officially assume the duties of Presidential protection until the time of President Theodore Roosevelt in 1901. It was the practice of earlier Presidents, instead, to hire their own security, and Hayes employed four people in that capacity. His son, Webb Cook Hayes, became the most important. Webb was deputized and followed his father everywhere he went. Acting as a personal bodyguard, Webb was always armed with a pistol. He was also the official "greeter" at social events and stood next to his father whenever White House visitors met the President.

During Rud's term in office, there were many people who arrived at the White House asking to see him. The idea of that being allowed seems laughable these days. A man who thought he was a prophet who controlled the destinies of Presidents, for instance, sent many letters threatening to kill Hayes. He was eventually apprehended and sent to jail. The "White House Cranks," as they were called, were said to be numerous, according to a newspaper report, and "almost every day one of them appeared." During Hayes's term in office, thirteen people were arrested for loitering around the White

House, and eleven were sent to an asylum. Among them were two women who were both convinced Hayes wanted to marry them. According to the Quebec Daily Telegraph, "numerous other cranks called at the White House but were sent away, being considered harmless."

One day when the president had received "many visitors," including Senators, Representatives, and Cabinet Members, he asked if there was anyone else waiting to see. His secretary told him there were two people and one of them was "crazy." Hayes asked him to "send in the sane one." When the visitor entered the president's room, he explained he was "Emperor of the World" and he had "come to take possession of the White House and the government." As reported in the Copper County Michigan, Evening News, Hayes rang a bell to summon his secretary and said, "If this is the sane one of the two, please have him taken away and send in the maniac." According to Hayes Presidential Center Director Christie Weininger, "President Hayes today is remembered less for what he did during his single term in office than for an election that threatened to tear the country apart. It's a story that seems to resonate with modern-day visitors to the center. They're very interested in how divisive the country was then. Somehow knowing that we've been there before and survived, I think, gives some comfort and some hope to people.

Ch. 15 - Finger-Pointing

Sam Tilden returned from a European trip in October of 1877 with newfound determination. The Washington Post reported that the failed Democratic nominee blamed his loss on "a great fraud, which the American people have not condoned and never will condone. Never, never, never. I did not get robbed. The people got robbed. It was a robbery of the dearest rights of an American citizen." Many Democrats continued to accuse Hayes of being "His Fraudulency," throughout his presidency. When two members of the Louisiana Returning Board were indicted in the summer of 1877 for altering election returns, it was taken as proof that his election had indeed been illegitimate. There's a saying of unknown origin – "Be careful when you point a finger at someone else because it usually means there's three fingers pointing back at you!" The Democrats were about to get a rude awakening from pointing the finger at the other party.

Montgomery Blair had trouble deciding on choosing a political party. He was a Democrat before 1854, a Republican from 1854 to 1865, and then switched back to being a Democrat in 1865. The Maryland legislator called for a lawsuit charging southern corruption in an attempt to overturn the 1876 Presidential election results. On May 17, 1878, the House of Representatives passed a resolution to investigate the "alleged false and fraudulent" elections in Louisiana and Florida. Clarkson Nott Potter, a three-term Congressman representing New York's 10th Congressional District from 1869 to 1873, the 11th District from 1873 to 1875, and 12th District from 1877 to 1879, was appointed as the head of the commission. The Democrats hoped Hayes would be implicated and, in any case, the investigation would damage the Republican Party in the coming 1880 Presidential election. Potter had an ulterior motive. He coveted the governorship of New York and felt he needed Tilden's support to win it. The House adopted Potter's resolution and set up an 11-man commission consisting of Democrats and anti-Hayes Republicans. Although the committee was stacked with political enemies of President Hayes, the investigation would actually serve not to embarrass the President but to unify the Republicans and divide the Democrats. Some, like Blair, wished to oust the president. Most wanted simply to injure Hayes politically. Congressman Alexander Stephens of Georgia characterized the investigation as "most unwise, most unfortunate, and most mischievous." (160)

Hayes was confident of his innocence claiming, "One thing you may be sure of, I was not a party to covering up anything." He denounced the as a partisan proceeding, vowing never to leave office except through the constitutional process of impeachment, if it came to that. Rud also predicted accurately that the Potter Committee would stir up more trouble for the Democrats than it would for the Republicans.

The committee uncovered conflicting evidence that reflected poorly on election and campaign officials of both parties. For ten months beginning in May 1878, the Potter Committee subpoenaed all telegrams sent by political operatives during the election dispute. A total of 29,275 had been sent, but all but 641 had been routinely destroyed by Western Union. The remaining telegrams were in code, known as cipher, which was commonly used with business and political communication of the time.

The committee heard bombshell testimony on June 4, 1878. James E. Anderson, the Republican Supervisor of Election Registrations in

East Feliciana Parish, Lousiana, claimed he had been promised a patronage job if he ensured that the parish election results were "fixed" for Hayes. Anderson showed a copy of a letter signed by Treasury Secretary John S. Sherman, then a Senator, attesting to the deal to throw out Democratic votes. But Anderson's testimony soon unraveled. Sherman forcefully denied the charge and the correspondence was soon proven to be a forgery. Anderson had a reputation for drinking and admitted that he had perjured himself during earlier testimony in New Orleans, damaging his credibility.

According to the New York Tribune, "Anderson has made a most humiliating exhibition of himself and demonstrated the weakness of the revolutionary cause he has been brought in to sustain." That revelation, combined with the lack of credible witnesses against the Republicans, caused the Potter Committee's investigation to begin to flounder. On the other hand, Hayes and his administration fully cooperated with the committee, releasing all requested documents. Hayes's openness, combined with Anderson's unimpressive testimony, undermined the legitimacy of Democrats seeking to reverse the election results.

Within a month, the Potter Committee had become a travesty, spending days focusing on minute details in depositions. Several Democrats, embarrassed by the entire process, joined with Republicans to pass a resolution on June 14 denying that Congress, the courts, or any commission the ability to reverse the 1876 election results. By late June, public sentiment reflected an observation by Sherman that the Potter inquiry would "fizzle out."

A different investigation, though, was just beginning. Everything changed when revelations about corruption emerged but not of the sort the committee had hoped to find. New York Tribune Editor

Whitelaw Reid learned that a Senate committee had possession of a series of cipher telegrams that had passed between Colonel William T. Pelton, Tilden's nephew; Manton Marble, the editor of the Democratic New York World; and election officials in the three Southern states with disputed returns. Roughly 750 of these telegrams found their way into Reid's hands.

In August of 1878, the Tribune started printing selections from the telegrams, making the most of the discovery by translating bits and pieces and publishing them over time. On October 7, the Tribune unveiled the first major disclosure, showing an offer from Marble, whose code name was Moses, and another from C. W. Wooley, code name of Fox, to bribe election officials. Using bold headlines and extra pages, the newspaper explained who wrote the telegrams and how it acquired and deciphered them. So that there would be no questions about accuracy, the Tribune published the original coded telegrams, the key to the code, and the translated messages. Then in October of 1878, the paper published telegrams sent by Tilden's agents offering bribes to vote-counters in three of the contested states: $50,000 for Florida, $80,000 for South Carolina, and $5,000 for the single vote from Oregon.

The Tribune's exposé forced the Potter Committee to investigate the cipher telegrams. In January of 1879, Pelton and Smith Weed Mead, a New York Assemblyman with a tongue-twister name, both confessed to their involvement in a bribery scheme to buy the election for Tilden. The dispatches revealed that on the very day Pelton arrived in South Carolina, he transmitted proposals for bribing the returning board. According to the New York Tribune, negotiations were conducted for six days and then Weed transmitted the following:

"Majority of Board have been secured. Cost is $80,000, to be sent as follows: One parcel of $65,000 dollars, one of $10,000, and one of $5,000. All to be $500 and $1,000 bills. Notes to be delivered as parties accept. Do this at once and have cash ready to reach Baltimore Sunday night. Telegraph decidedly whether this will be done."

Pelton admitted that his uncle had chastised him in November of 1876 for his role in the South Carolina bribery attempt. On the other hand, Marble claimed that the telegrams were "danger signals" and not discussions of vote buying. In February, the Democratic nominee himself appeared before the committee to deny participating in the bribery conspiracy and no direct evidence has ever linked him to it. Asserting his innocence, Tilden claimed that he knew nothing about the proposed bribes but admitted that when he found out about the activity of his agents, he immediately ordered them to stop.

There were, however, several factors that raised the possibility of Tilden's collusion. Pelton lived with his uncle at 15 Gramercy Park, from where he sent and received the cipher telegrams. The system of ciphers was the same code that Tilden used in his business transactions. Some of the telegrams were addressed to "Russia" which was the code name for Tilden, from his personal friends. Those with whom Pelton negotiated assumed that he was acting on behalf of his uncle, who was presumed to be the source of his funds. Nevertheless, the Potter Committee unanimously declared Tilden's innocence since no evidence of actual payments was uncovered. The committee quickly faded from the spotlight and is mostly forgotten today as yet another sad episode in an era where election fraud was rampant. In attempting to reverse the results of the Centennial election, the Potter Committee unwittingly gave the public a glimpse of the corruption and graft which flowed through American politics, fueling additional public cynicism about the political process.

Toward the end of December, telegrams emerged allegedly showing that the Democrats had used bribery to try to steal the Elector in Oregon, E.A. Cronin. A Democratic operative had been dispatched to Portland with a copy of "The Household English Dictionary," to be used in decoding secret telegrams related to the bribe scheme. One such telegram was, "Certificate of elector will be issued to a Democrat. Must purchase a Republican elector to recognize and act with Democrats and secure the vote and prevent trouble. Deposit $10,000 to his credit." If the bribe had been accepted, Tilden could have gotten his one-vote victory that way.

Tilden denied emphatically all knowledge of all such dispatches. The attempts to implicate him in corrupt transactions were not successful and he was again cleared of any personal wrongdoing. However, his political opponents endeavored to make sure the public didn't forget about the "Cipher Dispatches" in subsequent campaigns. No longer could he pose as the untarnished "reformer" above the normal fray of politics, his principal call to fame. These revelations did immeasurable damage to Tilden's reputation, likely ruining his chances for the Democratic Presidential nomination in 1880. They also removed any possibility that the Democrats could claim the moral high ground and use the fraud issue against the Republicans in the next election.

Thirty years later, speaking on the Senate floor so it would be read into the Congressional Record, South Carolina Senator Benjamin "Pitchfork Ben" Tillman, a former leader of the Red Shirts, proudly talked about how the disenfranchisement of Black voters was like "a second Declaration of Independence" boasting:

> "We set up the Democratic Party with one plank only, that this is White man's country, and White men must govern it. Under that banner, we went to battle. We stuffed ballot boxes because desperate diseases require desperate remedies. It was then that we shot them. It was then that we killed them. It was then that we stuffed ballot boxes because this disease needed a strong remedy. I do not ask anybody to apologize for it. I am only explaining why we did it." (160)

Ch. 16 - Lemonade Lucy

The hardest part of being the First Lady, according to Lucy, was reading negative comments about her husband. "I keep myself outwardly very quiet and calm," she admitted, "but inwardly sometimes there is a burning venom and wrath." She forced herself to hide her anger "under a smiling and pleasant exterior" when politicians, newspaper reporters, and members of the public criticized Rud. (161)

Lucy, on the other hand, was almost universally admired. Her pleasant exterior was extolled in a New York Graphic article on March 18, 1878 article saying has "has the reputation of fascinating her visitors because she is so vivacious and so responsive that everybody leaves her presence with a vague idea that he is the one person whom she was longing to see."

Rud always valued Lucy's opinions. She kept up-to-date with politics and, in fact, would often attend Congressional debates. She would wear a checkered shawl so that her husband could easily spot her. President Hayes famously quipped, "I don't know how much influence Mrs. Hayes has with Congress, but she has great influence with me." (166) Lucy loved entertaining guests at the White House. An article in the New York Herald proclaimed that she was, "A most attractive and lovable woman. She is the life and soul of every party. For the mother of so many children, she looks youthful."

Lucy was an abolitionist and supported the Republican Party in its anti-slavery efforts. As was traditional for the time, her primary role was as a wife and mother. The first President's wife to be a college graduate, she held progressive views and was committed to charitable causes. She was known to visit prisons, mental health facilities, and the National Deaf-Mute College, now Gallaudet University, in Washington. Surprisingly, though, she never took a stance on women's suffrage and her husband was not an advocate, either.

Lucy went out of her way to help poor people in Washington. Upon learning of a family or individual in dire need, she would ask for the situation to be carefully investigated, and then directly aid with cash from her own account, or from money collected from wealthy Cabinet members. In January of 1880 alone, she dispensed nearly a thousand dollars, a substantial sum of money at the time. On a regular basis, she would send flowers from greenhouses to the local Children's Hospital and visit those at the National Soldier's Home. Lucy was the first President's wife to maintain and allow public access to an independent schedule of public appearances.

How did Lucy feel about her husband's controversial removal of federal troops in the South? She expressed confidence that it would give Blacks "a better and fairer prospect of happiness and prosperity now than ever." She freely admitted that the President had very little choice, though, lacking support to continue keeping them there. (167) Rud and Lucy went from having three children at the beginning of the Civil War to having eight in all. Unfortunately, three did not survive their childhood. (168) Their firstborn, Birchard Austin, went on to become a prominent attorney in Toledo.

Webb Cook, their second son, turned out to be a national hero. A career military officer, he served in the Spanish American War, Philippine Insurrection, Boxer Rebellion, and World War I. Webb was presented with the Medal of Honor for his actions during the Philippine Insurrection. With Rud serving in the Civil War from the time he was five years old, Webb would spent six months of the year at his father's encampments. He became close with the commander of the unit, General George Crook, whom he regarded as his godfather. Crook taught him how to hunt, fish, and survive off the land.

At the outbreak of the Spanish American War, Webb was commissioned a Major in the First Ohio Cavalry, accompanying Major General W. R. Shafter as part of the First Expedition against Havana, Cuba. He later joined his regiment at Chickamauga Park until he embarked with the Fifth Army Corps for Santiago. He served through the campaigns of Santiago de Cuba and the invasion of Puerto Rico. Despite wounds received during the crossing of the San Juan River, Webb took part in the assault on San Juan Hill on July 1, 1898. (169) Leading the charge was, of course, future President Teddy Roosevelt. When the insurrection in the Philippines broke out, Webb was commissioned Lieutenant Colonel of the 31st U.S. Infantry. After a 33-day voyage aboard a ship, he arrived in Manila in late November of 1899. Within hours, Webb led a rescue party to free U.S. soldiers garrisoned at Vigan Island. (170) It was this act of heroism that earned him the Medal of Honor, the first time a President's son was so-honored. It wouldn't happen again until Theodore Roosevelt Jr. would receive the Medal during World War II. Webb's citation read:

> "Pushed through the enemy's lines alone, during the night, from the beach to the beleaguered force at Vigan, and returned the following morning to report the condition of affairs to the Navy and secure assistance."(159)

Webb also participated in the Boxer Rebellion, the China Relief Expedition, and the Russo-Japanese War. In WWI, he served as a special agent for the State Department until the French government's withdrawal from Paris. Commissioned a full Colonel when the U. S. entered the war, Hayes was sent to the Italian front where he served as a Regional Commander of the American Expeditionary Force.

After retiring from the military, Webb became Treasurer of the Whipple Manufacturing Company in Cleveland. Six years later, he was one of the organizers of the National Carbon Company, which later became Union Carbide. Webb continued for many years as a Vice President of the corporation until his retirement from civilian life.

Their third son and his father's namesake, Rutherford Platt went on to become a librarian, bank executive, and real estate developer. As has been mentioned, Joseph Thompson's brief life came to an end on June 24, 1863, while visiting his father's military site at Camp White.

Born September 29, 1864, in Cincinnati, while Rutherford B. Hayes was away fighting in the Civil War, their fifth son, George Crook, was named after General Crook. He sadly became the second of three Hayes children to die in infancy, on May 24, 1866, in Cincinnati.

Fanny, named after Rud's older sister who had died the prior year, was born on September 2, 1867, in Walnut Hills, near Cincinnati. She instantly became her mother and father's darling. The only daughter of Rutherford and Lucy, she was 10 years old when the family moved into the White House. Fanny would go on to devote her life to prison reform, working with inmates at the Reformatory Prison for Women in Framingham, Massachusetts.

During the White House years, sixth son Scott Russell and Fanny attracted much attention from the press and the public. Born February 8, 1871, Scott turned six years old just a month before his father became President. Scott's adult life was spent as a business executive, working in electrical and railroad manufacturing.

Fanny entered school in Fremont when the Hayes family took up permanent residence at Spiegel Grove in 1873. She attended Miss Augusta Mittleberger's boarding school in Cleveland where she was a classmate of the daughter of James A. Garfield. She then went to Miss Sarah Porter's school at Farmington, Connecticut with both Nellie Arthur, daughter of President Chester A. Arthur, as well as Molly Garfield. Fanny suffered from partial deafness her entire life.

The White House also became known for the Hayes dogs, the most celebrated of which was Gryme, a two-year-old greyhound. Hayes once wrote to Fanny that the "pets give a Robinson Crusoe aspect to our mode of life." Gryme was described by Rud as "Good-natured and neat in his habits and took all our hearts at once." The dog's clear favorite in the family was Lucy. "How happy old Gryme always was when she returned after an absence," wrote Hayes in his diary. One day, as Lucy sang the Star Spangled Banner, Gryme lifted his head and howled. Every time after that when she sang the National Anthem, Gryme would "sing" along with her.

Gryme would later accompany the Hayes family with two of his puppies when they returned to Spiegel Grove. Sadly, Gryme's life ended tragically when he was hit and killed by a train. The White House and the Hayes home in Ohio were flooded with letters of condolence. Hayes wrote, "The death of Gryme has made us all mourn. He was killed instantly by a train at Pease's Crossing. He stood on the track evidently expecting the train to turn out for him. All horse teams turned out for him."

The last of the Hayes children, Manning Force was the only one born at Spiegel Grove. He was born August 1, 1873 and his brief life came to an end barely a year after it began.

White House security guard William Henry Crook described Rud as "one of the best-natured men who ever lived in the White House" and someone who was "easily approached by anyone who had an excuse for meeting him." Although admirable, that kind of accessibility was also dangerous. Crook admitted, "Episodes of violent behavior were a frequent occurrence in the White House. We dealt with them quietly and they rarely got into the newspapers." (172) Hayes received so many assassination threats, he gave up the tradition of having concerts on the White House lawn. Access to the White House was curtailed and guards were stationed at external gates outside of the hours of 2:00 to 10:00 p.m. The entrance to the Executive Mansion's main door was provided with a guard station and all visitors had to show some identification before entering. (173)

The increased security measures were later relaxed after Lucy asked her husband to allow the "rolling of Easter eggs on the White House lawn," which later became an Executive Mansion tradition. Congress had passed a law in 1877 forbidding children from playing on the Capitol Hill grounds. In 1878, Rutherford and Lucy Hayes held that first Easter Egg Roll on the White House lawn.

The couple celebrated their twenty-fifth wedding anniversary on December 30, 1877 by renewing their vows and hosting a reception for friends and family. The gala affair was given front-page coverage in newspapers across the country. It had additional significance because they shared the day with daughter Fanny, whose formal christening took place at the White House.

Lucy also sponsored a wide range of musical and cultural events. On numerous occasions, she also invited Black groups to perform in the White House, including students of the Colored Industrial School, and famed singer Marie Selika Williams, introduced to her by Frederick Douglass. Able to play both the piano and guitar, Lucy hosted hymn-singing on Sunday evenings in the private quarters for friends and family. A talented contralto, her favorite hymns reportedly were "Jesus Lover of My Soul," and "Blest Be the Tie that Binds." Lucy wasn't the first President's wife to be called "First Lady." That distinction belongs to Mary Todd Lincoln. However, she did make the moniker famous. She was the first First Lady to have a bathroom and running water in the White House and the first to use a typewriter and phonograph. When the country's first telephone was installed in the White House during the Hayes Presidency, it was only connected to the Treasury Department and was assigned the telephone number "1."

Lucy is most remembered, though, as "Lemonade Lucy." Many photographs were taken of her serving pinkish lemonade at White House functions. The moniker was given to her by journalists, political cartoonists, and pundits to poke fun at the strict nature of the First Family of teetotalers. Lucy's maternal grandfather, an Ohio state legislator named Isaac Cook, had all his grandchildren sign a pledge to abstain from drinking. The decision to ban alcohol can be attributed to Lucy's moral, religious upbringing, but in reality, politics may also have been at play. She declared, "I have young sons who have never tasted liquor. They shall not receive from my hand, or with the sanction that its use in the family would give, the first taste of what might prove their ruin. What I wish for my own sons I must do for the sons of other mothers." (172) Lucy Hayes, to the delight of the Christian Women's Temperance Union, refused to allow anyone to serve alcohol at White House affairs.

The temperance movement emphasized how women could set a moral example for their families so, in her mind and theirs, it made sense that the First Lady should serve as a role model for the country. There was also, however, the desire to keep the temperance advocates in the Republican ranks rather than have them join the Prohibition Party. The temperance policy gained him support among religious groups. For the straight-laced Rud, it was a matter of having government officials conduct themselves with discretion and dignity at all times. Poking fun at the ban on alcohol at White House functions, Secretary of State William M. Evarts later noted, "The water flowed like wine." (160)

Lucy's compassion and sincerity endeared her to Washingtonians. She regularly visited Hampton Institute where she sponsored a scholarship for a Black student. She continued to show concern for the poor by contributing generously to Washington charities. Fond of children, the White House was open to her children's friends. Her young adult nieces and cousins were also frequent guests at the White House, often assisting in the hosting of White House social functions. The Hayes family was religious and lived an exemplary life. Lucy didn't allow smoking, dancing, or card-playing in the White House. The straight-laced Hayes was always bothered by the drunken behavior at receptions and other events in Washington. The Hayes' first official state dinner, after he became President, was to honor Russian Grand Duke Alexis and Grand Duke Constantine and there was plenty of wine at that event. That was enough for him. He sided with Lucy and decreed that no more alcohol would be served at the White House during his term. (161)

Politically astute and a champion of social causes, Lucy Hayes was considered a celebrity. She dressed simply and wore no make-up. Like her husband, she was an amiable person who offended very few people. By the end of Rud's term in office, Lucy was acknowledged to be one of the most popular President's wives the country has known." One newspaper, in fact, praised her compassion after a trip with the President to the former Confederacy saying, "Southern women, who hated the very name Northerner, put their arms around her neck and poured their bitterness and sorrow into her ears." (175) Hayes didn't regret his decision to refuse renomination by the Republican Party in 1880. He felt a strong sense of personal satisfaction claiming, "Nobody ever left the Presidency with less regret, less disappointment, fewer heart burnings, or any general content with the result of his term than I do. Full of difficulty and trouble at first, I now find myself on smooth waters and under bright skies." Looking back on his administration, he wrote:

> "I left this great country prosperous and happy. I left
> the party of my choice strong, victorious, and united.
> In serving the country, I served my party."

At that year's Republican National Convention, the choice for Presidential nomination was deadlocked between former President Ulysses Grant and Senator James Blaine of Maine. On the thirty-sixth ballot, Hayes loyalist James Garfield, former Civil War General and Republican Congressman from Ohio, was chosen as the compromise candidate. The ill-fated 20th President won the election by a small margin and then would be assassinated just four months after being inaugurated. He had resigned himself to the fact that his life would be in danger from the moment he took office admitting, "Assassination can no more be guarded against than can death by lightning. It is best to worry about neither." (176)

Rud and Lucy came close to being "ill-fated" themselves when they left Washington by train to return home to Fremont, Ohio after Garfield's Inauguration on March 4, 1881. The Boston Evening Transcript described how, during the journey, their train collided with another one going south. Both trains were wrecked and the engineer in the other locomotive killed. A greater tragedy was prevented by the conductor of the Hayes train, John M. Unglaub, who alertly reversed the engine as soon as he saw the oncoming train. Unglaub was badly injured but recovered. Hayes believed his quick action had saved their lives.

After returning to Spiegel Grove, Rud committed his retirement years to helping Blacks in the South. He focused on educational programs, which he believed could help create economically and socially prosperous Black communities. Hayes also reasoned that through education, racial inequality and tensions could be reduced. Hence, many of the initiatives he focused on were aimed at securing equal educational opportunities.

Lucy returned home and taught Sunday School, joined the Woman's Relief Corp, and entertained the many distinguished visitors to Spiegel Grove. She became national president of Woman's Home Missionary Society of the Methodist Church. She attended reunions of the 23rd Ohio Volunteer Infantry and spoke out against the plight of the urban poor and disenfranchised Blacks in the South.

What happened to Tilden? He retired to private life after the election. Although he was considered a Presidential possibility again in 1884, the campaign never came to fruition. He continued to remind people that he was the winner of the popular vote in 1876, saying, "I can retire to private life with the consciousness that I shall receive from posterity the credit of having been elected to the highest position in the gift of the people, without any of the cares and responsibilities of the office." (177) He died in 1886 of pneumonia at the age of 72. Part of Tilden's fortune, as directed in his will, supported the founding of the New York Public Library with a $4 million endowment. Inscribed on his grave is, "I Still Trust the People."

Lucy spent her last eight years at Spiegel Grove. As she sat by the bay window in her bedroom sewing, and watching Scott, Fanny, and their friends playing tennis on the south lawn of their mansion, she suffered a severe apoplectic stroke. Early in the morning of June 25, 1889 she died in her sleep. She was 57 years old. Flags were ordered flown at half-mast throughout the country to honor her. Rud was devastated by her death writing, "The soul had left Spiegel Grove." (178) Tributes to her were published in newspapers across the country. The most poignant remembrance may have been written by her son Webb who said, "My Mother was all that a Mother could be." (179) Rud's first birthday without Lucy was

October 4, 1889 when he wrote this diary entry expressing his remorse:

> "My birthday -- sixty-seven years old. It brings freshly and painfully to mind the absence from my side of my cherished Lucy. When I last was here in the spring at the centennial of the Government she was with me! Alas, how it weakens the hold of this life -- of earth upon me! How easily I could now let go of life!"

Rud mourned Lucy's death for four years before he passed away after suffering a heart attack on January 17, 1893 at the age of 71. His last words were, "I know I'm going to where Lucy is." (180) The two were buried together, along with their dog Gryme and two horses named Old Whitey and Old Ned, at Spiegel Grove.

W.E.B. Dubois was a recipient of financial support from the Slater Fund, which promoted Black education. Rud was one of its founders. The Boston Globe reported that when Dubois learned of Rud's death, he wrote to the Board of Trustees, "I am especially grateful to the memory of him, your late head, through whose initiative my case was brought before you and whose tireless energy and single-heartedness for the interests of my race, God has at last crowned." (181)

Today, Hayes is little remembered in the United States, but he is treated as a national hero in Paraguay, of all places. Hayes agreed to negotiate a long-held border dispute with Argentina. The decision gave Paraguay about 60 percent of its land. If you go to Paraguay today, you'll find a state named after the 19th President called "Presidente Hayes." The region celebrates "Presidente Hayes Day" on his birthday, October 4. They even have a soccer team named for Hayes in Ascuncion, the nation's capital, as well as a Hayes museum. In America, there is a Hayes Presidential Center in Fremont, Ohio, a Rutherford B. Hayes High School in Delaware, Ohio, and a Hayes Hall at Ohio State University.

Ch. 17 - The Jim Crow Era

The term "Jim Crow" originated in 1828 when a White New York comedian, Thomas Dartmouth "Daddy" Rice, introduced a song and dance routine in blackface, using a burnt cork to darken his face. According to Rice, his performance was inspired by an elderly Black man he had seen singing the song near a stage door one night in Cincinnati, Ohio. A popular hit in the 19th century, the routine was performed across the country as "Daddy Jim Crow," a caricature of a shabbily dressed, uneducated, poor Black vagrant.

Rice's act started the "Minstrel Show," a form of music and theatrical performance that focused on the mockery of Blacks. Jim Crow as entertainment spread rapidly across the United States in the years prior to the Civil War and eventually around the world. According to the Boston Post in 1838, "The two most popular characters in the world right now are Queen Victoria and Jim Crow." An embarrassing example of this influence came when America's Special Ambassador to Central America, John Lloyd Stephens, arrived in Merida on Mexico's Yucatan Peninsula in 1841. As he disembarked, a local brass band played "Jump Jim Crow" mistakenly thinking it was America's national anthem. (165)

The first name of "Jim" connotes a burglar trying to "jimmy" a lock and "Crow" refers to use of a crowbar. The meaning of "Jump Jim Crow" comes from the practice of farmers feeding their crows corn-soaked whiskey. The crows would get drunk, jump around, and then be beaten to death by the farmers. All of the references, of course, have racist connotations. The return to "home rule" cost Black Americans living in the South many of the hard-earned freedoms and civil liberties that had been won during Reconstruction.

Although outlawed, slavery was merely replaced with segregation of the races and was upheld by laws restricting the rights of Blacks. In turn, freedmen were considered servants now instead of slaves. The nomenclature was different. The result was pretty much the same.

The term Jim Crow was applied to the body of racial segregation laws and practices in the southern and border states after the Compromise of 1877. They mandated the separation of the races and unequal status for Blacks. The new laws perpetuated beliefs about the inferior nature of Blacks. The most significant Jim Crow laws required that public schools, public accommodations, and public transportation, including buses and trains, have separate facilities for Whites and Blacks. The facilities established for Whites were always superior.

W.E.B. DuBois described this period as, "After the Civil War, the slave went free, stood a brief moment in the sun, then moved back again toward slavery." He went on to explain:

> "Slavery was not abolished even after the Thirteenth Amendment. There were four million freedmen and most of them on the same plantation, doing the same work they did before emancipation, except as their work had been interrupted and changed by the upheaval of war. Moreover, they were getting about the same wages and apparently were going to be subject to slave codes modified only in name. There were among them thousands of fugitives in the camps of the soldiers or on the streets of the cities, homeless, sick, and impoverished. They had been

freed practically with no land nor money, and save in exceptional cases, without legal status, and without protection." (182)

Racial prejudice led to these discriminatory measures passed by state and local governments that sought to keep Blacks at a lower social and economic position. Jim Crow laws strictly enforced racial segregation in almost every aspect of southern life. The way people are brought up and what they're exposed to as children has tremendous influence on them. According to Dubois, "Children learn more from what you are than what you teach. (183)

Essayist Anaïs Nin put it in perspective when she said, "We do not see things as they are, we see things as WE are." (184) In other words, trying to convince people of the truth, as obvious as it may be to you, often doesn't work. They have their own truths and they may be deeply ingrained in them. So, "educating" adults to try to eliminate hatred and prejudice is not always a successful endeavor. That's why we need laws and other restrictions in a civilized society. If you can't change minds, you work on changing behavior.

The all-too-brief moment was gone when former slaves born to modest, often poor, circumstances could be elected to office and serve as living fulfillments of the American Dream. Small wonder, then, that after the Civil War, many Blacks who had served in the Union army, felt betrayed by the nation whose integrity they had fought to preserve. This was particularly true of the families who sacrificed their sons, fathers, and brothers in the war effort. All southern states instituted some form of Jim Crow laws. Blacks could not eat in the same restaurants, drink from the same water fountains, watch movies in the same theaters, play in the same parks, or go to the same schools as Whites. Blacks had to sit in the back of buses and streetcars and institutionalized White supremacy which gave second-class citizenship to Blacks was the law in most parts of the American South until the middle of the 20th century. Some people, in fact, have referred to the Civil Rights struggles of the 1950's and 1960's as the "The Second Reconstruction." The laws forced segregation of facilities and services, prohibited intermarriage, and denied suffrage. Blacks could not nurse Whites in hospitals. Signs like those on the next page could be seen everywhere throughout the South.

(Photos courtesy of National Archives)

In addition to discriminatory laws, there were certain unwritten social expectations. Segregation "de jure" means "by jurisdiction." In other words, there would be local and state ordinances that would require or ban certain behaviors. On the other hand, segregation "de facto" means "in effect." That usually refers to a custom or practice that isn't backed by legislation. There was a flood of the latter after the Centennial Election. For example, a Black man was not to shake hands with a White man and could not make eye-contact with a White woman or else he would risk being accused of highly inappropriate behavior. When speaking, Blacks were expected to address Whites as "Mr.," "Sir," or "Ma'am."

According to a report published by the NAACP, 2,522 Black Americans were lynched, burned alive, or hacked to death between 1889 and 1918. Lynching was the most violent form of discrimination. Offenses the victims were accused of were usually minor, such as attempting to register to vote or speaking out for equality. Often there were allegations of sexually assaulting a White woman or talking back to a White person. Rather than receiving a fair trial, many Blacks were lynched by White mobs. All that was required was an accusation rather than actual proof. Lynching was a major method used during this period to control Blacks and, in some cases, Whites who were sympathetic. The monopoly of the White southern state legislatures by die-hard segregationists, racists, and Redeemer Democrats, could hardly have been more disastrous in terms of economic justice. With the Jim Crow laws in full effect and no means of enforcing federal protections, former Black slaves were prohibited from learning a new trade or even how to read and write. Since the militant White supremacist organizations were now openly enforcing what only amounted to a new version of the old racial social order, the poverty that slaves had known in the past became a present reality, rendered explicitly legal and subject to brutal enforcement.

Blacks remained poor, and were forced to remain poor, literally on pain of death. Southern planters and capitalists now had access to a vast pool of almost-free labor again, in a manner and to an extent virtually indistinguishable from the slavery of the 1850s. Involuntary servitude had not been abolished but merely changed in form. Instead of a given slave belonging to or on a particular plantation as the chattel property of a particular, specific, individual master, the slaves of the 1870s and 1880s were now, as it were, "slaves at large." Northern officials gave varying reports on conditions of the freedmen in the South. One harsh assessment came from Rud's Secretary of the Interior Carl Schurz, who investigated the situation in the states along the Gulf Coast. His report claimed:

> "The number of murders and assaults perpetrated upon Negroes is very great; we can form only an approximative estimate of what is going on in those parts of the South which are not closely garrisoned, and from which no regular reports are received, by what occurs under the very eyes of our military authorities. As to my personal experience, I will only mention that during my two days sojourn at Atlanta, one Negro was stabbed with fatal effect on the street, and three were poisoned, one of whom died. While I was at Montgomery, one Negro was cut across the throat evidently with intent to kill, and another was shot, but both escaped with their lives. Several papers attached to this report give an account of the number of capital cases that occurred at certain places during a certain period of time. It is a sad fact that the perpetration of those acts is not confined to that class of people which might be called the rabble."

Schurz's report went on to describe White vigilante patrols in Alabama this way:

> "They board the boats; after the boats leave they hang, shoot, or drown the victims they may find on them, and all those found on the roads or coming down the rivers are almost invariably murdered. The bewildered and terrified freedmen know not what to do - to leave is death; to remain is to suffer the increased burden imposed upon them by the cruel taskmaster, whose only interest is their labor, wrung from them by every device an inhuman ingenuity can devise; hence the lash and murder is resorted to intimidate those whom fear of an awful death alone cause to remain, while patrols, Negro dogs and spies, disguised as Yankees, keep constant guard over these unfortunate people." (185)

Blacks were gradually evicted from public office, as the few that remained saw the sway they held over local politics considerably decreased. Socially, the situation was worse, as the Southern Democrats tightened their grip on the labor force. Vagrancy and "anti-enticement" laws were reinstituted. Anti-enticement laws imposed criminal fines for planters and other employers attempting to poach Black laborers already under an employment contract. These laws were designed to restrict worker mobility. It became illegal to be jobless, or to leave a job before the required contract expired. Economically, Blacks were stripped of independence, as new laws gave White planters the control over credit lines and property. Effectively, the Black community was placed under a system of subjugation that was very reminiscent of slavery.

Jim Crow laws blocked most Blacks from voting in public elections. Local authorities charged fees, called poll taxes, which most Blacks could not afford and required them to pass literacy tests not required of Whites. Deprived of a formal education, most Blacks who could not read and write well failed these tests. Some of them were designed so that virtually no one could pass. In addition to voting barriers in general elections, Blacks were excluded from Southern politics in other ways. Southern states introduced the "White Primary." The Democratic Party, the only real political party of power in the South, claimed that primaries to select candidates for various officers were private events. They banned participation by Blacks. By 1910, this practice was used in every Southern state. As a result of voting restrictions and exclusion from primaries, Blacks had little, if any, political influence in the South.

The rapid rise of terrorist White supremacist organizations rendered the act of attempting to vote, let alone trying to run for public office, potentially deadly. These measures were, unfortunately, very effective. In Louisiana, more than 130,000 Blacks were registered to vote in 1896. By 1905, that number dropped to just over 1,300. As late as 1900, in Louisiana only 0.5% of the Black population was allowed to register to vote. In North Carolina, no Blacks were registered to vote. "Grandfather" clauses were passed so that Whites didn't have to take tests. If your grandfather was registered to vote, you could also.

The 15th Amendment had prohibited denying men the right to vote based on race. It did not explicitly say, however, that it was also illegal to discriminate on the basis of trick questions. In later years, the southern states came up with many insidious ways to disenfranchise Black voters, like having them guess the number of jelly beans in a jar. Unless they were able to get the number exactly right, they would not be allowed to vote. They would also have to try to quickly answer a convoluted question such as, "Write every other word in this first line and print every third word in same line but capitalize the fifth word that you write."

Here's an actual sentence from Section 260 of Alabama's Constitution. It certainly qualifies as one of the more complex sentences ever written. A prospective Black voter would have to read this and try to explain the meaning to the satisfaction of a White registrar in order to be permitted to vote. It is not known whether any person was ever able to do it.

> "The income arising from the sixteenth section trust fund, the surplus revenue fund, until it is called for by the United States government, and the funds enumerated in sections 257 and 258 of this Constitution, together with a special annual tax of thirty cents on each one hundred dollars of taxable property in this state, which the legislature shall levy, shall be applied to the support and maintenance of the public schools, and it shall be the duty of the legislature to increase the public school fund from time to time as the necessity therefore and the condition of the treasury and the resources of the state may justify; provided, that nothing herein contained shall be so construed as to authorize the legislature to levy in any one year a greater rate of

state taxation for all purposes, including schools."
(186)

Shown below is part of a Literacy Test from the state of Louisiana. Designed to put the applicant through mental contortions, many of the test's questions are confusingly worded. If some of them seem unanswerable, that was intentional. Again, a White registrar would be the ultimate judge of whether an answer was right. A single incorrect answer would disqualify an applicant. There was no time allowed for thinking. The complete test had 36 questions that had to be completed in ten minutes. Among them were the following:

---

1. Draw a line around the number or letter of this sentence.

2. Circle the first, first letter of the alphabet in this line.

3. In the first circle below write the last letter of the first word beginning with "L"

   0   0   0

4. Cross out the number necessary, when making the number below one million.

   10000000000

5. In the space below, write the word "noise" backwards and place a dot over what would be its second letter should it have been written forward.

6. Spell backwards, forwards.

7. Print the word vote upside down, but in the correct order.

8. Place a cross over the tenth letter in this line, a line under the first space in this sentence, and circle around the last the in the second line of this sentence.

9. Draw a figure that is square in shape. Divide it in half by drawing a straight line from its northeast corner to its southwest corner, and then divide it once more by drawing a broken line from the middle of its western side to the middle of its eastern side.

10. In the third square below, write the second letter of the fourth word.

☐ ☐ ☐

11. Divide a vertical line in two equal parts by bisecting it with a curved horizontal line that is only straight at its spot bisection of the vertical.

12. Write every other word in this first line and print every third word in same line, but capitalize the fifth word that you write. (187)

Post-Script

A lot of people say the country is now divided as never before. The events described in this book, though, suggest that things weren't much different in the 1800's. People back then may have used overly-flowery language, seemingly as many words as possible to express themselves, and they certainly loved to use semi-colons. Otherwise, they were pretty similar to people today. That's both disturbing and comforting at the same time.

The election of 1876 marked the beginning of a long nadir for Blacks. Free from federal intervention, racists across the South engaged in a campaign of brutal violence and intimidation to keep Blacks isolated, removed from the mainstream, and unable to vote. Voting rights are critical. If you can't vote, you'll have no political representation and your interests will not to be served.

Since the Civil War, the struggle for racial justice in America has been agonizingly slow. It's been one of two steps forward and one step back. Sometimes, one forward and two back. What will tomorrow bring? More steps forward and steps backward? More swings of the pendulum? We've all got a chance to provide the answer.

Footnotes

1 https://npr.org/2013/01/14/169080969/segregation-forever-a-fiery-pledge-forgiven-but-not-forgotten Downloaded 11/14/20

2 https://listen.sdpb.org/post/segregation-forever-fiery-pledge-forgiven-not-forgotten Downloaded 12/5/20

3 https://csmonitor.com/Commentary/2021/0114/George-Wallace-Martin-Luther-King-Jr.-and-the-power-of-forgiveness Downloaded 1/5/20

4 https://.usatoday.com/story/news/politics/2020/07/18/rep-john-lewis-most-memorable-quotes-get-good-trouble/5464148002 Downloaded 11/2/20

5 https://epikfails.com/2017/04/19/presidential-pros-cons-part-five Downloaded 2/8/21

6 https://ohiohistory.org/learn/collections/history/history-blog/2016/february-2016/rosettaarmstead Downloaded 1/17/21

7 https://ohiohistory.org/learn/collections/history/history-blog/2016/february-2016/rosettaarmstead Downloaded 1/17/21

8 https://ohiohistory.org/learn/collections/history/history-blog/2016/february-2016/rosettaarmstead Downloaded 1/17/21

9 https://richlandsource.com/area_history/the-rosetta-armstead-case-a-fight-for-freedom-won-in-ohios-courts/article Downloaded 1/18/21

10 https://richlandsource.com/area_history/the-rosetta-armstead-case-a-fight-for-freedom-won-in-ohios-courts/article Downloaded 1/14/21

11 https://ohiohistory.org/learn/collections/history/history-blog/2016/february-2016/rosettaarmstead Downloaded 1/18/21

12 Sumner, 1893 p. 17

13 Hoffer, 2010 p. 314

14 Donald, 2009 p. 4.

15 Brewster, 2014 pp. 37-38

16 https://reason.com/2005/06/01/behind-the-jeffersonian-veneer-2 Downloaded 12/20/20

17 https://thoughtco.com/president-james-buchanan-the-secession-crisis-1773714 Downloaded 10/16/20

18 https://.lincolnabraham.com/abraham-lincolns-first-inaugural-address Downloaded 1/5/21

19 https://history.com/this-day-in-history/lincoln-replies-to-horace-greeley Downloaded 12/11/20

20 https://goodreads.com/quotes/67212-well-i-wish-some-of-you-would-tell-me-the Downloaded 2/5/21

21 Gould, 2014 P. 216

22 Gould, 2014 P. 217

23 Geer, 1984 p. 114

24 https://rbhayes.org/hayes/lucy-webb-hayes-and-her-influence-upon-her-era Downloaded 2/27/21

25 https://resources.ohiohistory.org/hayes/quotes.php Downloaded 10/10/20

26 https://rbhayes.org/hayes/the-role-of-lucy-webb-hayes-in-the-civil-war/ Downloaded 11/5/20

27 https://rbhayes.org/hayes/the-role-of-lucy-webb-hayes-in-the-civil-war Downloaded 2/21/21

28 https://rbhayes.org/hayes/the-role-of-lucy-webb-hayes-in-the-civil-war/ Downloaded 9/15/20

29 https://mentalfloss.com/article/69848/7-presidential-facts-about-rutherford-b-hayes Downloaded 10/17/20

30 https://shapell.org/blog/presidential-brothers-in-arms-rutherford-b-hayes-and-william-mckinley Downloaded 1/17/21

31 https://rbhayes.org/research/chapter-7-lucy-s-search-for-her-husband Downloaded 12/5/20

32 https://rbhayes.org/research/chapter-7-lucy-s-search-for-her-husband Downloaded 12/5/20

33 https://rbhayes.org/research/chapter-7-lucy-s-search-for-her-husband Downloaded 8/18/20

34 https://rbhayes.org/hayes/the-role-of-lucy-webb-hayes-in-the-civil-war Downloaded 2/5/21

35 Gould, 2014 P. 211

36 https://whitehouse.gov/about-the-white-house/first-families/lucy-ware-webb-hayes/ Downloaded 2/4/21

37 https://rbhayes.org/hayes/civil-war Downloaded 1/14/21

38 https://ironbrigader.com/2015/10/23/rutherford-b-hayes-recalls-incident-battle-cedar-creek Downloaded 2/26/21

39 https://lincolnportrait.com/physical_man.html Downloaded 1/7/21

40 https://presidentialham.com/u-s-presidents/abraham-lincoln-with-ham Downloaded 1/8/21

41 https://presidentialham.com/u-s-presidents/abraham-lincoln-with-ham Downloaded 1/8/21

42 https://presidentialham.com/u-s-presidents/abraham-lincoln-with-ham Downloaded 1/9/21

43 https://housedivided.dickinson.edu/sites/lincoln/letter-to-john-stuart-january-23-1841 Downloaded 10/14/20

44 Goodwin, 2005 p. 364

45 https://archives.gov/news/topics/emancipation-proclamation Downloaded 2/17/21

46 https://whitehouse.gov/briefing-room/speeches-remarks/2021/01/20/inaugural-address-by-president-joseph-r-biden-jr Downloaded 2/17/21

47 https://history.com/topics/american-civil-war/emancipation-proclamation Downloaded 10/6/20

48 https://history.com/topics/american-civil-war/emancipation-proclamation Downloaded 11/14/20

49 https://lincolncottage.org/black-reaction-to-the-emancipation-proclamation Downloaded 12/14/20

50 https://opinionator.blogs.nytimes.com/2013/01/29/hurrah-for-old-abe Downloaded 1/10/21

51 https://lincolncottage.org/black-reaction-to-the-emancipation-proclamation Downloaded 12/14/20

52 https://neaedjustice.org/social-justice-issues/racial-justice/corrected-confederacy-race-relations Downloaded 12/20/20

53 https://opinionator.blogs.nytimes.com/2013/01/29/hurrah-for-old-abe Downloaded 1/11/21

54 https://opinionator.blogs.nytimes.com/2013/01/29/hurrah-for-old-abe Downloaded 1/11/21

55 https://constitution.congress.gov/constitution/amendment-13 Downloaded 12/27/20

56 https://archives.gov/research/african-americans/freedmens-bureau Downloaded 2/3/21

57 https://archives.gov/research/african-americans/freedmens-bureau Downloaded 2/3/21

58 https://goodreads.com/work/quotes/178433-black-reconstruction-in-america-1860-1880?page=2 Downloaded 11/22/20

59 https://goodreads.com/work/quotes/178433-black-reconstruction-in-america-1860-1880?page=2 Downloaded 11/22/20

60 https://libquotes.com/ulysses-s-grant/quote/lbl5n1c Downloaded 12/1/20

61 https://.nps.gov/linc/learn/historyculture/lincoln-second-inaugural.html Downloaded 2/14/21

62 https://rogerjnorton.com/Lincoln.html Downloaded 2/27/21

63 https://findingdulcinea.com/news/history/2012/Abraham-Lincoln-Facts.html Downloaded 1/16/21

64 https://history.com/this-day-in-history/john-wilkes-booth-shoots-abraham-lincoln Downloaded 9/28/20

65 https://shapell.org/manuscript/rutherford-b-hayes-on-abraham-lincoln-assassination-april-15-1865 Downloaded 11/6/20

66 https://books.apple.com/us/book/grant-takes-command/id1040014296 Downloaded 1/22/21

67 https://quotes.yourdictionary.com/author/frederick-douglass/46354 Downloaded 2/14/21

68 https://.tsl.texas.gov/ref/abouttx/juneteenth.html Downloaded 10/4/20

69 https://presidency.ucsb.edu/documents/proclamation-157-declaring-that-peace-order-tranquillity-and-civil-authority-now-exists Downloaded 2/21/21

70 https://babel.hathitrust.org/cgi/pt?id=uc2.ark:/13960/fk3tt4fz9s&view=1up&seq=469&q1=gries Downloaded 10/20/20

71 https://listverse.com/2017/06/21/10-ways-american-slavery-continued-long-after-the-civil-war Downloaded 11/5/20

72 https://law.cornell.edu/uscode/text/42/1994 Downloaded 12/16/20

73 https://ballotpedia.org/Civil_Rights_Act_of_1866 Downloaded 11/22/20

74 https://americanpeople2.blogspot.com/2010/12/black-code-of-st-landrys-parish-1865.html Downloaded 2/3/21

75 https://thereconstructionera.com/when-the-white-league-militia-took-over-new-orleans-in-1874-it-pledged-to-end-the-stupid-africanization-of-government Downloaded 1/13/21

76 https://thereconstructionera.com/when-the-white-league-militia-took-over-new-orleans-in-1874-it-pledged-to-end-the-stupid-africanization-of-government Downloaded 2/3/21

77 https://origins.osu.edu/connecting-history/top-ten-origins-white-supremacist-violence Downloaded 12/14/20

78 https://jstor.org/stable/30234869?seq=1#metadata_info_tab_contents Downloaded 1/15/21

79 https://jstor.org/stable/30234869?seq=2#metadata_info_tab_contents Downloaded 12/16/20

80 https://potus.com/rutherford-b-hayes/ Downloaded 11/22/20

81 https://jstor.org/stable/30234869?seq=2#metadata_info_tab_contents Downloaded 12/16/20

82 https://thelionofanacostia.wordpress.com/2016/05/16/speech-of-frederick-douglass-at-the-1876-republican-national-convention/ Downloaded 1/19/21

83 https://books.google.com/books?id=UBpkVnw_AIIC Downloaded 9/27/20

84 https://bartleby.com/268/10/8.html Downloaded 11/28/20

85 Holt, 2008 p. 125

86 https://emilytaylorcenter.ku.edu/pioneer-woman/salter Downloaded 2/17/21

87 htts://vermonthistory.org/journal/misc/NominationRutherfordBHayes Downloaded 11/14/20

88 Hoogenboom, 1995 p. 260

89 https://rbhayes.org/hayes/1876-acceptance-speech Downloaded 2/16/21

90 https://rbhayes.org/hayes/1876-acceptance-speech Downloaded 1/11/21

91 https://presidency.ucsb.edu/documents/republican-party-platform-1876. Downloaded 12.3.20

92 https://cbsnews.com/news/election-1876-voter-fraud-suppression-partisanship Downloaded 2/15/21

93 https://toonopedia.com/milqueto.html Downloaded 9/21/20

94 Morris, 2003 p. 103

95 https://ourdocuments.gov/doc.php?flash=false&doc=34 Downloaded 11/15/20

96 DeGregorio, 1997 p. 69

97 Morris, 2003 p. 131

98 https://americanheritage.com/election-got-away Downloaded 12/15/20

99 https://inspiringquotes.us/quotes/QNzr_TsbdmpYG Downloaded 1/11/21

100 Morris, 2003 p. 159-160

101 https://inspiringquotes.us/quotes/QNzr_TsbdmpYG Downloaded 3/4/21

102 https://inspiringquotes.us/quotes/QNzr_TsbdmpYG Downloaded 3/4/21

103 https://infidels.org/library/historical/robert_ingersoll/indianapolis_ speech Downloaded 1/11/21

104 https://thereconstructionera.com/a-dead-radical-is-very-harmless-winning-the-election-of-1876 Downloaded 2/14/21

105 https://thereconstructionera.com/a-dead-radical-is-very-harmless-winning-the-election-of-1876 Downloaded 2/14/21

- 106 https://thereconstructionera.com/the-plan-to-suppress-the-black-vote-in-south-carolina-election-1876 Downloaded 2/16/21

108 Geer, 1984 p. 116

109 https://.americanheritage.com/was-presidential-election-stolen   Downloaded 1/5/21

110 https://coolidgefoundation.org/resources/ulysses-s-grant Downloaded *12/20/20*

111 https://constitution.congress.gov/constitution/amendment-20 Downloaded 12/28/20

112 https://rbhayes.org/clientuploads/RBHSpeeches/speech161. election_ day_ speech. html *Downloaded 2/14/21*

113 Morris, 2003, p. 104

114 Tagg, 1998 p. 62

115 Hessler, pp. 345

116 https://cmohs.org/recipients/daniel-e-sickles Downloaded 11/15/20

117 "Yankee King of Spain," Time Magazine June 18, 1945. June 18, 1945. Downloaded 10/5/20

118 Sternstein, 1966 p. 116

119 Morris, 2003 p. 20

120 Sterenstein, 1966 p. 117

121 https://rbhayes.org/hayes/disputed-election-by-ari-hoogenboom   Downloaded 1/8/21

122 ww.rbhayes.org/hayes/disputed-election-by-ari-hoogenboom   Downloaded 1/15/21

123 https://thereconstructionera.com/nov-8-1876-white-richmonders-celebrate-the-election-of-tilden-as-president Downloaded 2/12/21

124 https://historytoday.com/archive/feature/presidential-election-1876 Downloaded 1/3/21

125 https://thereconstructionera.com/hayes-asked-reporters-not-to-publish-claims-that-he-had-won-presidency-the-day-after-the-election Downloaded 12/3/20

126 https://rbhayes.org/hayes/disputed-election-by-ari-hoogenboom Downloaded 1/1121

127 https://saturdayeveningpost.com/2016/10/worst-presidential-election-u-s-history Downloaded 2/9/21

128 Holt, 2008 p. 229

129 https://thereconstructionera.com/illegal-votes-and-faithless-electors-in-the-election-of-1876 Downloaded 11/23/20

130 https://thereconstructionera.com/1876-winning-the-election-by-refusing-to-certify-the-vote-throwing-out-results Downloaded 11/13/20

131 Morris, 2013 p. 218

132 https://thereconstructionera.com/an-irish-immigrant-supporter-of-lincoln-writes-to-his-daughter-that-the-1876-election-is-a-fraud Downloaded 12/17/20

133 https://thereconstructionera.com/an-irish-immigrant-supporter-of-lincoln-writes-to-his-daughter-that-the-1876-election-is-a-fraud Downloaded 12/17/20

134 https://saturdayeveningpost.com/2016/10/worst-presidential-election-u-s-history Downloaded 2/9/21

135 https://thereconstructionera.com/illegal-votes-and-faithless-electors-in-the-election-of-1876 Downloaded 11/23/20

136 https://rbhayes.org/hayes/disputed-election-by-ari-hoogenboom Downloaded 12/3/20

137 https:// theclassroom.com/characteristics-democrats-republicans-during-1877 Downloaded 1/24/21

138 https://hrbhayes.org/hayes/disputed-election-by-ari-hoogenboom Downloaded 12/3/20

139 https://hrbhayes.org/hayes/disputed-election-by-ari-hoogenboom Downloaded 12/17/20

140 https://wsws.org/en/articles/2000/12/1876-d21.html Downloaded 1/15/21

141 https://goodreads.com/work/quotes/178433-black-reconstruction-in-america-1860-1880?page=2 Downloaded 11/25/20

142 Morris, 2013 p. 260

143 Crook, 1911 p. 119

144 https://rbhayes.org/hayes/disputed-election-by-ari-hoogenboom Downloaded 2/521

145 https://americanheritage.com/election-got-away Downloaded 2/16/21

146 Ayton 2017 p. 85

147 https://cbsnews.com/news/election-1876-voter-fraud-suppression-partisanship Downloaded 2/14/21

148 https://glc.yale.edu/testimony-henry-adams-regarding-negro-exodus *Downloaded 10/22/20*

149 https://theatlantic.com/magazine/archive/1893/10/the-hayes-tilden-electoral-commission/523971 Downloaded 1/15/21

150 Morris, 2013 p. 267

151 Barnard 2005, pp. 402–403

152 https://washingtonpost.com/politics/2021/01/16/presidents-and-inauguration-ceremonies/?arc404=true Downloaded 1/4/21

153 Ayton, 2017, p. 222

154 https://facinghistory.org/reconstruction-era/chamberlain-decries-end-republican-rule Downloaded 12/16/20

155 Ayton, 2017 p. 109

156 https://archive.nytimes.com/www.nytimes.com/learning/general/onthisday/harp/1102.html Downloaded 10/22/20

157 https://thereconstructionera.com/illegal-votes-and-faithless-electors-in-the-election-of-1876 Downloaded 1/14/21

158 https://azquotes.com/quote/595364 Downloaded 1/14/21

159 https://everydaypower.com/john-lewis-quotes Downloaded 2/3/21

160 https://oregonencyclopedia.org/articles/hayes_rutherford_b_visit_to_oregon 1880 Downloaded 11/19/20

161 Gould 2014 American First Ladies: The Lives and their Legacy, p. 150

162 https://cbsnews.com/news/election-1876-voter-fraud-suppression-partisanship

163 https://millercenter.org/president/hayes/hayes-1877-firstlady Downloaded 1/26/21

164 Gear, 1984 p. 112

165 https://rbhayes.org/hayes/hayes-children/ Downloaded 2/20/21

166 https://rbhayes.org/hayes/webb-cook-hayes Downloaded 11/7/20

167 https://rbhayes.org/hayes/webb-cook-hayes Downloaded 11/7/20

168 https://fampeople.com/cat-webb-hayes#:~:text Downloaded 2/11/21

169 Crook, 1911 p. 204

170 Garrison, Webb, A Treasury of White House Tales, Rutledge Hill Press, 1996, p. 111

171 https://whitehousehistory.org/lucy-hayes-temperance-and-the-politics-of-the-white-house-dinner-table#footnote-4 Downloaded 1/15/21

172 https://firstladies.org/blog/nineteenth-century-first-ladies-liquor-in-the-white-house Downloaded 10/14/20

173 Hoogenboom, 1995 p. 3

174 https://historyonthenet.com/authentichistory/1865-1897/1-reconstruction/4-1876election/index.html Downloaded 12/15/20

175 https://constitutionallawreporter.com/great-american-biographies/lucy-webb-hayes Downloaded 2/3/21

176 https://quotefancy.com/james-a-garfield-quotes/page/2 Downloaded 12/19/20

177 https://smithsonianmag.com/history/the-ugliest-most-contentious-presidential-election-ever-28429530 Downloaded 12/17/20

178 https://historyonthenet.com/authentichistory/1865-1897/1-reconstruction/4-1876election

179 https://rbhayes.org/collection-items/rutherford-b.-hayes-collections/hayes-webb Downloaded 1/12/21

180 https://goodreads.com/quotes/9937578-i-know-i-am-going-where-lucy-is Downloaded 11/17/20

181 https://bostonglobe.com/2021/02/15/opinion/racial-decency-irony-rutherford-hayes/ Downloaded 10/28/20

182 https://encyclopedia.com/social-sciences/encyclopedias-almanacs-transcripts-and-maps/black-reconstruction Downloaded 11/15/20

183 https://goodreads.com/quotes/74568-children-learn-more-from-what-you-are-than-what-you Downloaded 10/27/20

184 https://goodreads.com/quotes/5030-we-don-t-see-things-as-they-are-we-see-them
Downloaded 11/28/20

185 https://d1lexza0zk46za.cloudfront.net/history/american-documents/documents/cschurz-south-report-1865.pdf Downloaded 12/27/20

186 https://law.justia.com/constitution/alabama/CA-245810.html Downloaded 2/17/21

187 https://ferris.edu/HTMLS/news/jimcrow/question/2012/pdfs-docs/literacytest.pdf
Downloaded 1/7/21

Notes: Rutherford B. Hayes diary entries and letters from
https://rbhayes.org/research/diary-and-letters-of-rutherford-b.-hayes/

Lucy W. Hayes letters from https://rbhayes.org/research/civil-war-letters-of-lucy-webb-hayes

Bibliography

Ayton, Mel, *Plotting to Kill the President: Assassination Attempts from Washington to Hoover,* Potomac Books, 2017

Archdeacon, Thomas J., *The Erie Canal Ring, Samuel J. Tilden, and the Democratic Party.* New York History, 1978

Barnard, Harry, *Rutherford Hayes and his America.* American Political Biography Press, 2005

Berlin, Ira, *"Slaves Without Masters: The Free Negro in the Antebellum South."* Oxford University Press, 1981

Bigelow, John, *The Life of Samuel J. Tilden,* Show Biz East Productions, 2009

Brewster, Todd, *Lincoln's Gamble,* Simon & Schuster, 2014

Bruce, Robert V., *1877: Year of Violence.* Ivan R. Dee, 1959

Calhoun, Charles W., *The Presidency of Ulysses S. Grant.* University Press of Kansas, 2017

Chafe, William H., *Remembering Jim Crow: African Americans tell About Life in the Segregated South.* New York: W. W. Norton, 2001

Collier, Christopher, *Reconstruction and the Rise of Jim Crow, 1864–1896.* Benchmark Books, 2000

Conwell, Russell, *Life and public services of Gov. Rutherford B. Hayes.* B. B. Russell, 1876

Crook, William Henry. *Memories of the White House: The Home Life of Our Presidents from Lincoln to Roosevelt.* Little, Brown, 1911

Davison, Kenneth E., *The Presidency of Rutherford B. Hayes.* Greenwood Press. 1972

DeGregorio, William, *The Complete Book of U.S. Presidents,* Gramercy, 1997

Dodds, Graham G., *Take Up Your Pen: Unilateral Presidential Directives in American Politics.* University of Pennsylvania Press, 2013

Donald, David Herbert, *Charles Sumner and the Coming of the Civil War.* Naperville, IL: Sourcebooks, Inc., 2009

Du Bois, W. E. B., *"Black Reconstruction in America."* Transaction Publishers, 2013

Ewing, Elbert, W. R. *History and Law of the Hayes–Tilden Contest Before the Electoral Commission: The Florida Case, 1876–1877.* Cobden Pub. Co., 1910

Fleming, Walter L. *"Documentary History of Reconstruction: Political, Military, Social, Religious, Educational, and Industrial."* Palala Press, 201.

Flick, Alexander Clarence, and Gustav S. Lobrano, *Samuel Jones Tilden: A Study in Political Sagacity.* Dodd, Mead & Company, 1939

Eric Foner, *A Short History of Reconstruction,* Harper & Row, 1990

Foner, Eric, *Reconstruction: America's Unfinished Revolution, 1863–1877.* Harper Perennial Modern Classics, 2002

Geer, Emily Apt, *First Lady: The Life of Lucy Webb Hayes,* Kent State, 1984

Goldman, David J., *Presidential Losers.* Lerner Publications, 2004.

Goodwin, Doris Kearns, *Team of Rivals: The Political Genius of Abraham Lincoln,* Simon & Schuster, 2005

Gould, Lewis L., *American First Ladies: Their Lives and Their Legacy*, Routledge, 2014

Grant, Ulysses S., *Personal Memoirs.* Barnes & Noble, Inc., 1885.

Guenther, Karen, *Potter Committee Investigation of the Disputed Election of 1876.* The Florida Historical Quarterly, 1983.

Hayes, Lucy, Draft of *Lucy's Search for her Husband,* from www.rbhayes.org/research/chapter-7-lucy-search-for-her-husband, 1876, downloaded 12/16/20

Hayes, Rutherford B. & Williams, Charles Richard. *The Diary and Letters of Rutherford B. Hayes, Nineteenth President of the United States.* Ohio State Archeological and Historical Society, 1922

Haworth, Paul Leland, *The Disputed Presidential Election of 1876,* The Burrows Brothers Company, 1906

Hendricks, Nancy *America's First Ladies: A Historical Encyclopedia and Primary Document Collection of the Remarkable Women of the White House*, Random House, 2015

Hirsch, Mark D., *Samuel J. Tilden: The Story of a Lost Opportunity.* The American Historical Review, 1951

Hoffer, William, James Hull, *The Caning of Charles Sumner*. Baltimore, MD: Johns Hopkins University, 2010

Holt, Michael F., *By One Vote: The Disputed Presidential Election of 1876*, University Press of Kansas, 2008

Hoogenboom, Ari, *Rutherford B. Hayes: Warrior & President*, University Press of Kansas, 1995

Horton, James O., and Lois E. Horton, *Slavery and the Making of America*. Oxford University Press, 2005

Kelley, Robert, *The Thought and Character of Samuel J. Tilden: The Democrat as Inheritor*. The Historian, 1964

Keith, LeeAnna, *The Colfax Massacre: The Untold Story of Black Power, White Terror, and the Death of Reconstruction*, Oxford University Press, 2008

Kelley, Robin D. G., and Earl Lewis, *To Make Our World Anew: A History of African Americans*. Oxford University Press, 2000

Lane, Charles, *The Day Freedom Died: The Colfax Massacre, the Supreme Court, and the Betrayal of Reconstruction*. Henry Holt & Co., 2008

Lynch, John R., *"The Facts of Reconstruction."* The Neale Publishing Company, 1913

Morris, Roy, Jr., *Fraud of the Century: Rutherford B. Hayes, Samuel Tilden, and the Stolen Election of 1876*. Simon & Schuster, 2003

National Association for the Advancement of Colored People, *Thirty Years of Lynching in the United States: 1889–1918*. Negro Universities Press, 1969

Oldaker, Nikki with John Bigelow, *Samuel Tilden the Real 19th President" Elected by the Peoples' Votes*. Show Biz East Productions, 2006

Packard, Jerrold, *American Nightmare: The History of Jim Crow*. St. Martin's Press, 2002

Polakoff, Keith Ian, *The Politics of Inertia: The Election of 1876 and the End of Reconstruction*. Louisiana State University Press, 1973

Rehnquist, William H., *Centennial Crisis: The Disputed Election of 1876*. Alfred A. Knopf, 200.

Republican Party Platforms, *Republican Party Platform of 1876*
https://www.presidency.ucsb.edu/node/273305. Downloaded 12/2/20

Richardson, Heather Cox, *The Death of Reconstruction*. Cambridge, Harvard University Press, 2001

Rehnquist, William, *Centennial Crisis: The Disputed Election of 1876*. Knopf, 2004

Reid, Whitelaw, *Ohio in the War: The history of her regiments, and other military organizations*. Moore, Wilstach & Baldwin, 1868

Robinson, Lloyd, *The Stolen Election: Hayes Versus Tilden—1876*. Forge Books, 2001

Severn, Bill, *Samuel J. Tilden and the Stolen Election*. I. Washburn, 1968

Simkins, Francis Butler, *Pitchfork Ben Tillman, South Carolinian*. Louisiana State University Press, 1967

Sternstein, Jerome L., *The Sickles Memorandum: Another Look at the Hayes-Tilden Election-Night Conspiracy*, Journal of Southern History Vol 32 No. 3 Aug. 1966

Stevens, Albert C., *The Cyclopaedia of Fraternities*, Hamilton, 1907

Stowell, David O. *Streets, Railroads, and the Great Strike of 1877*. University of Chicago Press, 1999

Sumner, Charles, *Memoir and Letters of Charles Sumner: 1845–1860* edited by Edward Pierce, 1893

Tagg, Larry. *The Generals of Gettysburg*, Campbell, CA: Savas Publishing, 1998

Trefousse, Hans L., *Rutherford B. Hayes*. Times Books, 2002

U.S. Electoral Commission, *Electoral Count of 1877. Proceedings of the Electoral Commission and of the Two Houses of Congress in Joint Meeting Relative to the Count of Electoral Votes Cast December 6, 1876, for the Presidential Term Commencing March 4, 1877*. 44th Cong. 2d Sess. Washington: GPO

White, Richard, *The Republic for which it Stands: The United States During Reconstruction and the Gilded Age, 1865-1896*. Oxford University Press, 2017

Woodward, C. Vann, *Reunion and Reaction: The Compromise of 1877 and the End of Reconstruction*. Little, Brown, and Co., 1951

Wormser, Richard, *The Rise and Fall of Jim Crow*. St. Martin's Press, 2003

About the Author

Formerly a consultant who delivered more than 3,000 leadership and professional skills training seminars for many Fortune 500 companies and an Adjunct Professor at Boston University's School of Management, Len Sandler holds a B.S. in Psychology, an MBA, and a Ph.D. in Organizational Behavior. He is now retired and lives in Plymouth, MA, with his wife Marilyn. They have four children - Lori, Melinda, Scott, and Craig - along with three grandchildren - Elizabeth, Louisa, and Oscar.

Len is also the author of:

- *Becoming an Extraordinary Manager: The Five Essentials for Success*
- *See You on the High Ground: The Jared Monti Story*
- *Because of You We Live! The Untold Story of George & Simone Stalnaker*
- *The Incredible Battle of Castle Itter*
- *Mind Your Own Business: How to Jump-Start Your Career!*

Made in the USA
Middletown, DE
03 September 2023